BASIC SERVICES FOR URBAN POOR

INSTITUTE OF SOCIAL SCIENCES
URBAN STUDIES SERIES

1. Urbanisation in Developing Countries: Basic Services and Community Participation
Edited by **Bidyut Mohanty**

2. Urbanisation in India: Basic Services and People's Participation.
by **K. C. Sivaramakrishnan, Biplab Dasgupta, M. N. Buch**

3. Basic Services for Urban Poor: A Study of Baroda Bhilwara, Sambalpur and Siliguri
by **Archana Ghosh, S. Sami Ahmad, Shipra Maitra**

4. Urban Poverty, Basic Services and Environment
by **P. K. Dave, Laurie Baker**

Urban Studies Series No. 3

Basic Services for Urban Poor

A Study of Baroda, Bhilwara, Sambalpur and Siliguri

Archana Ghosh
S. Sami Ahmad
Shipra Maitra

INSTITUTE OF SOCIAL SCIENCES
and
CONCEPT PUBLISHING COMPANY

ISBN 81-7022-551-5

First Published in 1995

Published and Printed by
Ashok Kumar Mittal
Concept Publishing Company
A/15-16 Commercial Block, Mohan Garden
New Delhi 110 050

Layout by
Institute of Social Sciences
B-7/18 Safdarjung Enclave
New Delhi 110 029

Foreword

This publication, the third in the urban studies series of the Institute of Social Sciences, is the outcome of an extensive field study by the research team of the urban studies department of the Institute. It carries forward at the micro level the issues pertaining to the delivery of basic services raised in the previous publications in the series.

The interim findings of the study were presented at two regional seminars organised by the Institute in Bhubaneswar (November 1992) and Baroda (April 1993). Issues arising from the discussions, and suggestions and recommendations made at these seminars have been incorporated in the finalisation of the study.

I am grateful to the Friedrich Ebert Stiftung, Delhi office, and its resident representative, Dr. Heinz Bongartz, for their support for this project.

New Delhi
November 1994

George Mathew
Director

Acknowledgement

The present volume is the outcome of the research project, "Urban Poverty, Basic Services and Local Participation", undertaken by the research team in the Urban Studies Unit in the Institute of Social Sciences. The theme of the research study was conceived by the team in early 1992, with the objective of studying the access of the urban poor communities to certain basic amenities and the involvement of the communities in the development programmes.

After long deliberations with many other experts in the field of the urban studies, it was decided that the study would be based on evaluation of government-sponsored basic services programmes specially designed for slum localities. To evaluate the responses of the communities and their actual involvement in the programmes, Urban Basic Services (UBS) programme was decided to be given special emphasis. The UBS programme which was initiated in 1986 as a pilot project mainly in lower order class I cities and middle order towns has changed its nomenclature as Urban Basic Services for the Poor (UBSP) since 1990 with continued emphasis on participatory planning and services development. The revised programme however differs to some extent from the earlier programme (UBS) in terms of institutional structures, financing pattern, training programmes of the functionaries etc. To assess the impact of the participatory programme in the slum community it was however felt to be more appropriate to concentrate on those cities where the programme had been going on for quite some time. Therefore the cities which had undertaken the programme in its earlier form, that is, the UBS were selected for in-depth study.

The scope of the study was kept limited to slums in four cities belonging to four states, two each from the eastern and western part of the country.

The book runs into six chapters. In addition to the four case studies of four cities presented separately, there is an introductory chapter and a concluding chapter. The introductory chapter introduces the subject of the research and gives a background of the study and its objective, scope, methodology etc. The concluding chapter gives a comparative assessment of the four case studies and discusses the issues emerging out of the analyses.

The successful completion of the research project and the publication of this volume has been possible due to kind support and assistance received from many individuals and institutions. First and foremost was the generous advice and valuable comments extended by Prof. Amitabh Kundu of the Jawaharlal Nehru University. Ms. Marty Rajandran, Urban Project Coordinator in UNICEF country office in New Delhi was generous with ideas and comments. Mr. T. K. Banerjee. Joint Director, Institute of Local Self-Government and Urban Studies, Calcutta, Prof. L. N. P. Mohanty, National Institute of Habitat Management, Bhubaneswar, Prof. Chetan Vaidya, University of Baroda, and Prof. Iqbal Narain, Institute of Development Studies, Jaipur helped us in all possible ways by providing the logistics and guidance at the State level. The exhaustive household level survey would not have been possible without the field support of our local representatives – Mr. Niladri Mukherjee in Siliguri, Ms. Prerana Vaidya in Baroda, Mr. Srikant Panigrahi in Sambalpur and Mr P. R. Sharma in Bhilwara. In each city the officials of the State and local level institutions have been extremely supportive and helpful in providing information and assistance. We express our gratitude to all these friends and well-wishers.

We are grateful to Ms Suhasini Ramaswamy for her editorial assistance. Thanks to Mr. Deep Chand Maity who spent his precious time for computer data processing and Mr P N Kuttappan in the Institute for word processing and making the layout of the book. Last but not least, we express our special gratitude to all the respondents in our field survey in all the four cities, without whose willing participation the study would not have been possible. We hope this study will bring out their predicaments in daily life and help the policy makers take constructive decisions about their future.

Archana Ghosh
S. Sami Ahmad
Shipra Maitra

Contents

LIST OF TABLES

Baroda

Bhilwara

Sambalpur

Evaluation and Conclusion

Chapter I

INTRODUCTION

The theory of economic growth under perfect competition leading to the optimum allocation of economic resources, has long been discarded by imperfections in the society. The policies for increasing economic growth measured in terms of per capita income fail to take the distributional aspects into account leading to widening inequality in the system. A large number of Third World nations achieved the overall UN income target (i.e. $ 275 per capita per year in 1985) during the fifties and the sixties but the standard of living of the masses did not change much. In the seventies development has been redefined in terms of the "reduction or elimination of poverty, inequality and unemployment within the context of a growing economy" (World Bank, 1990). It is now being realised that low productivity, low levels of living and low income are three mutually reinforcing phenomena that constitute the basis of underdevelopment. According to Myrdal, (1968) they constitute a process of "circular and cumulative causation" in which low incomes lead to low levels of living which keeps productivity low, which in turn perpetuates low income and so on.

Indicators of Poverty: Changing Perspective

A major objection towards using the per capita GNP as a measure of economic development is that it fails to include the low level of living as reflected by the lack of basic services. Proper housing conditions, clean drainage and sewerage systems, per capita consumption of water and electricity, increasing enrolment in schools, low child mortality rates are some of the indicators that reflect the conditions of living describing the nature of economic development.

Basically, such indicators fall into two groups – those that seek to measure development in terms of a normal or optimal pattern of interaction among social, economic and political factors and those that measure development in terms of quality of life.

One of the major studies on the first group of composite indicators was carried out by the United Nations Research Institute on Social

Development (1970). The study was concerned with the selection of the most appropriate indicators of development and an analysis of the relationship between these indicators at different levels of development. The result was the construction of a composite social development index, taking nine social and seven economic indicators. The choice of indicators shows that thcy wanted to measure development in terms of structural change rather than in terms of human welfare. The World Bank (1990) also argued that improvement in the health, education and nutrition of the people was important not only in their own right but also to promote growth in income.

Direct provision of health, nutritional and educational services is particularly relevant for the low income communities. The evidence from other countries suggests that rapid and politically sustainable progress on poverty alleviation has been achieved by pursuing a two-fold strategy – to promote the productive use of labour through market incentives, social and political institutions, infrastructure and technology and to provide basic social services such as primary health care, family planning, nutrition and primary education to the poor.

The two elements are mutually reinforcing; one without the other is not sufficient. In Brazil and Pakistan, for instance, growth has raised the incomes of the poor, but social services have received very little attention. As a result, mortality among children remains unusually high and primary enrolment unusually low and the poor are not in a position to take advantage of economic opportunities. Some other countries, by contrast, have long stressed the provision of social services, but growth has been too slow. In Sri Lanka, for example, primary enrolment rates are very high and under 5 mortality rates are exceptionally low, but the potential for raising the level of living of the poor has gone to waste for lack of economic opportunity (World Bank, 1990). Progress has been the greatest in the countries that have implemented both parts of the strategy. In Indonesia and Malaysia this approach has brought about a substantial reduction in poverty along with rapid improvements in nutrition, under 5 mortality and primary enrolment.

Poverty as measured by low income tends to be at its worst in rural areas, even allowing for the often substantial differences in cost of living between town and countryside. The problems of malnutrition, lack of education, substandard housing and so on, are also as a rule, more severe in rural areas. Urban incomes are generally higher than rural incomes and urban services are sometimes more accessible. Despite this, poor town dwellers may suffer more than rural households from certain aspects of poverty. The urban poor, typically housed in slums or squatter settlements, often have to contend with appalling overcrowding, bad sanitation and contaminated water.The sites are illegal. Pollution is a constant threat.

Many of the slum dwellers are migrants from rural areas in search of better paid jobs. The effect of migration on poverty depends crucially on whether urban employment opportunities are better or worse than in rural areas.

Growth in urban employment and wages is the broad determinant of the pace of poverty reduction through its direct influence on the existing urban poor and through the opportunities it creates for rural migrants. Government can affect the urban demand for labour by altering the incentives and regulations that workers and their employers face and by providing or abstaining from providing adequate urban infrastructure.

The informal sector plays a very important role in providing jobs in urban areas. It is very diverse in its income structure and activities. It is dominated by one-person firms and small-scale entrepreneurs that employ a few apprentices (often relatives) and hired labourers. These firms are not covered by government labour regulations, and there are no restrictions on entry. But many in the informal sector pay indirect taxes and fees – such as, license fees for small vendors. Wages are generally lower than in the formal sector. There is also a high degree of inequality and many entrepreneurs do much better than workers in the formal sector. Activities range from efficient manufacturing, transport and trading entrepreneurs to marginal work such as collecting and recycling trash. Most of the sector's production is for consumption – especially by low income households and little is saved as marketable surplus.

Participatory Approach

In almost every developing country in Asia, the gap between the demand and supply of urban services, with respect to low-income communities, continues to widen. Urban services refer to physical services such as provision of water, garbage collection and disposal, electricity as well as social services such as health care, child care, education and so forth. Rapid urban growth has posed many problems, particularly in terms of the ability of city governments to deliver adequate urban services. Gradual realisation of the ineffectiveness of the service-delivery model (i.e. government provided services) has prompted experimental and innovative efforts to mobilise people's resources towards improving the urban environment. Self help and community participation have been age-old traditions by which people in rural areas in the developing countries (particularly in Asia) have satisfied their basic needs. In the cities, however, such methods of delivering basic services have only recently been developed and with varying degrees of success. This scheme is of benefit to the government in various ways. Increased participation on the part of the people can reduce the overall cost of social transfers. People-based programmes can provide government with a great deal of information on the social and economic needs of the population. Instead of costly data gathering programmes, channels are created through which information can funnel upwards. Participatory service organisations may help governments to identify potential leaders who can assist in the development process.

From the point of view of low-income communities, participation in urban services may provide physical and welfare benefits that otherwise would not be available and they promote a sense of neighbourliness within the community which is often missing in urban areas. In addition, participation in urban service delivery may open the possibilities of employment for residents of low-income communities.

The participatory approach towards delivery of basic services has been practised in many Asian countries including India for a considerable period. It has been regarded as an important instrument in poverty alleviation programmes.

The earlier poverty alleviation programmes were concerned with the supply aspect of basic services. The participatory approach tends to emphasise the demand aspect from the grassroots level. The formation of neighbourhood committees in slums will specify the nature of the demand for basic services through preparation of a mini-plan for each area. Community participation is sought in not only specifying the demand for urban services but also supervising the utilisation of such services.

Participation can be divided into two stages – planning and implementation. At the planning stage, the plans are formulated at the grassroots level and guided by the higher level authorities including the central government. Residents' participation at this stage is very necessary in formulating the area development plan. The area-specific needs are reflected in these mini-plans that are monitored at the higher authority level in order to co-ordinate it with the overall development. Residents' participation may be realised either directly or through resident organisations. These organisations are either resident - participatory or resident - representative organisations.

At the implementation stage, resident participation may be in sharing of cost. Cost sharing may be achieved in many ways by making these residents who will benefit bear the cost, by donating according to the residents' interest, direct contribution of labour, contribution of monetary equivalent of one's share of labour and the like. Residents' participation varies according to the nature of the project. For small-scale co-operative projects, residents may carry out the project by directly contributing labour. For larger projects, where the residents lack the ability to carry out such programmes, participation is generally restricted to the partial planning stage (Yeung and McGee, 1986).

The Asian Scene

In Asian countries, this new approach towards delivering community services began in the seventies. Korea became one of the world's most successful developing countries with rapid economic growth and modernisation. The physical infrastructure was rapidly expanded as a prerequisite for industrial development. Corresponding improvement in urban services was inadequate. The deliberate bias in the government's policy in favour of diverting resources towards the expansion of the industrial sector resulted in accelerated economic growth but at the same time increased economic inequality. In order to correct this overemphasised urban industrial bias, the New Community Movement (*Saemaul Undong*) was formally launched in rural Korea and gradually expanded in urban Korea. The new policies accorded with local residents' self-help aspirations become positively re-evaluated. New programmes began to mobilise local resources committed to improve poor people's living standards, particularly their housing conditions. Thus local self-help resources were incorporated into a legitimate area of municipal policies, expanding the changes of better urban services becoming accessible to the poor. The latest housing improvement programme, for instance, has extended long-term housing loans, improved loan eligibility, liberal item exemptions and improved administrative and legal procedures designed for speedy execution of neighbourhood-sponsored housing development projects to the low-income group. Gradually, the movement has taken over many functions, such as road construction, installation of sewerage lines and extending piped water to large cities (Suh, 1981).

The government provides 70 to 80 per cent of the housing finance as loan through local bodies. The residents sometimes rent parts of their dwelling in order to repay loans.

The participatory approach has been experimented with in the Philippines too. Strategies to involve communities in service delivery have been used in certain government programmes in the Philippines. However, the extent to which community participation is encouraged is not fully determined. Community participation has been observed in the provision of certain physical infrastructure. But community leaders are generally political vote-seekers, so a sustainable movement towards community participation has not been evolved. It has not been institutionalised in the service delivering agencies (Castillo, 1983).

In Malaysia, the participatory approach was first adopted by the family planning associations, focusing on population activities, particularly family life education for youths. Gradually it was directed towards various social problems faced by the young factory workers. The concept of the community gives priority to the community of young workers rather than the geographical coverage with the residents of the area although not necessarily excluding them. The workers play the roles of both educators and students simultaneously. They participate at all levels of programme implementation, that is, from determining their needs and areas of action to planning, implementation and review. A working relationship with other agencies is established to maximise resources through collaboration. But major financial support comes from the government. Other fund-raising activities are running small sales, selling greeting cards and venturing into various economic activities.

In Indonesia, the government plays a very important role in delivering social services. The programmes are channeled downwards from various government departments and are coordinated by local organisations for community security. There are several local community organisers at the local level, with special functions, such as, improving economic opportunities or helping women. The service-delivering model is so structural that it is difficult for a person with little education to understand the necessary procedures for requesting services (Economic and Social Commission of Asia and the Pacific, 1981).

In Hong Kong also the dependence on the government to cope with community problems is quite overwhelming. Government functions in Hong Kong are performed by a tightly organised and centralised bureaucracy headed primarily by expatriate officials, influenced rarely by political pressure from society. The widening gap between the people and government is not alleviated by the local governments as they do not exist. There are however voluntary Mutual Aid Committees (MACs) an outgrowth of a government experiment based initially on a genuine public concern over the inadequate provision of public security services. However, the MACs limit their activities to relatively less important services like recreational, cultural and sport needs, whereas housing, transportation and medical services are more critical needs. They are not active in organising self-help activities. Rather they are very much dependent on the government for their activities. Residents' participation in these activities tends to be low. Hong Kong has reached a level of development where basic needs in urban services, for example, water, drainage, electric power and so on, are no longer problems. Residents are concerned instead with the quality cost and availability of reviews at higher levels of technical sophistication and organisational complexity. These, the residents consider, are beyond the capability of the MACs.

Experience from different countries shows that participatory urban services are strongly dependent upon people's active involvement. Expansion of the residents' awareness of the need for and scope of such activities is urgently required. If more people can be involved at all stages of service provision, including planning, implementation and evaluation, it is more likely that the service will be provided.

The Indian Scenario

The poverty level in India as in most developing countries, is defined in terms of a level of consumption considered essential for subsistence. The poor are identified as those who do not have adequate income to secure a predetermined level of minimum consumption. The Task Force on projections of minimum needs and effective consumption demand was set up by the Planning Commission in 1977 to formulate a qualitative index of poverty. It defined the poverty line "as the mid point of monthly per capita expenditure class having daily calories intake of 2400 per person in rural areas and 2100 per person in urban areas." At 1976-77 prices the mid-points were Rs. 61.8 in rural areas and Rs. 71.3 in urban areas. These figures have been upgraded from time to time. On the basis of the above official definition of the poverty line, the number of poor in the rural and urban areas has been assessed from time to time. The basic data for this purpose have been drawn from the periodic rounds of NSS surveys of private consumer expenditure. These are now obtained through quinquennial surveys of consumer expenditure.

According to the estimate of the National Commission on Urbanisation (1988), there were nearly 57 million urban poor in the country in 1987-88 and as of now, it is estimated that nearly 60 million of the people living in the urban areas belong to the category of urban poor. The study on the urban poor by the National Institute of Urban Affairs (1988) reveals that 68 per cent of them are women and children. Urban poverty manifests itself in the proliferation of slums, rapid growth of the informal sector, inadequate supply of civic services, underutilisation of the labour force and so forth. About two-thirds of the poor urban households are engaged in the informal sector. Generally the average capital investment on a worker in the formal sector is about 25 to 30 times higher than that in the informal sector (Linn, 1983). The percentage of casual labour in the informal sector increased from 13.2 percent to 14.5 percent (National Sample Survey Organisation, 1986). Child labour accounts for 8 per cent of total employment in the informal sector.

In India's development strategy, removal of poverty became a dominant objective initially in the Fifth Five-Year Plan (1974-79). The earlier plans mentioned the existence of large scale poverty in the country, but there was no proper analysis of the dimension of the problem. The Fifth Plan noted that the consumption levels of the bottom 30 per cent of the country's population with their share of only 13.46 per cent of the total private consumption, remained far below the minimum of Rs. 40.6 (1972-73 prices) per capita per month required to stay just above the poverty line. It however made no distinction between rural and urban poverty. It stressed the need to raise the share of the bottom 30 per cent in total private consumption to about 21.98 per cent. It suggested to the economic growth processes and national level programmes such as the Minimum Needs Programme, public procurement and distribution of essential goods.

The Sixth Plan (1980-85) started a more definite approach to poverty issues in the country. It observed that the growth process was not enough for the removal of poverty. Specific policy measures were needed to influence the composition of output in favour of mass consumption goods. It observed that nearly 51 per cent of the rural population and 41 per cent of urban population were living below the poverty line in 1979-80. Different programmes were suggested for urban areas and rural areas in order to reduce each of the abovementioned percentages to 30. But characteristically, the Sixth Plan showed a distinct bias towards rural poverty by implementing various rural poverty alleviation programmes.

The Seventh Plan (1985-90) constitutes the first conscious attempt to address urban poverty issues directly. It observes that the persistent migration from rural areas has led to the rapid growth of slums in many urban settlements. This has led to overcrowding in relatively unskilled and low paid jobs in the informal sector. The problem of urban poverty would require a major thrust towards employment generation and skill formation.

From the era of the Fifth Plan there has been a perceptible change in the approach to urban poverty issues in India. From a welfare and service-oriented strategy there has been a shift towards poverty alleviation through expansion of employment opportunities and raising of the productivity levels of those engaged in jobs with low productivity.

There has been a change in the approach to the management of urban services also. From a trickle-down service-delivering mode the gradual shift is towards increasing community participation at all stages of service provision – planning, implementation and evaluation (National Institute of Urban Affairs, 1988).

Urban Poverty Alleviation Programmes in India

The National Commission on Urbanisation has classified the current urban poverty alleviation programmes in the following manner:

1. Shelter and physical environment related programmes
2. Nutrition supplement programmes including public distribution
3. Programmes for employment generation
4. Programmes for the development of citizen participation and development of institutional capacities of service agencies.

1. Slum clearance was the key approach in the shelter-related programmes during the First and Second Plans. The resistance of

the local population to be relocated, paucity of resources and maintenance problems were the main reasons behind abandoning this approach. This has been replaced by the programmes of slum improvement and sites and services scheme. Various housing schemes based on income criteria are also in operation. The government has introduced a hire purchase scheme in housing where the economically weaker section gets special privileges in terms of low interest rates and some direct subsidy.

The water supply and sanitation programme has made some progress, but is still insufficient in the face of growing congestion in urban areas. These programmes are highly capital intensive and are carried out at the central and state government levels leaving maintenance to be taken care of by the local bodies.

2. The public distribution system aims at providing a balanced diet at reasonable prices in the poverty-stricken, malnourished parts of the country. But actually the offtake from the public distribution system is greater in urban areas than in rural ones. The Integrated Child Development Services (ICDS) aims at providing nutritional food to children of the rural and tribal areas where the incidence of malnutrition among children is very high. Among the general programmes of child development, the spread of free education is aimed at covering all the children of the urban poor (National Commission on Urbanisation, 1988).

3. Various state governments run various income-generating programmes in slums. The central government launched income-generating programmes known as Self-Employment Programme for the Urban Poor (SEPUP) in urban areas in 1986.

   The Nehru Rozgar Yojana (NRY) was launched in 1989. It has been designed to provide employment to the underemployed and unemployed poor residing in urban areas. This employment is of two types: one relating to the setting up of self-employment ventures and the other to wage employment through shelter upgradation works and creation of public assets in the low income neighbourhoods of urban local bodies. Specifically, it consists of three schemes: (i) micro enterprises, (ii) urban wage employment, and (iii) housing and shelter upgradation. (i) The first scheme is applicable to all urban settlements in the country excluding areas falling under cantonment boards (SEPUP was merged with it afterwards). (ii) The second is applicable to all urban settlements with a population below one lakh. But in states like Sikkim and the North Eastern Hill Area, class I cities (population above one lakh) will come under this scheme provided that the state governments ensure that this will not lead to enhanced inmigration from rural areas, nor reduce the pace of development in other areas. (iii) The third scheme is applicable to all cities with a population between one and 20 lakhs with a relaxation for towns with a population of less than one lakh in the case of the North Eastern Hill States end Sikkim and for similar towns in the hill districts of other states and for newly industrialising townships.

The urban poor constitute the broad target group of NRY. Within this target group, women and beneficiaries belonging to scheduled castes and scheduled tribes constitute special target groups. It is expected that broadly 30 per cent of the beneficiaries setting up self-employed ventures should be women. Further, funds proportionate to their share in the urban population will be earmarked for beneficiaries belonging to scheduled castes and scheduled tribes.

4. The most significant effort on the part of the government to foster active community participation on a sustainable basis in the urban sector is through the Urban Community Development (UCD) projects which had their origin in the rural community development projects started in 1952. In 1958, the first pilot project in urban community development was initiated in Delhi with the assistance of the Ford Foundation. The Third Five Year Plan mentioned the need for each city to mobilise its own resources to create better conditions for its citizens and emphasized the need for urban community development.

UCD is designed to function as part of the local body and is reviewed as a link between the people and the municipal corporation. The objective is to strengthen local voluntary organisations and establish bustee (slum) level agencies in order to cover activities normally not covered towards creation of stronger communities with their own leaders who can plan finance and carry out self-help projects. At present UCD projects are in operation in 18 towns and cities.

The initiation of the Urban Basic Services (UBS) Programme in 1985 and the Self-Employment Programme for the Urban Poor

(SEPUP) in 1986 was a major step in this direction. In 1985, the UCD, Low Cost Sanitation and the Small and Medium Town Development Projects were merged into a new programme called the Urban Basic Services (UBS). Here the emphasis is on evolving a mechanism under which basic services particularly those related to child and maternal health, basic education, income earning opportunities for women and the like which affect the quality of life can be developed, utilised and maintained in an effective participatory manner. The National Commission on Urbanisation has supported these programmes as a 'compelling necessity' in the context of present day 'urban reality.'

The UBS aimed at institutionalising community participation and bringing various government organisations, NGOs and urban slum dwellers together in providing the basic services. It tried to involve the local community at all stages of development namely, planning, implementation and monitoring of the programme activities.

Community participation at every step is essential for shaping local demand, better utilisation of the services supplied and maintenance of the facilities provided.

During the Eighth Plan, further convergence of various programmes has been sought under the name of Urban Basic Services for the Poor (UBSP). This has been described as the most important component of the Urban Poverty Alleviation Programme to be converged at the local level with other programmes such as EIUS, Low Cost Sanitation Programmes and NRY. UBSP is presently being implemented in 618 towns spread over all the major states. Its prime objective, besides the service delivery, is to empower the local people, especially the women through development of leadership and make the community self-reliant in sustaining the development.

The role of UNICEF needs special mention here. Pursuing a participatory and community development approach, UNICEF has been able to reach a significantly larger proportion of the poor and improve their habitat and accessibility to basic services. There are many examples in different parts of the world where this approach has made its impact, the Hyderabad Urban Community Development project being one of them. This approach has helped urban communities in improving their own living conditions at costs which are low, affordable and within the means of the poor.

UNICEF has given substantial financial support in promoting various programmes such as the UCD, small and medium town development and low cost sanitation. It has been a major funding partner in launching UBS, contributing 40 per cent of the project cost. The rest of the finance was shared by the central and state governments. However, this financial assistance has been discontinued since UBSP has been launched. UNICEF is now providing financial support for training facilities for the project officials.

The Present Study

A number of studies have been conducted on the availability of basic services in urban areas. In 1987-88, the National Institute of Urban Affairs (NIUA) conducted an all-India study on basic services for the urban poor based on a household survey in 79 UBS towns. There are many more town level studies focused on these aspects. These studies generally focused on access to basic services by the slum dwellers, rather than their involvement in the delivery and utilisation of these services.

The present study specifically emphasises the UBS programmes in selected cities and the extent and nature of community participation in managing their supply. It also describes to a certain extent other community development programmes running simultaneously in these areas.

Four cities, where UBS is in progress, have been selected in this study. They are Baroda (or Vadodara), Bhilwara, Sambalpur and Siliguri. Each of them has experienced rapid population growth associated with lack of adequate civic services. The main objectives may be described as follows:

- To analyse the regional dimension of urban poverty with special focus on the availability of basic services to the urban poor
- To analyse various policy measures and programmes initiated by the Government of India for providing basic social and physical amenities to the urban poor.
- To assess the extent of people's participation in poverty alleviation programmes at the local government and the beneficiary levels with special reference to the Urban Basic Services programme.
- To suggest measures for improving the living conditions of the urban poor as well as expanding the area of community participation.

The economic profile of the surveyed cities provides a glimpse into the pattern of urbanisation and consequent provision of basic services in these settlements. The city of Baroda experienced phenomenal industrial growth during the sixties. It is the second major industrial centre in Gujarat next to Ahmedabad. It is also recognised as the prime educational centre. It is linked with the major growth centres within and outside the state through National Highways and a railway network. The economic strength of the city attracts migrants from both within and outside the state. In 1981, the migrants formed approximately 24 per cent of the total city population of Baroda. This has increased to 30 per cent in 1991. The city's share in the total urban population of the state has also increased from 5.8 per cent in 1961 to over 7 per cent in 1991. It acquired metropolitan status in the 1991 census. Simultaneously the number of slums also has been increasing continuously.

Bhilwara is situated in a belt rich in minerals and cotton. After Independence, it has emerged as one of the important industrial centres of Rajasthan with considerable potential for further growth and development. Bhilwara's population has increased from 43,499 in 1961 to 183,791 in 1991 – an increase of more than 300 percent in 30 years.

Today, Bhilwara is the ninth most populous urban centre in Rajasthan. The gap between population growth and economic development however persists resulting in an increasing growth of slums. There are fifty such slums in Bhilwara scattered over various parts of the city.

Sambalpur municipal town is one among the principal urban centres of the state, where on the whole, the level of urbanisation is low. From a small urban centre till 1971, Sambalpur became a class I city in 1981. It does not have an industrial base like the previous two cities, but thrives as an important market place for the hinterland. The two National Highways running through the cities have also improved its position promoting a flourishing transport sector and also a vibrant service sector. With increasing population growth, the slum population consists of more than half of the total city population. The number of slums in Sambalpur has nearly doubled during 1981-91.

Siliguri was declared an urban area in 1951 with a population of just over six thousand. Within a span of 40 years, the city population grew to more than two lakhs, making Siliguri the most urbanised settlement in the whole of North Bengal, which is otherwise the least urbanised area in the state. Siliguri maintains a vital link for the trade between India and Sikkim, Bhutan, Nepal and Tibet. The Assam rail link in the 1950s made this town a gateway to North-East India. The National Highway No. 31 passes through the city. It is basically a market town. Since 1960, it has become an important centre for wholesale trade. It offers strong potential for industrialisation as well.

A significant component of population growth in Siliguri has been the inflow of ordinary and extraordinary migration. Extraordinary migration is caused by the inflow of refugee populations from time to time. The strategic location of the town as well as its strong economic base as an important trade centre have been instrumental in attracting refugee and non-refugee migrants from within and outside the country.

All the four cities display certain common characteristics. Within a span of three decades they have experienced urban concentration too fast to be matched by the adequate flow of basic services. The economic strength of these urban centres has rapidly changed the size of their settlements, creating gross deficiencies in the supply of essential services. The thrust of urban growth has created pressure on the existing assets of the city consequently impoverishing the city-base. Rapid migration from inside and outside the respective states has overstressed existing health, sanitary, environmental and educational facilities and services. Congestion and the lack of access to industrial and commercial locations have become serious problems. Unemployment and poverty have escalated because the labour force has been expanding steadily. The urban infrastructure that has been assembled slowly over several years has suddenly become inadequate for the city dwellers lowering per capita availability of services. All these lead to the need for institutional adjustment as well as community participation in service provision. In the short run, self-help services have met some of the basic needs of low-income populations. But the longer term viability and strength of this approach will have to depend on the acceptance and popularity of innovative methods by residents and policy options that government planners and administrators follow.

Methodology

The present study on urban poverty, basic services and local participation is based on a primary survey of 1600 households in 68 slums spread over the four cities of Baroda, Bhilwara, Sambalpur and Siliguri.

The number of sample households is spread equally in the four cities, each city having 400 households. The number of slums, however, is not equally distributed. The slums, where the centrally sponsored Urban Basic Services (UBS) scheme is going on are selected. The number of slums is approximately half of the total UBS slums in each city. These slums are representative of the city in terms of geographical location and social variations.

The number of households to be covered in each sample slum has been decided according to its share in the total population of the sample slums. The proportional distribution can be described as follows:

$$h_i = \frac{Hi}{H} \times 400$$

Where h_i = Number of sample households in slum i

H_i = Number of total households in slum i

H = Total number of households in the sample slums in each city.

The households are evenly spread within each slum in order to represent the general socio-economic character of the slums.

The primary data-base has been generated from a three-part structured questionnaire regarding various aspects of basic services and poverty alleviation programmes. The first part is related to the socio-economic background of the slum households. The second part consists of questions on basic services, (education, housing, electricity, water supply, sanitation and health) as well as on participatory activities. The third part deals with information on income generation programmes.

Information has also been collected from two other sources:

(i) Extensive talks with officials of municipal corporations, other government officials and people from different voluntary organisations which have been directly involved in the city development programme.

(ii) general observation of the sample slums by the surveyors. The data-base has been generated both at the organisation level constituting the supply of, and at the household level, consisting of the demand for basic services in order to examine the nature of community participation.

The study presents the results of a comparative analysis of four cities beginning with a conceptual background and city profile. Each of the following four chapters presents an overview of the existing service-delivery programmes in the individual cities followed by a detailed discussion of household survey. The last chapter draws together common themes and issues that run throughout the individual studies. It also suggests some recommendations towards more effective utilisation of the participatory approach.

NOTE

Recently, the Lakdawala Committee set up by the Planning Commission has recommended certain changes in its report (1993) in the measurement of poverty. The committee suggests that a minimum living standard should be adopted in measuring poverty by taking bath food and non-food consumptions on the basis of the observed consumer behaviour. The report of the committee is still under consideration.

REFERENCES

Castillo, G. T. (1983), *How Participatory is Participatory Development? A Review of the Philippine Experience*, Philippine Institute for Development Studies, Makati, Philippines.

Economic and Social Commission for Asia and the Pacific (1981), *Migration, Urbanization and Development in Indonesia*, ESCAP, Bangkok, Thailand.

Linn, J. F. (1983), *Cities in the Developing World*, Oxford University Press, New York.

Myrdal, Gunnar (1968), *Asian Drama*, Pantheon, New York.

National Commission on Urbanisation (1988), *Report*, Vol. II, NCU, New Delhi.

National Institute of Urban Affairs (1988), *Approach to Urban Poverty: A Position Note*, NIUA, New Delhi.

National Institute of Urban Affairs (1991), *Basic Services and the Urban Poor*, NIUA, New Delhi.

National Sample Survey Organisation (1986), *Sarvekshana*, April, Central Statistical Organisation, New Delhi.

Suh, S. M. (1981), *Reality of the Poor and Public Policy*, Korea Development Institute, Seoul, South Korea.

United Nations Research Institute on Social Development (1970), *Content and Measurement of Socio-Economic Development*, UNRISD, Geneva.

World Bank (1990), *World Development Report*.

Yeung, Y. M. and T. G. McGee (eds) (1986), *Community Participation in Delivering Urban Services in Asia*, International Development Research Institute, Ottawa, Canada.

Chapter II

BARODA

CITY PROFILE

Baroda is one of the most industrialised cities of the country and the second major industrial centre in Gujarat, next to Ahmedabad. The city experienced phenomenal industrial growth during the sixties. The setting up of industries like the Gujarat Refinery in 1965, Gujarat State Fertiliser Corporation in 1967, Indian Petrochemical Corporation in 1969, along with the oil find in Ankleshwar near the city in 1960 improved its economic importance. Several other major industrial units and a number of small scale ancillary industries came on their heels. The city at present has over 500 registered industries with a multiple of medium and small scale and cottage industries.

In addition, Baroda is also recognised as the seat of learning of the state with a number of prime educational centres being situated in the city. Its locational advantage of links with major growth centres in and outside the state through National Highways and a railway network has boosted its economic importance. The setting up of three industrial complexes by the Gujarat Industrial Development Corporation (GIDC) and three more estates by private and cooperative establishments added more importance to the city.

As a consequence, the city experienced a tremendous population growth during the last ten decades mainly owing to influx from rural and small urban centres within and outside the state. The city had a migrant population numbering 1,75,685 in 1981 which was nearly 24 per cent of the total population of 734,473 at that time. Though the 1991 migration figures are not available yet, unofficial estimates show that they are nearly 3,04,453 or 30 per cent of the current population of 10,21,084 in the Baroda municipal area. The overall city population which grew by 50 to 58 per cent during the two decades previous to the last, showed however, a significant decline in the growth rate to 39 per cent. Table 2.1 shows that the city's share in total urban population in the state has increased from 5.8 per cent in 1961 to over seven per cent in 1991 although it has maintained a constant proportion in the district urban population over these decades.

Table 2.1
Trend in Urbanisation in the State of Gujarat, Baroda District and City

Year	Total urban population (thousands)			Per cent decadal variation in urban population			Per cent of city's population in relation to urban population	
	State	District	City	State	District	City	State	District
1961	5371	397	310	-	-	-	5.8	77.9
1971	7497	603	467	41.00	51.75	50.94	6.8	77.5
1981	10602	951	745	41.42	57.58	57.11	6.9	77.3
1991	14164	1316	1021	33.60	38.45	39.02	7.21	77.6

Source: Census of India, 1991a.

The city has acquired its metropolitan status in the 1991 census and its population is expected to touch 18 million by the end of the century (ORG 1990).

The state's first metropolitan city Ahmedabad having reached the saturation point in terms of industrial growth and employment potential, Baroda along with Surat has become the alternative pull centre. During the last two decades Ahmedabad experienced considerably lower urban growth than Surat and Baroda although the rates of urban growth have reduced to a significant extent in all three metropolitan centres during the last decade (Table 2.2).

Table 2.2
Trend in Growth of Metropolises in Gujarat

Urban centres	Total population	Growth rate		Density
		1971-81	1981-91	
Ahmedabad	28,72,865	45.94	28.94	12525
Surat	14,96,943	92.63	62.03	8426
Baroda	10,21,084	57.11	39.02	6784

Source: Census of India, 1991a.

The city has grown physically from an area of 21.37 sq.km in 1901 to 108.22 sq.km in 1961, reaching 150 sq.km at present. Exorbitant growth in urban population has put tremendous pressure on space and nearly 6784 persons live in one square kilometre area as against 394 in the district and 210 in the state.

The rapid growth of the city population has led to phenomenal increase in slums and slum population. The number of slums recorded a continuous increase from only 20 in 1920 to 255 in 1982 and 336 in 1992. There has been a 32 per cent growth in the number of slums during the last 10 years. The slum population at the same time has grown from 94,705 in 1982 to an estimated figure of 2,21,052 in 1992. Therefore, while the city population grew by 39 per cent during the last decade, the slum population registered an increase of more than 100 per cent.

If the *chawls* and other very low quality housing are also considered, the population without adequate shelter and basic services will be more than the estimated figure.

Basic Services and Response of Local Government

Tremendous population pressure has made the existing infrastructure for providing basic services utterly inadequate. Although Baroda is an ideal example where the participatory development process has been adopted by the city authorities (municipal corporation, and other sectoral authorities), industrial houses and the NGOs, a substantial portion of households is still deprived of very minimum basic facilities such as water supply, drainage, roads, and so forth. A very recent survey by the United Way of Vadodara reveals that only 70 per cent of the sample households (4167 selected from all over the city from all strata of population) covered had access to adequate drinking water, only 53.2 per cent had individual bathrooms and 59.8 per cent had individual toilets. While 76 per cent households had electricity connections in their houses, sewage connection was available only to 66 per cent of them. More than 23 per cent of the sample households lived in *Kachcha* houses, only 31.5 per cent of those had adequate water, 8.5 per cent could have the facility of a separate bathroom and 15 per cent a separate toilet and only 35 per cent of them had electricity connections (United Way of Vadodara, 1991).

It is important to note the role of the Baroda Municipal Corporation (BMC) in this regard. The Corporation, which is the primary authority in providing basic services to its population and is one among the oldest local governments, has been facing a tremendous pressure on its available resources for providing essential services. Although municipal revenues have increased from a paltry amount of Rs.3.44 lakhs in 1911 to as high as 6802.31 lakhs in 1990 it has become utterly inadequate to serve the growing population. Because of high revenue expenditure the city authority cannot incur the huge capital expenditure required to meet the rising demand for urban services in the city. The trend in the municipal expenditure patterns of 1987-88 and 1990-91 in Table 2.3 shows that the establishment cost and the maintenance cost of municipal assets are the two heads of expenditure which together constitute more than 62 per cent of the total expenditure of the corporation in both the reference periods. It is also noticed that expenditure on these two accounts has more than doubled during this period. In contrast the expenditure on capital projects which is considered to be for the development and construction of new

Table 2.3
Income and Expenditure of Baroda Municipal Corporation: 1987-88 and 1990-91

	1987-88 (Rs in lakhs)	Per cent to total	1990-91 (Rs in lakhs)	Per cent to total	Per cent increase 1987-88 to 1990-91
Establishment	1036.91	30.98	2213.97	32.55	113.42
Contingency	33.57	1.01	84.44	1.24	151.53
Maintenance	1088.49	32.53	2178.05	32.02	100.1
Primary education	558.43	16.69	968.57	14.24	73.44
Loan charges	474.9	14.19	642.28	9.44	35.24
Capital projects	154.20	4.61	715.00	10.51	363.68
Total own expenditure	3346.51	100.00	6802.31	100.00	103.26
Loan expenditure	621.70	-	1320.76	-	112.44
Total own income	3503.29	-	6712.31	-	91.60
Loan income	383.53	-	1106.00	-	188.52

Source: Baroda Municipal Corporation, Unpublished Records.

infrastructure, though registered an increase of 363.68 per cent from 1987-88 to 1990-91, constituted merely 4.61 and 10.51 per cent respectively of the total municipal expenditure in these two reference periods. Table 2.3 further shows that while total municipal expenditure has grown by 103.26 per cent, its income has increased only by 91.6 per cent and the corporation has had to fall back upon more and more loan income which has grown during this period by more than 188 per cent.

Shelter and Basic Services Programmes for the Poor

Despite the resource constraints, however, the city administration has undertaken several initiatives to improve the shelter and basic services condition of the poor and the city population, especially from state government grants and loan income from different agencies such as Housing and Urban Development Corporation (HUDCO), Life Insurance Corporation (LIC), and the state government. It has also taken recourse to open market borrowing and loans from the World Bank for specific development projects for the poor. The local government has undertaken two types of approaches for ameliorating the conditions of the poor by improving their quality of life. Under the first approach there are local programmes specific to the local needs, planned and implemented by the local body in cooperation with other sectoral authorities. They are financed by a mix of the local body's own revenue income, loan income and grants from the state government. These are mainly infrastructure development projects with no grassroots level participation. The others are basically participatory programmes to be implemented by involving the people at every stage through some structured institutional framework at the community level.

Though the main focus of this study is the participatory programmes mainly the UBS, it is necessary to have a glance at other programmes to assess the situation of basic services in the poor localities of the city. Baroda Municipal Corporation is one among the very few local bodies which has undertaken Low Cost Housing Projects for the poor. It has constructed 1160 slum quarters under the slum clearance scheme of Government of India. As many as 1464 tenements were constructed under the low cost housing programme for flood affected people in 1970 which were allotted on a hire-purchase basis on monthly instalments of Rs. 19. It has also provided 3494 housing units for economically weaker sections (EWS) and low income group (LIG) under HUDCO assisted programmes. The Corporation had created a special Revolving Fund for generating housing stock under which 328 LIG houses were constructed. In addition under the International Year of Shelter for Homeless (IYSH) programme it has resettled more than 1000 slum households under the site and services scheme by giving them land plots with proper drainage and water supply facilities, where the slum dwellers themselves have constructed *pucca* houses by self-help.

It has also undertaken several basic services schemes like the Basic Sanitation Scheme and the Environmental Improvement of Urban Slums Project. Family Welfare and Universal Immunisation Programmes and the Integrated Child Development Services (ICDS) have also been undertaken to improve the health condition of the poor especially women and children.

Participatory Development Programmes of UCD and UBS

Baroda has a long tradition of participatory development initiatives undertaken by the local body and non-governmental organisations. The first such community based programme, the Baroda Urban Community Development Project was initiated here in 1965 under the guidance and financial assistance from the American Friends Service Society and was later handed over to the Baroda Citizens Council (BCC) one of the oldest non-governmental organisations in the city. The BCC since then has been continuing the programme and at present serves 18 slum localities covering 12,209 households with a population of 56,268 with provision for non-formal education, health, economic welfare, basic amenities and suchlike, and helps in developing local leadership. While working with the people in slums, the Council insists on the active participation by the community in contributing finance or offering material and human support.

Baroda Municipal Corporation is implementing two such programmes based on self help - the Urban Community Development (UCD) Programme and the Urban Basic Services (UBS) Programmes. The Urban Community Development Programme which was started in the latter part of 1980 now caters to 80,000 population in slums.

The Urban Basic Services Programme on the other hand, is a new addition to the development programmes in the city. Adopted in 1987, the UBS programme like the UCD ensures the provision of health care for children and women, education and basic services facilities like water supply and sanitation besides conducting training programmes for capacity building and skill formation. The programme at present covers a population of 42755 in 29 slums.

The main objective of the programme at the local level is to make people understand their problems and try to solve them with the guidance of community organisers who work as the contact between the local government and the people.

Organisational Set up and Financing of UBS

Organisation of the UBS programme starts from the grassroots level. In order to reach the ultimate beneficiaries 29 Neighbourhood Committees (NHCs) have been formed in 29 UBS project slums in Baroda. Each NHC or Basti Committee consists of 15 members who are the resident community volunteers (RCVs). Each RCV represents 20 to 25 houses in his/her locality. Through regular meetings the NHCs take up the matter with the local authority with the help of the community organisers (COs) and try to solve them with active community participation.

The Basti Committee in each slum helps in organising various programmes such as medical camps, sewing classes, immunisation camps, adult literacy classes, study centres and so on. It helps in identifying the beneficiaries and also tries to arrange for equipments needed for their programmes.

At the local government level there is an Advisory Committee or Project Management Committee whose members include the department heads of the BMC and some experts in specific fields. The Advisory Committee through its regular quarterly meetings monitors the programmes. Besides, the BMC Commissioner also convenes a meeting every week in which the UBS programme is discussed. The elected municipal corporators also take interest in the UBS in their respective wards and discuss the problems with the project officials. The Project Director at the municipal level is in charge of the functional responsibility.

The project officer (PO) of the BMC coordinates the activity with the help of the seven community organisers.

The programme during the last five years since its inception has provided social services such as health, education facilities; physical services like sanitation and drinking water supply; and economic services such as income generating activities for women, training for women and so on, for all round development of the slum households (For achievements of the programme see Appendix 1.1).

Financing of the programme was the responsibility of the UNICEF, central and state governments and the BMC until very recently. The financing pattern has changed from 1992 for the Eighth Plan period. Now UNICEF is only actively involved in training the functionaries at different levels and many new schemes have been brought under the new programme. The funding pattern also has changed from a lump sum amount per city to per capita allocation for the new project areas under the revised programme of Urban Basic Services for the Poor or UBSP.

Table 2.4
Expenditure Pattern of UBS Project

	Activities	1987 to March 1991 (Rs)	April '91 to March 1992 (Rs)	Total up to March '92 (Rs)	Percentage total Expenditure
1.	Health	85,732	30,377	1,16,109	8.37
2.	Education	5,118	75,829	80,947	5.83
3.	Income generation activities for women	68,366	51,239	1,19,605	8.61
4.	Training/orientation/refresher courses	4,715	-	4,715	0.34
5.	Sanitation	2,18,261	3,780	2,22,041	15.99
6.	Drinking water	25,200	-	25,200	1.81
7.	Equipment/supplies	68,062	310	68,372	4.92
8.	Others	8,044	-	8,044	0.58
	Total	4,83,498	1,61,535	6,45,033	46.46
Salary of project staff		4,52,187	2,63,892	7,16,079	51.57
Administrative expenditure		14,747	12,683	27,430	1.97
Total expenditure		9,50,423	4,38,110	13,88,533	100.00
Total grants received		10,06,188	6,34,822	16,40,010	
Balance		55,765	1,96,712	2,52,477	

Source: Baroda Municipal Corporation, Unpublished Records.

Although around Rs.14 lakhs have been spent for the programme since its inception in 1987 till March 1992 the expenditure on various social and physical components has been very minimum. The financing pattern of the programme shows that out of the total expenditure only 46.46 per cent or Rs. 6.4 lakhs have been spent for different development components. Sanitation has been given the highest priority among all the services as the figures show. It must be highlighted that the administrative expenditure and the salary of the project staff accounted for more than half or 53.54 per cent of the allocated fund (Table 2.4).

THE SURVEY

It is against the background of the city and the approach to its problems that the present section provides an analysis of the findings from the household survey conducted in Baroda slums. The objective of the survey was to assess the access of the households to basic services in UBS project slums and the nature and form of awareness and involvement of the community in the basic services programmes, especially the UBS.

Information was collected from three different sources during the survey: (i) household survey through 3-part structured questionnaire schedules, (ii) extensive talks with officials of municipal corporation, other government officials and people from different voluntary organisations which have been directly involved in the city development programmes, and (iii) observations of the slums by the researcher.

For the household survey 400 schedules were canvassed in 16 slums. For the questionnaire survey a two-stage sample was used. The first stage comprised the selection of 16 slums out of 29 under the UBS programme since its introduction in the city. The UCD slums and slums under the revised UBSP Programme started recently were not considered because the situation in these slums might not be comparable with the UBS slums so far as the basic services were concerned. In the selection of the slums due consideration was given to secure a fair cross sectional representation over land status, topographic, social and economic characteristics. In the second stage 400 households were selected at the slum level. The number of households in each locality was decided according to its share in the total population of the surveyed slums (for example, if slum A has a population which is 20 per cent of the total population of 16 slums taken together, then the same per centage or 80 households were selected from slum A). The respondents were selected for the questionnaire survey using the systematic sampling technique. The Table 2.5 shows the distribution of surveyed households over selected slums.

Table 2.5
Distribution of 400 Sample Households over Selected Slums

Sl. No.	Name of the slums	Total no. of households	Number of sample households
1.	Bajaniwas	200	15
2.	Bapa Nagar	200	15
3.	Chatriyanagar	380	29
4.	Dewalipura	190	15
5.	Govind Nagar	700	55
6.	Hanuman Tekra	125	10
7.	Harijanwas	120	10
8.	Jalaram Nagar	500	39
9.	Jasoda Nagar	600	47
10.	Jayaram Nagar	445	35
11.	Jayajaitri Nagar	350	27
12.	MES School	150	12
13.	Mujhmunda	435	34
14.	Ramdev Nagar	480	37
15.	Rangawadpura	114	10
16.	Opp. Sewage Canal	130	10
		5119	400

The analysis of the survey data first gives a short profile of the social, demographic and economic characteristics of the sample households in our survey. It discusses the accessibility of basic services to the households and their responses to the UBS programme at slum level and also at the household level, across different income classes. To highlight the trend in the availability of services to slum households during the last one decade efforts have been made to compare the present survey findings with those of two other such exercises done by two other agencies in Baroda slums at different points of time. In 1982, Operations Research Group (ORG) analysed the data from a survey conducted by the BMC in all the 255 slums in the city at that time. The second was done by the National Institute of Urban Affairs (NIUA) in 1988 on the basis of its own survey in 9 slums of Baroda among 213 households as part of its all India study on Basic Services for the Urban Poor. Although the sample sizes varied from one study to another, the purpose and nature of these two studies, however, were almost similar to our study in so far as the aspects of basic services were concerned

Socio-demographic Characteristics of Sample Households

The sample households in our survey consisted of five members on an average with little inter-slum variation (Table 2.6). The average size of our sample family though not much different from that of an average household of 5.2 (NIUA, 1988) in a slum on an all India basis, was a little higher than the average family size of the slums of Baroda which was 4.4 in 1982 (ORG 1986). In fact the ORG survey showed that there had been a decline in family size from 4.8 in 1976 to 4.4 in 1982.

Our survey shows that out of 400 households, 92 per cent are Hindus while the remaining 8 per cent comprise Muslims and Sikhs. The surveyed slums are dominated by Scheduled Castes and Scheduled Tribes (SCs and STs) with more than three-fourths or 78 per cent of the surveyed households belonging to these categories. This characteristic is clearly in contrast with the all-slums average of the SC/ST population in Baroda, which was only 33 per cent of the total population in 1982 (ORG 1986).

Table 2.6
Social Background of Sample Households

Slum Pocket	No. of sample households	Total no. of persons	Average size of household	Per cent		
				Language (Gujarati)	Religion (Hindu)	General Caste
Bajaniwas	15	78	5	93	87	13
Bapa Nagar	15	78	5	100	100	20
Chatriyanagar	29	144	5	38	93	34
Dewalipura	15	68	5	100	100	20
Govind Nagar	55	260	5	67	96	24
Hanuman Tekra	10	43	4	100	100	0
Harijanwas	10	46	5	100	100	0
Jalaram Nagar	39	182	5	59	79	5
Jasoda Nagar	47	225	5	30	100	23
Jayaram Nagar	35	173	5	100	100	0
Jayajaitri Nagar	27	127	5	81	89	33
MES School	12	70	6	0	0	100
Mujhmunda	34	180	5	50	88	41
Ramdev Nagar	37	189	5	95	100	11
Rangawadpura	10	57	6	100	100	20
Opp. Sewage Canal	10	47	5	80	100	40
All Slums	400	1967	5	69	92	22

Source: Field Survey, Baroda, ISS, 1992.

The migrant population in our sample is more than 51 per cent (Table 2.7). Many of them were old migrants who had come here more than ten years ago and the majority came when the city's industrialisation process started with great momentum in the sixties. Though the average migrancy length is 9 years, 67 per cent of those migrant households came to the city more than ten years ago. Therefore it may be said that the exorbitant growth in the number of slums and slum population as observed during the last decade was more due to natural increase than migration into the city.

Many of the migrants came here in search of employment as 40 per cent households reported 'job' as the sole reason for coming to the city. Another major reason was education. However, reasons such as family migration, education, natural calamities, like drought and floods also forced many of them to come to the city.

Table 2.7
Nature of Migrancy among Sample Households

Slum pockets	Migrants (per cent)	Migrancy length (years)	Per cent above 10 years of migrancy	Per cent migrancy reason (job)	Per cent migrant	
					Within state	Outside state
Bajaniwas	40	15	100	40	27	13
Bapa Nagar	40	10	50	20	7	33
Chatriyanagar	90	10	62	69	31	59
Dewalipura	40	10	17	47	33	7
Govind Nagar	42	10	83	27	11	33
Hanuman Tekra	70	8	14	60	60	10
Harijanwas	30	10	33	30	30	0
Jalaram Nagar	64	10	72	46	36	28
Jasoda Nagar	77	5	69	68	39	38
Jayaram Nagar	3	10	0	0	3	0
Jayajaitri Nagar	59	10	75	41	56	4
MES School	17	10	50	8	17	0
Mujhmunda	53	10	78	41	12	41
Ramdev Nagar	59	10	68	49	54	5
Rangawadpura	30	7	67	30	30	0
Opp. Sewage Canal	30	8	100	20	10	20
All Slums	51	9	67	40	25	26

Source: Field Survey, Baroda, ISS, 1992.

It is not that the migrant households consisted only of Gujarati people from neighbouring districts. Baroda slums show typical characteristics of a slum in a metropolitan city with inmigration from all parts of the country. In our sample out of total 204 migrant households 49.5 per cent belonged to different parts of the state of Gujarat, while the remaining 50.5 per cent comprised people from states such as Maharashtra, Uttar Pradesh, Rajasthan and others (Table 2.8).

Table 2.8
Distribution of Migrant Households in Surveyed Slums over Place of Origin

State	No. of migrant households	Per cent
Gujarat	101	49.50
Maharashtra	26	12.74
Uttar Pradesh	48	23.53
Rajasthan	18	8.82
Bihar	7	3.43
Others	4	1.96
Total	204	100.00

Source: Field Survey; Baroda, ISS, 1992.

A majority of the surveyed slums or 56 per cent of them have more than 50 per cent migrant population and in some cases it is above 90 per cent. The slums which are very old and situated on private lands usually have a lower migrant population.

The age and sex composition of the 1967 members of the sample households is seen in Table 2.9. The number of children is slightly more than the adult members. Children constituted 53.78 per cent of the total population.

The number of females among both children and adults is much lower than that of males, resulting in a sex ratio of 870 which is substantially lower than the all India average of 932 and even lower than that of the city which was estimated to be 898 in 1991. Moreover in contrast to the increase in sex ratio of the city population from 889 in 1981 to the present level, there has been in fact a decline in the sex ratio in the slums from 894 in 1982 to the present level of 872. The decline in the sex ratio in the slums may be because of decreasing family migration which seems to have contributed significantly to the overall decline in the migration to the slums during the last decade as observed earlier.

Table 2.9
Age-Sex Composition of Population in Surveyed Slums

Slum pockets	No. of sample house-holds	Total no. of persons	No. of adults		No. of children		Sex ratio
			Male	Female	Male	Female	
Bajaniwas	15	78	18	19	24	17	1056
Bapa Nagar	15	78	22	17	15	24	773
Chatriyanagar	29	144	32	29	42	41	906
Dewalipura	15	68	17	15	25	11	882
Govind Nagar	55	260	56	55	88	61	982
Hanuman Tekra	10	43	11	10	14	8	909
Harijanwas	10	46	10	11	14	11	1100
Jalaram Nagar	39	182	43	40	47	52	930
Jasoda Nagar	47	225	57	50	71	47	877
Jayaram Nagar	35	173	53	39	43	38	736
Jayajaitri Nagar	27	127	32	31	38	26	969
MES High School	12	70	13	12	18	27	923
Mujhmunda	34	180	42	38	55	45	905
Ramdev Nagar	37	189	48	43	54	44	896
Rangwadpura	10	57	13	16	15	13	1231
Opp. Sewage Canal	10	47	7	10	15	15	1429
All Slums	400	1967	474	435	578	480	870

Source: Field Survey, Baroda, ISS, 1992.

Educational Background of Slum Households

Educational status of adult members of our sample households is not very poor in Baroda. Fifty-five per cent of male adults are literate though their educational standard is limited to high school level. Twenty-five per cent of them are high school educated, 27 per cent up to primary and middle, and only 3 per cent are have been educated above high school level (Table 2.10).

The level of literacy among the female members however is much more disturbing. Nearly 80 per cent female adult members out of a total of 435 are illiterate, and of those having any formal education, 5 per cent are educated only up to primary level, 8 per cent up to middle school level and only 3 per cent have reached above that standard. It is, however, noted that higher education is equally limited for both male and female members.

Table 2.10
Educational Background of Adult Members in Sample Households

Level of education	Per cent male	Per cent female	Total
Primary School	11	5	8.0
Middle School	16	8	12.0
High School	25	4	13.0
Above High School	3	3	3.0
Illiterate	45	80	62
Total	100	100	100

Source: Field Survey, Baroda, ISS, 1992.

Employment Profile and Economic Background of the Slum Households: Impact of Income Generation Programmes

The level of workforce participation is quite low among the slum households in Baroda city. Only 22.5 per cent out of a total 1917 are engaged in some employment activities and 95 per cent of them are male adults (Table 2.11). The per centage of working female adults in the work force is incredibly low at only 5 per cent which indicates that out of a total adult female population of 435 only 22 or 5 per cent are engaged in any type of earning activities. The percentage of female workers in slums is much lower than the city average in Baroda, which was 8.77 per cent as recorded in the 1991 census.

It is also important to note that among the females who are employed 65 per cent have irregular employment and 35 per cent are self-employed and engaged in household activities and no one has any kind of regular employment.

A brighter picture emerges so far as the male employment status is concerned. Forty-two per cent male workers are in regular employment. The per centages of adult male members engaged in self-employed activities and irregular employment are 35 and 37 respectively.

The type of employment of the male work force shows that a majority are engaged in different industrial establishments in the city either as regular workers or as irregular workers (Table 2.12).

Table 2.11
Percentage Distribution of Employed Adults over Sex and Type of Work

Slum pockets	No. of sample house-holds	Total no. of persons	Adult working		Adult self-employed		Adult regular employed		Adult irregular employed	
			Male	Female	Male	Female	Male	Female	Male	Female
Bajaniwas	15	78	100	0	12	0	53	0	35	0
Bapa Nagar	15	78	100	0	24	0	12	0	65	0
Chatriyanagar	29	144	100	0	6	0	71	0	23	0
Dewalipura	15	68	88	12	7	50	20	0	73	50
Govind Nagar	55	260	88	12	46	14	2	0	52	86
Hanuman Tekra	10	43	100	0	0	0	40	0	60	0
Harijanwas	10	46	100	0	0	0	100	0	0	0
Jalaram Nagar	39	182	95	5	10	50	62	0	29	50
Jasoda Nagar	47	225	100	0	16	0	51	0	33	0
Jayaram Nagar	35	173	97	3	35	0	19	0	46	100
Jayajaitri Nagar	27	127	97	3	18	0	32	0	54	100
MES School	12	70	100	0	38	0	15	0	46	0
Mujhmunda	34	180	95	5	16	50	62	0	22	50
Ramdev Nagar	37	189	100	0	31	0	51	0	18	0
Rangawadpura	10	57	100	0	25	0	67	0	8	0
Opp. Sewage Canal	10	47	55	45	33	60	33	0	33	40
All Slums	400	1967	95	5	22	35	42	0	37	65

Source: Field Survey, Baroda, ISS, 1992

Table 2.12
Distribution of Male Workers over Types of Jobs

Self-employed Type	No.	Regular worker Type	No.	Irregular worker Type	No.
Petty trade	51	Factory worker	97	Casual factory worker	70
Vehicle Puller		Service	46	Irregular service	16
(*Rickshaw* and Auto rickshaw, hand cart etc.)	21			Daily labour	27
Washerman, Mason				Vehicle puller	12
Tailors etc.	6				
Others	9	Others	27	Others	17
Total	97		170		142

Source: Field Survey, Baroda, ISS, 1992

Ninety-seven out of total of 170 regular employed are working in different industries and another 70 are also employed in these establishments as irregular workers. A substantial portion of the slum workers who earn their livelihood from self-employment activities is engaged in small trading activities.

Because of the low employment potential the economic level of the households is very poor. The income and expenditure profile of the households in the surveyed slums draws attention to their appalling economic condition although Baroda is one among the highly industrialised cities in India and it has already been noted that a large section of the working population in our surveyed slums is engaged in these industries as regular and irregular employees.

Table 2.13
Distribution of Households over Income-Class

Monthly income range (Rs.)	Number of households	Per cent household
101-250	12	3.00
251-500	164	41.0
501-1000	174	43.50
1001-2000	50	12.5
Total	400	100.00

Source: Field Survey, Baroda, ISS, 1992.

Not a single household among the 400 surveyed has a monthly income of more than Rs.2000. The distribution of households among different income classes is seen in Table 2.13. More than 84 per cent of the surveyed households have monthly income ranging between Rs.251 to Rs. 1000. The average household income per month of a family comes to only Rs.658 which makes the per capita income per month only Rs. 137 (Table 2.14). The average monthly household income in the slums is even less than half of that of the city which was Rs.1471 in 1991 (United Way of Vadodara). Their monthly expenditure profile shows that the average monthly household expenditure ranges between Rs. 526 at the lowest to Rs. 894 at the highest across the slums and in 10 out of 16 slums per capita monthly expenditure is much lower than the all-slums average of Rs.142. Out of 400 sample households 305 or 76.3 per cent live below the poverty line if we go by the Planning Commission estimate of the per capita poverty line expenditure of Rs.209 and below per month. Not a single slum could be placed above the poverty line if the slum level average per capita expenditure was considered.

The disturbing scene of employment profile and economic background of the members of the slum households in Baroda can be analysed in the perspective of different employment generation programmes. The corporation under the aegis of the UBS programme in the slums has been organising different training programmes for women and also arranges for small loans to the trained women to start income generation activities. Though the municipal records show that 53 training classes have been conducted mainly for women in different skills such as knitting, sewing, tailoring, etc., and 1849 persons have been trained, this has not apparently improved their employment potential. They could not utilise their acquired skills to start their own activities either owing to lack of financial capacity to buy necessary equipments or of space in their homes for the purpose. Out of 1849 trained persons only 255 or 13.79 per cent received some loan or seed money for starting their business during the last four years since the inception of the UBS programme. (see Appendix 1).

Table 2.14
Income and Expenditure Profiles of Sample Households

Slums Pocket	No. of sample house-holds	Total no. of persons	Average reported household income (Rs)	Average reported household expenditure (Rs)	Per capita monthly Income (Rs)	Per capita monthly Expenditure (Rs)	Per cent households below poverty line*
Bajaniwas	15	78	726	801	140	154	66.7
Bapa Nagar	15	78	574	566	110	109	80.0
Chatriyanagar	29	144	628	716	126	144	72.4
Dewalipura	15	68	488	526	108	116	86.7
Govind Nagar	55	260	556	559	118	118	89.1
Hanuman Tekra	10	43	469	526	109	122	80.0
Harijanwas	10	46	714	889	155	193	50.0
Jalaram Nagar	39	182	761	828	163	177	61.5
Jasoda Nagar	47	225	683	674	143	141	74.5
Jayaram Nagar	35	173	745	717	151	145	77.1
Jayajaitri Nagar	27	127	695	737	148	157	70.4
MES High School	12	70	595	668	102	114	91.7
Mujhmunda	34	180	784	718	148	136	79.4
Ramdev Nagar	37	189	761	828	149	162	73.0
Rangawadpura	10	57	901	894	158	157	70.0
Opp. Sewage Canal	10	47	451	526	96	112	100.0
All Slums	400	1967	658	698	137	142	76.3

* Percapita monthly expenditure below Rs. 209.
Source: Field Survey, Baroda, ISS, 1992.

The recently launched employment generation programme of the Nehru Rozgar Yojana (NRY) has also been introduced in the city. Our survey reviewed that the NRY with all its components of Scheme of Urban Micro Enterprise (SUME), Schemes of Housing and Shelter Upgradation (SHASU) and Scheme of Urban Wage Employment (SUWE) has been taken up by the city government in 1989 and 375 persons out of a total of 4000 applicants received loans also. However, among all the UBS project slums only 39 persons have received such loans so far. In our survey of 400 sample households a very negligible proportion (only 4 %) had access to this loan and more surprisingly very few people have ever heard of the programme.

As NRY is a city-wide programme catering to all the urban poor and is not exclusively earmarked for the slum population, it appears that slum households got very little access to the facility. Lack of awareness on the part of slum dwellers has hindered them from asking for the loan.

The system of inviting applications for loans through advertisement in local dailies for identifying beneficiaries also keeps the slum population out of the system.

The involvement of CO in beneficiary identification is important in this regard. As they are aware of the grassroots level scenario and needs of the people, they can in consultation with the NHC sponsor names for loans to the BMC.

The BMC records on the other hand show that a major portion of allocated funds under different components of NRY has remained unutilised. Out of a total allocated fund of Rs. 40.70 lakhs from 1989 only 7.5 per cent could be utilised. (Appendix 1.2).

There is need for convergence of the UBS with the SUME component of NRY. The training programmes for men and women can then be streamlined so that after completion they can have access to these low-interest loan facilities to buy the necessary equipment and start utilising their skills to supplement their family incomes.

Access to Housing and Basic Services

Housing Scenario

Compared to slums in other metropolitan cities the housing condition of slum households is relatively better in Baroda. Although only 3 per cent households own *pucca* houses which are concentrated primarily in three out of 16 sample slums in our survey, the per centage of households with *kachcha* houses is 56. A substantial portion of sample households (41%) live in semi-*pucca* houses (Table 2.15).

Three of the four slums where the average income is higher than the all-slums average have more *pucca* houses and the per centage of households with *kachcha* houses is also less in these slums. The slums with higher average incomes not only have more *pucca* houses but they also have a larger number of rooms in each household. While 10 out of 16 (62.5%) sample slums have the majority population living in one room, in the rest of the six slums a majority of households have two room tenements and in four out of these six slums more than 67 per cent households have monthly household income averages higher than all the slums.

Ownership status of the houses among the slum households indicates that 96 per cent own their huts and only 3 per cent are living as tenants and in 13 out of 16 sample slums there are no tenants at all. However the land ownership does not rest with them as most of the slums are on encroached land which belongs to different government and private agencies.

Electricity facility is available in 69 per cent houses. Excepting in three slums where per centage of electrified households is very low (below 20%), in all other slums per centages ranged between 56 and 100. However only 10 per cent households indicated that they did not have electricity connections because of poor economic condition. Some of the slums do not have electricity connections as they have narrow roads too small to facilitate electricity connections to be drawn inside.

It must be noted, however, that the housing scenario for poor households in terms of all the indicators in Baroda slums is better for the sample households in our survey when we compare our survey findings with two other surveys conducted during the last decade, as mentioned earlier. The per centage of households living in *kachcha* houses which was 83 in 1988 during the NIUA survey is reported to be 56 in our survey (ISS) in 1992 (Table 2.16). In the same way the per centage of households with semi-*pucca* houses was 16 per cent in 1988 as against 41 per cent as shown in our survey. The per centage of households who owned houses was only 62 in the 1988 survey. Access to electricity was restricted to merely 4 per cent households in 1982; it is available to 69 per cent households during our survey in 1992. Moreover the average number of rooms per household is more in our survey: while 83 per cent households in all slums used to live in

Table 2.15
Access of Housing and Electricity to Surveyed Households

Slum pocket	No. of sample households	Type of housing (per cent household)			Average no. of rooms per house	Ownership status (per cent household)		Average money paid to get the house (Rs)	Per cent electrified	Average monthly expenses on electricity (Rs)
		Pucca	Semi-*pucca*	*Kachcha*		Owner	Tenant			
Bajaniwas	15	20	40	40	2	100	0	3167	60	31
Bapa Nagar	15	0	33	67	2	80	13	0	0	0
Chatriyanagar	29	0	7	93	1	100	0	7000	59	36
Dewalipura	15	0	13	87	2	100	0	0	80	50
Govind Nagar	55	0	49	51	1	98	0	7000	56	39
Hanuman Tekra	10	0	60	40	1	100	0		80	22
Harijanwas	10	10	70	20	1	100	0	10000	60	24
Jalaram Nagar	39	0	59	41	1	97	0	0	90	41
Jasoda Nagar	47	0	30	70	1	100	0	3300	74	36
Jayaram Nagar	35	0	46	51	2	100	0	0	74	54
Jayajaitri Nagar	27	0	22	78	1	100	0	0	74	32
MES School	12	0	42	58	1	75	25	10500	8	7
Mujhmunda	34	0	56	44	1	100	0	0	100	52
Ramdev Nagar	37	19	46	35	2	97	0	1750	86	44
Rangawadpura	10	0	60	30	2	100	0	4000	60	112
Opp. Sewage Canal	10	0	30	70	1	30	70	0	20	9
All Slums	400	3	41	56	1	96	3	5840	69	46

Source: Field Survey, Baroda, ISS, 1992.

one-room tenements in 1982, in our observations the figure is 68 per cent and nearly 32 per cent households have more than one room in their huts. The improvements in the housing situation might have been possible because of different shelter programmes undertaken by the BMC and other agencies during the last decade and certain sections of households have definitely benefitted from these programmes.

Despite this, however, a majority of the poorer households, particularly those living in *kachcha* houses in our survey, have very dilapidated huts with old tin sheets as roofs and the floors and walls are made of mud. The loan facility under the Housing and Shelter Upgradation Scheme under NRY though undertaken by the BMC has not yet reached the poorer households. This scheme which contains a substantial loan amount along with a grant to be repaid with interest by the borrower household within a stipulated period might have restricted the poorer section of the sample households from approaching the authorities for this facility.

Table 2.16
Status of Housing Facilities in 1982,1988 and 1992

(Per cent Households)

Sl.No.	Housing Facility	1982 (ORG)	1988 (NIUA)	1992 (ISS)
1.	*Type of Housing*			
	a. Pucca	-	1	3
	b. Semi-pucca	-	16	41
	c. Kachcha	-	83	56
	d. One room	83	-	68
2.	*Ownership status*			
	a. Owner	-	62	96
	b. Tenant	-	14	3
	c. Not identified	-	22	-
3.	House having electricity	4	12	69

Source: ORG, 1986; NIUA, 1991; Field Survey, Baroda, ISS, 1992.

Water Supply

Water supply is available to almost all the households in our survey. A majority of them (87%) depend on common water source (Table 2.17) and only 12 per cent have independent water sources. Except in

Table 2.17
Water Supply Situatic

(*Per cent Household*)

Slum pockets	No. of sample house-holds	Water supply source		Type of source availability				If not inside per cent response 'Near'	Quality of water response 'Fit for drinking'	Duration of supply response 'Adequate'
		Indepen-dent	Common	Piped	Hand pump	Inside	Outside			
Bajaniwas	15	47	53	100	0	47	53	100	100	87
Bapa Nagar	15	0	100	0	100	0	87	38	67	0
Chatriyanagar	29	0	100	100	0	0	100	52	100	100
Dewalipura	15	0	100	93	7	0	100	53	67	0
Govind Nagar	55	0	100	49	51	0	100	51	73	13
Hanuman Tekra	10	0	100	100	0	0	100	10	100	30
Harijanwas	10	20	80	60	0	20	80	25	100	50
Jalaram Nagar	39	0	100	97	0	3	97	55	100	18
Jasoda Nagar	47	11	89	68	26	11	89	71	83	28
Jayaram Nagar	35	0	91	46	49	3	86	67	97	94
Jayajaitri Nagar	27	4	96	89	7	0	100	52	81	11
MES School	12	0	100	100	0	0	100	67	100	0
Mujhmunda	34	94	6	91	3	94	6	100	88	88
Ramdev Nagar	37	0	100	68	14	0	100	49	97	43
Rangawadpura	10	0	70	0	100	0	100	20	100	0
Opp. Sewage Canal	10	0	100	70	30	10	90	67	100	0
All Slums	400	12	87	72	24	14	86	49	89	40

Source: Field Survey, Baroda, ISS, 1992.

one slum where 94 per cent of the slum households have an independent supply, in other slums a majority have to depend on taps and handpumps provided by the municipality. Though handpumps have been provided under the UBS programme, they are insufficient to serve the people with adequate water. Therefore the households with higher incomes have opted for independent sources. It was observed that the slums with high average monthly household incomes have more independent water supply sources. In the four slums where independent water supply connections existed, the monthly household income was above Rs.700 which was much higher than the all-slums average of Rs.658.

The water supply situation as revealed in our survey however does not show any significant change over time. Though water is available to all the households in our survey, the per centage of households served by tap water is the same as observed in the NIUA survey of 1988 (see Table 2.18). More households, in our survey, have (24%) handpumps as their source of water at present, as against 19 per cent in 1988. However, the number of handpumps has been quite inadequate as it is observed that the per centage of households being deprived of adequate water is more in the latter survey.

Table 2.18
Status of Water Supply in 1982, 1988 and 1992

(Per cent Households)

	Water Facilities	1982 (ORG) Per cent	1988 (NIUA) Per cent	1992 (ISS) Per cent
1.	*Source*			
	a. Independent	4	-	12
	b. Common	96	100	87
	c. Served by water supply	84.6	100	100
2.	*Type of Source*			
	a. Tap water	-	72	72
	b. Handpump	-	19	24
3.	Fit for drinking	-	100	89
	Supply adequate	-	49	40

Source: ORG, 1986; NIUA, 1991; Field Survey, Baroda, ISS, 1992.

Sanitation

Environmental sanitation which is the most important requirement in the crowded slum settlements is the most neglected and inadequate in all urban centres. This is also true in Baroda slums. It is surprising to note that 91 per cent of the surveyed households do not have any provision for latrines and only 9 per cent have their own latrines (Table 2.19). It was also observed during the survey that in many localities community toilets have been provided by the municipality but people do not use those facilities because either they are not regularly cleaned or there is no regular water supply in them.

Table 2.19
Toilet Facility

Slum pockets	No. of sample house-holds	Per cent households with			Average installation expenditure for independent toilet (Rs)
		Independent toilet	Common toilet	No provision	
Bajaniwas	15	47	0	53	2071
Bapa Nagar	15	0	0	100	0
Chatriyanagar	29	0	0	100	0
Dewalipura	15	0	0	100	0
Govind Nagar	55	0	0	100	0
Hanuman Tekra	10	0	0	100	0
Harijanwas	10	0	0	100	0
Jalaram Nagar	39	0	0	100	0
Jasoda Nagar	47	9	0	91	1200
Jayaram Nagar	35	0	0	100	0
Jayajaitri Nagar	27	0	0	100	0
MES School	12	0	0	100	0
Mujhmunda	34	32	0	68	1750
Ramdev Nagar	37	27	0	73	2700
Rangawadpura	10	50	0	50	1150
Opp. Sewage Canal	10	0	0	100	0
All Slums	400	9	0	91	1774

Source: Field Survey, Baroda, ISS, 1992.

Drainage and Garbage Disposal

Drainage conditions are also equally precarious and there are not much inter-slum differences so far as these facilities are concerned. While 87 per cent households in 12 slums reported there was no provision,

Table 2.20
Drainage and Garbage Disposal Facilities

(Per cent households

Slum pockets	No. of sample house-holds	Source of drainage		Open drainage/Sewage type		Garbage disposal mode				Cleaning 'YES'
		Open	No Provision	Kachcha	Pucca	Bin	On the Street	Outside House	Sweeper	
Bajaniwas	15	53	47	53	0	0	60	40	0	0
Bapa Nagar	15	0	100	0	0	0	53	47	0	0
Chatriyanagar	29	0	100	0	0	0	59	41	0	0
Dewalipura	15	0	100	0	0	0	73	27	0	0
Govind Nagar	55	0	100	0	0	0	78	20	0	0
Hanuman Tekra	10	0	100	0	0	0	70	30	0	0
Harijanwas	10	0	100	0	0	0	60	40	0	0
Jalaram Nagar	39	3	97	3	0	0	77	15	5	0
Jasoda Nagar	47	2	98	2	2	6	72	19	0	2
Jayaram Nagar	35	0	100	0	0	0	91	9	0	0
Jayajaitri Nagar	27	0	100	0	0	0	81	7	11	0
MES School	12	0	100	0	0	0	67	17	17	0
Mujhmunda	34	94	6	94	0	0	76	0	12	3
Ramdev Nagar	37	24	76	24	0	0	57	43	0	0
Rangawadpura	10	0	100	0	0	0	80	20	0	0
Opp. Sewage Canal	10	0	100	0	0	0	50	50	0	0
All Slums	400	13	87	13	0	1	72	23	3	1

Source: Field Survey, Baroda, ISS, 1992.

only some type of *kachcha* drains existed in the other 4 slums catering to 13 per cent households (Table 2.20). Garbage disposal facilities are available to only one per cent households, while 95 per cent reported they either threw it on the street or anywhere outside the house. The UBS progress report of the corporation though shows that a sufficient number of dustbins have been provided. They are either not being used by the households or are broken.

While a substantial per centage of households (31.6) reported access to public toilets as per the ORG survey in 1982, in our survey no one responded using public toilet facility (Table 2.21). It is not because more people are going in for private toilet facility. They do not have any facility at all. The per cent households with no provision of toilets has consistently become higher from 60.44 per cent in 1982 to 81 in 1988 and 91 in 1992.

Throwing garbage on to the street or anywhere outside the hut has also remained the mode of garbage disposal for a majority of households in 1992 as it was during the NIUA survey in 1988.

The UBS financing pattern and the performance schedule of the municipality also showed that the highest per centage of development funds had been used for providing sanitation facilities. This however does not seem to have brought about the expected change in the immediate environment in the slums.

Table 2.21
Status of Sanitation Facilities in 1982, 1988 and 1992

(Per cent households)

Sanitation Facilities	1982 (ORG)	1988 (NIUA)	1992 (ISS)
1. *Toilet facility*			
a. Independent	8.00	4	9
b. Public	31.6	10	0
c. No provision	60.4	81	91
2. *Drainage facility*			
a. Open	-		1
b. No provision	-		87
3. *Garbage disposal*			
a. Bin	-	0	1
b. Sweeper	-	0	3
c. Outside	-	70	23
d. On the street		30	72

Source: ORG, 1986; NIUA, 1991; Field Survey, Baroda, ISS, 1992.

Non-Formal Education and UBS

Providing pre-school education to children and adult education facilities to illiterate adults are important objectives of the UBS. The observations from our survey indicate that out of 1058 children more than 68 per cent go to schools, either primary school or Balwadi/Anganwadi (Table 2.22). Anganwadi centres have been provided under the Integrated Child Development Services (ICDS) scheme in almost all the slums, including the UBS project slums. These centres provide non-formal pre-school education to children along with supplementary nutrition, immunisation, health check-ups referral services and so on in an integrated manner. Ready to eat food also is supplied to children. Despite this, irregular attendance by the children especially girls in the Anganwadis is a common phenomenon.

The drop-out rate among female children is high and it is more so at higher levels. In almost all the slums the per centage of female children going to primary schools is much lower than that of males though an equal per centage of female and male children go to Anganwadi schools. A large per centage of female children (44 per cent) do not go to school at all, while this per centage in the case of male children is only 23 (Table 2.22). A major section of surveyed households responded that they were not sending the children to school because of high expenditure. It may be mentioned here that though pre-primary and primary schools are available in each locality and such education is supposed to be free, the expenditure on books, stationery and uniforms is sufficient to deter the poorer households from sending their children to school.

Despite the low level of literacy among the adult members the use of adult literacy classes is also minimum. A very negligible per centage of the adult population attends adult literacy classes. According to the municipal records 18 Adult Literacy Centres (ALCs) have been opened under the UBS Programme, and they have catered to 490 beneficiaries. Though engagement of the female adults in economic activities is minimum as it has already been noted, the attendance in ALCs is very minimum. Therefore in the absence of sufficient motivation on the part of the beneficiaries the facilities provided remain underutilised.

Table 2.22
Children's Education

Slum pockets	No. of sample house-holds	Total no. of Children		Per centage of children in			
				Primary schools		Balwadi/Anganwadis	
		Male	Female	Male	Female	Male	Female
Bajaniwas	15	24	17	38	24	17	12
Bapa Nagar	15	15	24	40	29	33	25
Chatriyanagar	29	42	41	50	17	17	17
Dewalipura	15	25	11	40	36	36	18
Govind Nagar	55	88	61	34	28	22	30
Hanuman Tekra	10	14	8	36	25	7	0
Harijanwas	10	14	11	29	9	7	18
Jalaram Nagar	39	47	52	49	19	13	13
Jasoda Nagar	47	71	47	32	23	31	9
Jayaram Nagar	35	43	38	50	53	30	21
Jayajaitri Nagar	27	38	26	47	35	32	23
MES School	12	18	27	50	19	22	41
Mujhmunda	34	55	45	47	16	31	40
Ramdev Nagar	37	54	44	39	34	20	25
Rangawadpura	10	15	13	33	62	27	8
Opp. Sewage Canal	10	15	15	27	20	7	33
All Slums	400	578	480	41	27	24	23

Source: Field Survey, Baroda, ISS, 1992.

Health Facilities

General Health

Access to health care facilities is an important indicator of quality of life of the households and one of the most important emphases of UBS. The slum households in our survey have greater access to government hospitals and very few take the help of private doctors. However many of the households take recourse to both the facilities (Table 2.23). While 78 per cent of them regularly avail themselves of government health care facilities, only 7 per cent responded that they depended exclusively on private doctors and hospitals.

Table 2.23
Availability of Health Care Facility

Slum pockets	No. of sample house-holds	Health service available (percentage distribution)			Per cent takes health care facility		Average expenditure on health (Rs)
		Govt. hospital	Private doctor	Other	Yes	No	
Bajaniwas	15	93	7	0	93	7	48
Bapa Nagar	15	87	13	0	67	33	75
Chatriyanagar	29	97	3	0	79	21	46
Dewalipura	15	20	0	80	60	33	52
Govind Nagar	55	100	0	0	89	11	59
Hanuman Tekra	10	100	0	0	90	10	45
Harijanwas	10	80	20	0	90	10	53
Jalaram Nagar	39	95	5	0	92	5	47
Jasoda Nagar	47	96	4	0	47	53	41
Jayaram Nagar	35	97	0	3	83	14	61
Jayajaitri Nagar	27	100	0	0	81	19	42
MES School	12	0	0	0	83	83	50
Mujhmunda	34	97	0	3	71	29	59
Ramdev Nagar	37	97	3	0	92	8	53
Rangawadpura	10	100	0	0	90	10	42
Opp. Sewage Canal	10	100	0	0	70	30	47
All Slums	400	78	7	15	79	22	51

Source: Field Survey, Baroda, ISS, 1992.

Mother and Child Care Facility

Mother and Child care are the two most important components of UBS. It provides such facilities to pregnant mothers and children. Immunisation facilities for children are also provided through the Universal Immunisation Programme run by the BMC with the financial assistance of central and state governments and UNICEF. The per centage of fully immunised children below one year in our sample is 79 (Table 2.24). There is significant inter-slum variation also. In 10 slums 100 per cent children are immunised in the other six slums such per centages are considerably low. The total per centage of immunised children though considerably high falls short of the target of 100 per cent coverage in 1991-92 as envisaged by BMC in its annual action plan.

Table 2.24
Immunisation of Children

Slum pockets	No. of sample household	Total No. of children below 4 years	Per centage immunised
Bajaniwas	15	4	100
Bapa Nagar	15	6	100
Chatriyanagar	29	7	43
Dewalipura	15	3	100
Govind Nagar	55	12	100
Hanuman Tekra	10	4	100
Harijanwas	10	1	100
Jalaram Nagar	39	12	67
Jasoda Nagar	47	16	100
Jayaram Nagar	35	8	100
Jayajaitri Nagar	27	5	100
MES School	12	7	43
Mujhmunda	34	8	100
Ramdev Nagar	37	14	57
Rangawadpura	10	6	33
Opp. Sewage Canal	10	4	50
All Slums	400	117	79

Source: Field Survey, Baroda, ISS, 1992.

Consciousness about health is also not very high among women members. Prenatal checkups, and other medical facilities are provided to the women through the UBS programme. However 69 per cent women go for prenatal checkups - 61 per cent of them in government hospitals, another 6 go to other doctors and 31 per cent of them do not take recourse to any prenatal check-up whatsoever.

Only 64 per cent women preferred government hospitals for child delivery, 55 per cent of them had the help of a doctor during delivery. Surprisingly, a substantial per centage (29) of women opted for home delivery and 39 per cent of them under the help of household members. All the slums revealed almost similar characteristics in terms of all the indicators of health care facilities for women.

Regarding family planning, it was observed that 67 per cent of 909 adult members in our 400 sample households did not adopt any family planning measures. It was surprising to note that the 33 per cent adults who used any type of family planning device, consisted of 28 per cent male and only 4 per cent female (1 per cent households did not respond.)

It is important to note that more than non-availability of family welfare facilities, the personal bias of the adult members has guided their decisions on family planning measures. Lack of awareness was also an important factor as reported by 34 per cent of adult members. More than 38 per cent of the adult women reported that their husbands did not allow them to adopt any such device.

It is however noted that the sample households in our survey have better access to health facilities than those reported in the other two surveys in 1982 and 1988 (Table 2.25). Government health facilities are being availed of by more households in our survey (78%). In 1982 it was only 43.9 per cent. The per centage of women going for health checkups, which was 6.1 per cent during the NIUA survey in 1988 is 69 as reported in our survey. In fact per centages of women going to government hospitals for child delivery and getting a doctor's help during delivery were reported to be much less (30 and 44 respectively) in 1988. Incidence of home delivery was reported to be as high as 57 per cent by the NIUA survey, as against the present level of 24 per cent in our sample.

Table 2.25
Status of Health Facilities in 1982, 1988 and 1992

Health Facilities	1982 (ORG)	1988 (NIUA)	1992 (ISS)
1. *General health* (per cent households)			
a. Visit to govt. hospitals for treatment	43.9	44	78
b. Private doctor	19.4	79	7
c. Others	36.7	27	22
2. *Mother and childcare*			
a. children immunised (fully + partially) (per cent children below 4 year)		79	79
3. *Mothercare* (per cent women)			
a. going for prenatal checkup	-	61	69
b. Govt.hospital as place of child delivery	-	30	64
c. Home as place of child delivery	-	57	24
d. Other hospitals	-	13	12
e. Doctor as help during child delivery	-	44	55
f. Trained Dai as help	-	-	3
g. Untrained Dai	-	42	-
h. Household member/neighbour as help	-	6	39
i. others	-	8	3
4. *Family planning* (per cent)			
a. husband using FP measure	-	-	28
b. Wife	-	-	4
c. None	-	-	67

Source: ORG, 1986; NIUA, 1991; Field Survey, Baroda, ISS, 1992.

Income-class Variations and Availability of Basic Services

The analysis of our survey data in the previous section shows that there are not very significant inter-slum differences so far as employment and access to basic amenities are concerned. But there are differences in these indicators across income classes in the case of some basic amenities.

The higher the income class, the higher has been the share of regular job-holders. The proportion of self-employed people has been the lowest in the highest income group. The proportion of persons in irregular job has been highest in the poorest income group. For all income classes taken together, the distribution of workers in the regular and irregular jobs has been almost the same. The share of females in the work-force is very low as has already been noted. Across the income class, the proportion of male workers does not change much, and the per centage of female workers is much less in higher income classes. Among the economically weaker sections, the per centage of female workers is the highest in irregular jobs. In the higher income group, the per centage of female workers is the same in both self-employed and regular job categories. Females of the economically weaker households have not been absorbed in these two categories (Table 2.26).

A strong income-class bias is noticeable in the availability of basic services. In terms of per capita space, the structure of houses and related facilities, higher income classes have access to better facilities. The average number of rooms has increased from 1 to 2 from the lowest to the highest income class leading to a slightly lower level of congestion. The per centage of households having pucca houses is increasing with increasing level of income (Table 2.27).

Housing amenities like electrification has improved with improved economic conditions. Though for a majority of the slum dwellers water is supplied from common sources, the relatively better-off go for independent sources. For them, supply of water from a common source is inadequate whereas in the lower income-classes, more people think it is adequate. Sanitation facilities in the slums are gravely unsatisfactory. Almost 92 per cent of the slum dwellers have no toilet provision. There are a few independent toilets but these belong to higher income classes.

A disparity in educational facilities is evident from the fact that for all income-classes the per centage of male school-going children is

Table 2.26
Distribution of Adult Workers over Types of Employment Across Income-Class

Income class (Rs)	No. of sample households	Total no. of persons	Percent of working persons	Per cent workers					
				Self-employed		Regular employed		Irregular employed	
				Male	Female	Male	Female	Male	Female
Rs. 101 - 250	12	45	27	18	0	0	0	82	100
Rs. 251 - 500	164	771	22	24	0	25	0	51	100
Rs. 501 - 1000	174	872	22	25	29	51	0	23	86
Rs. 1001 - 2000	50	279	24	8	50	61	50	32	0
	400	1967	23	22	18	41	6	37	82

Source: Field Survey, Baroda, ISS, 1992.

Table 2.27
Housing Conditions and Housing Amenities across Income-Class

Income class (Rs)	No. of sample house-holds	Average No. of rooms	Type of construction (percentage distribution)			Percent Household with				
			Pucca	Semi *Pucca*	*Kachcha*	Electri-fied	Water sup-ply source (Indp.)	Water fit for drink-ing	Water adequate	Indepen-dent toilet
Rs. 101-251	12	1	0	33	67	17	0	100	25	0
Rs. 251-500	164	1	0	34	66	66	6	85	34	1
Rs. 501-1000	174	2	2	47	51	72	16	92	48	11
Rs. 1001-2000	50	2	16	46	38	74	4	16	6	30
	400	3	41	56	1	69	12	89	40	9

Source: Field Survey, Baroda, ISS, 1992.

greater than that of their female counterparts (Table 2.28). In Balwadi schools, however, there is not much variation in these per centages. Participation of the female child in Balwadi schools has increased with the increase in income. The proportion of children not going to school has steadily declined with rise in income. This has been true for both male and female children. But the per centage of female illiterate children is nearly double that of their male counterparts.

Table 2.28
Children's Education Across Income Class

Income class (Rs)	No. of sample house-holds	Total no. of children		Per centage distribution of children in			
				Primary school		Balwadi/Anganwadi	
		Male	Female	Male	Female	Male	Female
Rs. 101 - 250	12	12	10	25	40	8	0
Rs. 251 - 500	164	224	191	42	29	19	18
Rs. 501 - 1000	174	262	218	43	27	27	24
Rs. 1001 - 2000	50	80	61	33	18	26	33
	400	578	480	41	27	24	23

Source: Field Survey, Baroda, ISS, 1992.

In the case of social services, however, these income class differences are not very acute. Slum dwellers have not shown any preference for private doctors across the income class. Government hospitals are still the major supplier of medical services. In case of child delivery, however, the relatively better off people seek private medical help other than the government hospital.

Family planning measures are not adopted by the majority of slum dwellers irrespective of their income-status.

The income-class-wise expenditure pattern of the households on basic amenities, however, show that a major portion of their household income is spent on basic amenities, mainly on health and education. While poorer households spend proportionately more on health, the higher income classes spend more on education of children especially for primary and above primary education. This signifies that even though health facilities are available through government hospitals, people have to spend on medicines. But the expenditure on physical infrastructure such as water, sanitation, garbage disposal and so forth is negligible. As a majority of households live in their own houses, recurring expenditure in terms of rent and tax on houses is also minimum (Table 2.29).

Table 2.29
Income Class wise distribution of Expenditure on Urban Services

Income class (Rs)	No. of sample house-holds	Reported average monthly expenditure on urban services (Rs)	Average expenditure on education (Percentage)			Average monthly expenditure on (percent to total reported expenditure)				
			Fees	Uniform	Books etc.	Rent/ House tax	Electri-city	Water supply	Sanita-tion	Health
Rs. 101 - 250	12	79	4.1	14.6	12.7	0	29.2	0.0	0.0	39.3
Rs. 251 - 500	164	143	3.5	14.0	10.5	.7	39.2	0.0	0.0	32.2
Rs. 501- 1000	174	340	20.6	25.6	11.5	1.2	23.8	0.0	0.9	16.5
Rs. 1001 - 2000	50	369	20.2	44.7	11.1	1.6	6.2	0.0	0.0	16.2
All Income Classes	400	176	12.4	23.0	8.5	.9	26.1	0.0	0.2	28.9

Source: Field Survey, Baroda, ISS, 1992.

Awareness of the Community and Participation in UBS

Against the background of the analysis on availability of basic services it is worthwhile to discuss the extent of community awareness and participation of the sample households in the organisation, planning, management of the UBS programme. Our survey results show that the response of the local people and their involvement in the programme have not been very encouraging (Table 2.30). Only 57 per cent responded that they were aware of the UBS programme and only 55 per cent said that they knew the community organiser (CO) of the area. In 3 out of 16 slums not a single household responded having heard of the programme at all. It was also noted during the survey that awareness about the programme was restricted only to the people living in surrounding areas where the corporation signboard indicating the ongoing UBS programme has been put up. People staying in other parts of the same slum were generally not aware of the programme at all. Only 31 per cent of the respondents said that they knew about NHC existing in their areas. However 72 per cent respondents who were aware of NHC also knew the local volunteer but only 35 per cent of them responded they knew anything about the NHC meeting or when it was held.

The low level of awareness culminated in very low level of participation in community activities. Participation at the organisational level in the day-to-day activities of the NHC was seen to be very low. Thirty-one per cent of them responded that they sometimes communicated with the CO about their problems. However 71 per cent respondents discussed their problems often with the RCVs.

Only 15 per cent households responded that they had ever been involved in the selection of volunteers for NHC. More than 70 per cent of them had never had any occasion to interact with the community organiser to discuss their problems and find solutions. The majority of them did not even know when the community organiser visited the area. Sixty five per cent of our respondents replied that they had never attended any community meeting organised by BMC or NHC. The UBS cell in the BMC organised several community meetings on different aspects of the programme to make the people aware of the programme and a substantial portion of its total expenditure from its inception till 1991 March has been spent on such meetings in different project slums. Our survey findings however indicate that most of the people did not take much interest in such activities.

Table 2.30
Community Awareness and Participation among Surveyed Households

(Percent household)

Slum pockets	No. of sample house-holds	Aware of		Interact with CO for civic amenities	Aware of NHC	Involved in NHC selection	Knowledge		Discuss problems with RCVS
		UBSP	CO				of NHC meetings	of NHC volunteer	
Bajaniwas	15	100	87	13	60	13	80	100	100
Bapa Nagar	15	20	27	7	7	0	7	7	7
Chatriyanagar	29	100	97	28	3	10	3	3	3
Dewalipura	15	93	100	87	80	40	100	100	100
Govind Nagar	55	80	78	75	44	9	49	49	47
Hanuman Tekra	10	90	80	10	80	20	80	90	90
Harijanwas	10	0	0	0	0	10	0	0	0
Jalaram Nagar	39	46	46	18	31	18	38	46	46
Jasoda Nagar	47	0	0	0	4	0	11	100	98
Jayaram Nagar	35	97	97	100	91	69	94	100	97
Jayajaitri Nagar	27	7	4	0	0	0	0	96	96
MES School	12	42	33	33	33	0	17	100	100
Mujhmunda	34	71	62	3	0	0	0	100	97
Ramdev Nagar	37	62	62	8	38	5	41	100	100
Rangawadpura	10	60	70	70	50	50	60	90	90
Opp. Sewage Canal	10	0	10	0	10	10	0	10	10
All Slums	400	57	55	31	31	15	35	72	71

Source: Field Survey, Baroda, ISS, 1992.

It must be noted however that participation was very much associated with awareness. In those slums where awareness was high interaction of the community was also found to be relatively high.

The survey results further show that irrespective of the income-class, there is general awareness about the UBS programme. Yet interaction with the community organiser is more in the lower income groups. On the other hand, relatively better-off people are aware of neighbourhood committees. It is again the higher income groups who are more involved in the selection process of the RCVs by way of attending more meetings. They participate more actively in the discussions with the RCVs about local problems. Participation at the grassroots level in the slums seems to be confined to the relatively affluent class (Table 2.31).

In such cases the roles of CO and RCVs are important. To motivate the people at the grassroots level with the help of RCVs is one of the primary functions of the CO. The RCVs are also trained for that. During the last four years 219 volunteers have been imparted training on such courses. However from 1990 no such training courses have been organised as reported by the municipality.

Lack of incentive of the UBS volunteers may be one of the reasons for low level of motivation on their part. The volunteers in UCD programmes and also in the recently launched World Bank programme, get sufficient remuneration for their work whereas the UBS programme does not ensure such incentives.

Insufficient number of community organisers is also another reason for lack of regular contact with the people, each of the 7 COs employed in the UBS cell is in charge of a number of slums covering a large area consisting of a number of households. They are sometimes overburdened and cannot visit the area regularly and maintain contact with the people.

Because of this, response of the households in taking advantage of the facilities such as Anganwadi, ALCs, child and mother care facilities, and using them properly has not been very encouraging and this is evident among all households accross all income-classes. Immunisation facilities which are provided under UBS as also under the universal immunisation programme were availed of only by 79 per cent of 117 households who have children below four years of age.

Table 2.31
Community Awareness and Participation Across Income-classs

(Percent household)

Income Class (Rs)	No. of sample house-holds	Aware of		Know about		Interact with CO for civic amenities	Involved in NHC Selection	Discuss problems with RCVs
		UBS	CO	NHC Meetings	NHC Volunteers			
Rs. 101 - 250	12	67	33	42	67	58	0	42
Rs. 251 - 500	164	53	30	70	50	30	11	70
Rs. 501 - 1000	174	58	36	71	57	30	18	70
Rs. 1001 - 2000	50	60	46	88	62	24	16	86
All Income Class	400	57	35	72	55	31	15	71

Source: Field Survey, Baroda, ISS, 1992.

The per centage of children going to Balwadi centres is low. The attitude of adults towards literacy centres is particularly important. In spite of very high illiteracy among the women members of our surveyed households the per centage of women using the facility is almost nil in most of the slums. In the absence of any noticeable workforce participation rate among women, their preoccupation with wage earning activities cannot be cited as an excuse for not attending ALCs. Lack of awareness about the programme and their ignorance about the effect of this functional literacy on their day-to-day life are the two important factors which inhibited them from going in for informal education.

Involving the community in the planning and implementation process is the most important objective of the UBS. Neighbourhood committees at the grassroots level are to serve as the vehicle to achieve the objective. People's felt needs are to be expressed through the 'mini-plans' chalked out by the NHCs in consultation with the CO and the implementation is to be achieved through self-help approach.

In Baroda, although according to municipal reports 29 such NHCs have been formed consisting of 297 volunteers each representing 20-25 houses in his/her area, it was observed during the survey that in some cases these NHCs were either non-existent or were not functioning (e.g. Chatriyanagar, Mujhmunda). It was also ascertained from the municipal sources that the decentralised planning process which should start at the NHC level through formation of area-wise miniplans has not yet been attempted in the city. The action plans for the UBS are formulated at the BMC under the instructions from the state government and the UNICEF which was till recently a major financing partner. Though local level needs are considered during the exercise, NHCs are not involved in the process.

Involvement of the community in sharing the financial responsibility was also found to be absent in the slums. The system of creating a Revolving Fund with allocation from the UBS fund to be supplemented by people's contributions and managed by the local NHC is almost non-existent in Baroda. The fund is usually created to help the NHC to bear the day-to-day maintenance expenditure of the facilities like repairing of handpumps, buying of cleaning materials and also giving small loans with very low interest to the local people for starting small ventures and in times of exigency.

In many other such project towns for example, in our other survey town Sambalpur in Orissa, a Revolving Fund has been formed by all the NHCs and has been functioning well. In some of the slums additional funds have also been allocated based on the performance level of the NHC. This has helped in managing the day-to-day maintenance expenditure in a particular slum.

In Baroda such revolving funds were not generated by the NHC in any of our surveyed slums and for small repairing and maintenance also the NHCs had to depend on the Corporation alone.

Inter-Slum Comparison of Basic Services and Community Participation

Findings from the aggregate data of 400 households analysed in the previous section reveal that although there are no significant income differences among slum households, the households in higher income ranges have better availability of certain facilities which exist in the locality. Even community awareness and participation in the activities vary to some extent with income classes.

The slum level average data also corroborate the same findings so far as basic services are concerned. To assess the position of slums in terms of per capita income, five components of basic services (education, housing, water, sanitation and health), community awareness and participation, we have ranked 16 slums in descending order from 1 to 16 for each component. While for per capita income ranks have been assigned according to the slum level average of monthly per capita income, for other selected services weighted values have been added and the highest scoring slum has been assigned rank 1 (see Appendix 1.3 for variables and explanations).

Scores for all five components of basic services have been worked out and then a composite index has been computed and slums have been ranked accordingly. In the same way scores and ranks for community awareness and participation have also been worked out separately.

Table 2.32 gives the ranks of slums in terms of each of the selected indicators, namely, per capita average monthly income, education, housing, water supply, sanitation, women and child health, community awareness and participation and then in terms of a composite index. To find out whether there is any significant relationship between indicators, the coefficients of rank correlation have been computed.

Table 2.32
Ranks of Slums on the Basis of Some Selected Indicators

Slum pockets	RANKS								
	A	B	C	D	E	F	G	H	
	Average percapita income	Education	Housing	Water supply	Sanitation	Women and child health	Community awareness	Community participation	Composite Index
Bajaniwas	9	10	5	2	2	10	3	4	4
Bapa Nagar	12	6	13	16	15	9	14	16	15
Chatriyanagar	10	5	15	3	14	11	11	13	12
Dewalipura	14	13	14	13	10	14	2	2	11
Govind Nagar	11	2	8	14	9	1	7	8	7
Hanuman Tekra	13	15	3	11	11	2	4	7	8
Harijanwas	3	16	1	5	13	6	16	14	9
Jalaram Nagar	1	3	6	6	7	7	10	11	6
Jasoda Nagar	8	14	10	7	5	15	12	12	13
Jayaram Nagar	4	12	9	4	6	3	1	1	1
Jayajaitri Nagar	7	11	11	12	8	4	13	10	10
MES School	15	9	12	8	12	16	9	5	14
Mujhmunda	6	7	7	1	1	5	8	9	3
Ramdev Nagar	5	4	2	9	3	8	6	6	2
Rangawadpura	2	1	4	15	4	12	5	3	5
Opp. Sewage Canal	16	8	16	10	16	13	15	15	16

Source: Field Survey, Baroda, ISS, 1992.

Some important observations have emerged from the above table The average per capita income level of the slums has a significant bearing on the availability of services mainly housing, sanitation and health facilities. The slums which rank higher in per capita income hold similar or near-equivalent positions in terms of accessibility to these services. A significantly high positive correlation exists between per capita income and housing (.63) and also sanitation (.57). Health Services including mother and child care also show a reasonably high positive correlation with income (.33). These observations suggest that with increase in income people do try to spend more on better quality of these services.

However, for facilities like water supply and education, income sensitivity was minimum as the ranks of slums in terms of these two services indicate. Increase in income had hardly any effect on the availability of a community facility like water. On the other hand for education it has been observed that irrespective of income-class variation people in all slums spend a significant portion of their earnings on children's education. Quality of housing on the other hand has very important bearing on services like sanitation. With improved quality of housing, the chances for acquiring an independent toilet go up at the next stage. High positive correlation (.53) was found between ranks of slums in terms of housing and sanitation. Therefore it is necessary to improve the housing condition of the slum households and the shelter component of the NRY should be emphasised to facilitate people to spend for better facilities.

Surprisingly, however, ranks of slums according to community participation or in terms of awareness towards the programme did not exhibit much similarity with ranks of slums according to average per capita monthly income. The slums ranking high in income category were not ranking quite high in terms of awareness towards the programme and also not in terms of participation.

But it is important to note that involvement of the community in the activities is very much positively related with awareness of the community about the programme. A significantly high correlation (.6) was found to exist between the ranks of slums in terms of these two indicators. Therefore awareness creation is important to motivate the people to participate in activities.

Community awareness, however, does not ensure better availability of basic services. If the ranks of slums in terms of composite index of all the five services under consideration is taken into account, it is observed that there is no significant association between this index and the community awareness. Wide variation exists between the ranks of the slums in terms of these two indicators. In the same way participation has also not shown any significant relationship with the composite index of basic services.

CONCLUSION

In the light of the above analysis of our field survey data some broad observations regarding three key areas of the UBS programme in Baroda may be made with some policy implications.

Basic Services – In the provision of basic services the effect of UBS in Baroda has been a mixed one. Facilities like health and child care have improved while sanitation has been totally neglected. There has been a steady improvement in the per centage of women seeking antenatal services and trained medical attention at birth, though the coverage is still not universal. The social services like pre-school education for children immunisation, etc., have gained momentum, however informal education for adults has received minimum response. Income class variations in the availability of services is also noticeable. Higher income classes have better access to certain facilities.

Convergence – So far as convergence of different programmes is concerned it has been observed that the local government or the BMC has adopted some measures to avoid overlapping of programmes. The Anganwadis opened under the ICDS programmes are being used for UBS purposes. The child care and immunisation needs of the community are being catered to through the Universal Immunisation Programme. However, urban poverty cannot be tackled with the provision of some social and physical amenities only. The income generating programme like NRY has not been given due importance yet. All the three components of NRY which tackle urban poverty by both generating more employment and income also inculcate participation on the part of beneficiaries in the form of resource generation by contributing labour and money. Convergence of NRY with UBS is very important to attack urban poverty in an integrated manner.

Community Participation – The response of the community towards participation in the development process has not been a very encouraging one. Awareness among the people especially among those who do not hold any position in the NHC like RCVs, Balwadi teachers, etc., is minimum. The women who are the main focus of the programme have been neglected. Except for some training courses for skill formation, participation of women is minimum in the day-to-day activities of the programme.

The decentralised planning process which should start at the NHC level, in which mini-plans are to be integrated at the local level, has not been effectively implemented. The BMC is formulating the plan after taking into consideration the needs of a particular locality. Although BMC has a long history of decentralised administration system, where day-to-day municipal functions and even revenue collection are delegated down to the ward level units, in the case of UBS the power is restricted to the UBS cell in the Corporation.

Participation is also limited so far as sharing the financial responsibilities is concerned. The system of creating a Revolving Fund is extremely useful for the success of UBS. But this has not been created in UBS slums. It is essential to create such funds for small activities in the locality and helping poor women with small loans for starting small income generation ventures. Involvement of NGOs in savings mobilisation for creating such funds in Baroda is also important. There is the example of the Baroda Citizens Council (BCC) in developing habits of savings among slum households through the formation of Community Savings and Loan Association (CSLA). With a minimum saving of Rs. 10 per month at 6 per cent rate of interest a member of CSLA is eligible for a loan up to Rs. 1500 after six months, repayable within 18 months along with 12 per cent interest (Vaidya and Shah, 1992). The system of collecting the monthly savings by BCC volunteers regularly makes the chances of defaulting minimum.

POLICY IMPLICATIONS

The UBS being a very structured programme with a stringent monitoring system, it has a suffocating experience at the local level. In the process of fulfilling specified goals within limited time periods and with limited resources, the basic philosophy of community development which is the foundation of the UBS programme is lost sight of. There must be some flexibility in selecting the goal and the community should be given sufficient scope to express its priorities and needs. The revised UBSP programme which allows wider flexibility is expected to remove this difficulty.

In a participatory community development programme like UBS the involvement of local elected members is essential. After the introduction of the 74th Constitution Amendment Act, 1992, the representation of women members will be more in local bodies and in some states 30 per cent seats are already reserved for women. As the focus of UBS is women and children, the involvement of women members in the Advisory Committee at the local level is necessary.

To ensure community awareness and people's involvement, the UBS staff like PO and COs at the local level must be more concerned and have sufficient training to communicate with people and help the community understand its problems and needs and find ways for solving those. The human factor is very important in a people oriented programme. Wherever these programmes like UCD/UBS have been successful, the role of the community organiser, project officer has been commendable. A professional attitude among the staff is also needed. Trained social workers may be recruited at the municipal level to work in the UBS cell and the municipal employees who would work in the department must be well trained and they should be allowed to work without much disruption by untimely transfer or political interference.

Appendix 1.1

Progress of UBS from 1987 to December 1991 in Baroda

Sl. No	Type of Activities	No. of Units	No. of beneficiaries
A.	**Health Activities**		
1.	Growth charts introduced	138	--
2.	Adults educated for health education such as ORT Home based diarrhoea, family planning, Immunization etc.	2615	51053
3.	Family planning operations done	86	
4.	Copper T cases done	21	
5.	Slide/film shows	147	5826
6.	Health check up camps	2866	15017
B.	**Educational Activities**		
1.	Children admitted to school	205	--
2.	Distribution of books and notebooks to children	1523	--
3.	Adult literacy classes	18	490
4.	Evening study centres	10	395
5.	Study tours	15	980
6.	Educational competitions held	61	1362
C.	**Economic Activities**		
1.	Sewing classes started	32	1370
2.	Knitting classes started	06	91
3.	Short term training programmes	13	325
4.	Typing classes started	02	63
5.	Beneficiaries under self-employment scheme	211	--
6.	Beneficiaries under bankable scheme	03	--
7.	Mahila groups given seed money	02	--
8.	Beneficiaries under NRY Scheme	39	
9.	Beneficiaries under scheduled caste subsidised scheme	36	
D.	**Water and Sanitation**		
1.	Hand pumps installed	30	--
2.	Standposts constructed	08	--
3.	Bathing cubicals constructed	20	--
4.	Community latrines constructed	09	--
5.	Stream water drainage line installed	09	--
6.	Latrines constructed at primary schools	11	--
7.	Sanitation education camps held	663	12911

Contd...

Sl. No	Type of Activities	No. of Units	No. of beneficiaries
8.	Ventilators installed	1325	--
9.	Dustbins distributed	1737	--
10.	Dustbins installed at slums	47	
E.	**Community Organisation**		
1.	Basti committee formed	29	--
2.	Basti meetings held/No. of volunteers participated	215	3613
3.	Volunteers trained	297	--
4.	Community halls under construction	04	--

Source: Baroda Municipal Corporation, 1992.

Appendix 1.2

Allocation and Disbursement under NRY Programme from 1989 to March, 1992

Allocation Head	Grant Amount (Rs)	Disbursement Amount (Rs)
Loan and Subsidy	34,78,010	1,32,955
Training	2,81,000	1,93,620
Administrative	2,30,700	5,809
Construction of Palika Karigar Kendra	80,000	--
Training of construction trade	3,44,000	

Source: Baroda Municipal Corporation, 1992

Appendix 1.3

Indicators used for Ranking the Sample Slums

No.	Description	Explanation
1.	Per capita income	Absolute figure
2.	Per capita expenditure	Absolute figure
3.	Literates	Per cent to total adult
4.	Adults educated upto primary school	Per cent to total adult
5.	Adults educated upto middle school	Per cent to total adult
6.	Adults educated up to high school	Per cent to total adult
7.	Adults educated above high school	Per cent to total adult
8.	Children going to school up to primary level	Per cent to total children
9.	Type of housing	Kachcha: 1; semi pucca: 2; pucca: 3
10.	Average No. of room per person	Absolute figure
11.	Electricity	Weight - Wholly or partly: 1; otherwise: 0
12.	Water supply source	Independent: 3; Common near: 2; otherwise: 1
13.	Quality of water supply	Fit for drinking: 1; otherwise: 0
14.	Duration of supply	Adequate: 1; otherwise: 0
15.	Toilet facility source	Independent with flush: 2; common: 1; otherwise: 0
16.	Drainage/sewage source	Pucca: 2, kachcha 1; otherwise: 0
17.	Mode of garbage disposal	In the bin: 1; otherwise: 0
18.	Cleaning	Yes: 1; No: 0
19.	Type of immunised children	Wholly or partly: 1; otherwise: 0
20.	Nearest health service available	Govt. hospital: 1; otherwise: 0
21.	Women check before child delivery	Yes: 1; No. 0
22.	Help during delivery	Doctor: 2; Trained Dai: 1; otherwise: 0
23.	Family planning measure utilisation	Yes: 1, No. 0
24.	Awareness of UBS	Yes: 1, No. 0
25.	Volunteer known	Knowing and duscussing problem: 2; knowing only: 1; otherwise: 0
26	Awareness of IGP	Yes: 1; No: 0
27.	Received Loan	Per cent household
28.	Loan amount	Absolute Figure

REFERENCES

Baroda Citizens Council (1990). *Life in Baroda in the '90s*, BCC in association with Operations Research Group, Baroda.

————, (1990). *25 years 1965-1990*, BCC, Baroda.

————, (1992). *Children in Different Circumstances*, BCC, Baroda.

————, (1992). *Annual Report, 1991-91*, BCC, Baroda.

Baroda Municipal Corporation 1990. *Year Book*, BMC, Baroda.

Census of India (1991a). *Provisional Population Totals: Rural-Urban Distribution*, Office of the Registrar General, New Delhi.

————, (1991b), *Provisional Population Totals: Workers and their Distribution*, Paper 3 Series 1, Office of the Registrar General, New Delhi.

Ganesan, N, (1989). *Urban Basic Services Programme in Andhra Pradesh*, RCUES, Hyderabad.

Gujarat Municipal Finance Board, (1990) *Statistics of Municipal Bodies - Gujarat State, 1983-84 to 88-89*, GMFB, Ahmedabad.

National Institute of Urban Affairs, (1991). *Basic Services and the Urban Poor*, NIUA, New Delhi.

Operations Research Group, (1986). *Report on Survey of Slums, Chawls and Khadkis -- Vadodara City - 1982*, ORG,Baroda.

Pandya, Sweta and Kacker, Rashmi, (1992) *Children in Difficult Circumstances*, Baroda Citizens Council, Baroda.

Rajyaguru, H M, *People of Slums*, (1988). Baroda Citizens Council, Baroda.

United Way of Vadodara, (1991). *Needs Assessment of Community Baroda*, United Way of Vadodara, Baroda.

Vaidya, Chetan and Shah, Rajesh, (1992). *Role of Non-Governmental Organisation in Housing and Urban Land Development in India: A Case of Baroda Citizens Council*, BCC, Baroda.

Chapter III

BHILWARA

CITY PROFILE

Bhilwara, the headquarters of the district of the same name, is in the south-eastern part of Rajasthan. Situated on the Ajmer-Khandwa section of the Western Railway, it has direct road and railway links with the state capital Jaipur. With Bhilwara district surrounded on the north by Ajmer, on the north-west, west and south-west by Udaipur and on the east and north-east by Bundi and Tonk districts, Bhilwara city is well connected with the headquarters of all these neighbouring districts. This transportational network, in turn, connects the city with other bigger regional and national level urban centres.

With the geographical location of 25°21′ N latitude and 74°39′ E longitude, Bhilwara city falls in the Mewar Region of Rajasthan which is situated on the eastern slopes of the Aravalli hills. The Aravalli hills guard the region from the impact of the Thar Desert, making it a transitional zone between two major climatic regions of India, the humid east and the arid west (Singh, 1971) which is suitable for agriculture and other economic activities. Therefore, the favourable location and opportunities for agricultural as well as industrial advancement of the surrounding areas have been significant factors in the economic development of Bhilwara.

Although, according to hearsay Bhilwara is 900 years old, the historical records testify its existence of three and a half centuries (Sehgal, 1975). The city witnessed the chequered events of war and power struggle during the fifteenth and sixteenth centuries involving the Delhi rulers and Ranas of Mewar. But the seventeenth and eighteenth centuries were marked with relative peace and prosperity. Among the several factors contributing towards the city's growth during this period, two stand out most significantly. First, Rana Amar Singh's treaty with Jahangir in 1615 AD and the subsequent inclusion of Bhilwara area under the *Khalsa* land by Maharana Raj Singh. Secondly, the organisation of an association of the merchants of the town as *Panch Mahajans* not only for local administration but also for reorganising and stimulating the business activities of the area (Bhattacharya and Lodha, 1969). These measures, from the very beginning, not only induced a sense of security and privilege among the merchants and artisans of the town, but also reorganized the trade and commerce. Subsequently, under the British rule, Bhilwara emerged as an important centre for business and commercial activities. It was famous for the excellence and durability of its tinned utensils which were largely exported (Imperial Gazetteer of India). Talking about the same period a British scholar went on record to say, "The chief commercial mart, Bhilwara, which showed not a vestige of humanity rapidly rose from ruin and in a few months contained 1200 houses, half of which were occupied by foreign merchants – Bales of goods, the produce of the most distant lands, were piled up in streets" (Erskine, 1908).

Bhilwara's commercial and industrial activities have remarkably expanded since the early 1920s with the city's emergence on the mineral map of India when it became an important centre of mica mining. The opening of the second cotton textile mill of Rajasthan in the city in 1938 added a new dimension to its industrial and economic development.

After Independence the process of development further accelerated in Bhilwara. In course of time, two types of industries – one based on cotton and the other on minerals, mica in particular, made headway. Presently it has two cotton textile spinning and weaving mills. One woolen textile mill, one vegetable oil plant apart from several flour mills and other agro-industries. Located in Bhilwara-Chittaurgarh industrial belt today, Bhilwara has emerged as one of the important industrial centres of Rajasthan with considerable potential for further growth and development.

Demographic Characteristics

Bhilwara is the ninth most populous urban centre in Rajasthan. Since 1981, when it crossed the one lakh population mark, it has attained the class I category in the urban class hierarchy. Therefore, in conformity with the convention of the Indian Census now it is referred to as a city. In fact, Bhilwara is the largest urban place and the only city in the district accommodating its 59.11 per cent urban population. The remaining 40.89 percent is shared by towns of different sizes (Tables 3.1 and 3.2). The massive concentration of population in favour of

Table 3.1
Growth in the Number of Urban Places and their Population in Bhilwara District, 1901-1991

Year	Class I		Class II		Class III		Class IV		Class V		Class VI		Class VII	
	No.	Population	No.	Population	No.	Population	No.	Population	No.	Population	No.	Population	No.	Population
1901	-	-	-	-	-	-	1	10,346	1	8,974	3	12,158	5	31,478
1911	-	-	-	-	-	-	-	-	2	16,692	3	12,744	5	29,436
1921	-	-	-	-	-	-	-	-	2	17,396	3	12,314	5	29,710
1931	-	-	-	-	-	-	1	10,402	1	9,298	3	13,323	5	33,023
1941	-	-	-	-	-	-	1	15,169	2	15,471	2	9,172	5	39,812
1951	-	-	-	-	1	29,668	1	11,609	3	17,005	2	9,223	7	67,505
1961	-	-	-	-	1	43,449	1	12,165	1	17,769	-	-	3	63,433
1971	-	-	1	82,155	-	-	1	15,334	2	18,817	-	-	4	116,306
1981	1	122,625	-	-	-	-	4	56,477	1	9,461	-	-	6	188,563
1991	1	183,791	-	-	1	23,646	6	94,093	1	9,419	-	-	9	310,949

Source: Census of India 1981, Census of India, 1991a.

Table 3.2

Percentage of Towns in each Class to Total Number of Towns and Percentage of Population in each Class to Total Urban Population, 1901-1991 in Bhilwara District

Year	Class I		Class II		Class III		Class IV		Class V		Class VI	
	Towns	Popln.	Towns	Popln.	Towns	Popln.	Towns	Popln.	Towns	Popln.	Towns	Popln.
1901	-	-	-	-	-	-	25	47	25	28.51	50	24.33
1911	-	-	-	-	-	-	25	44.79	25	26.94	50	28.27
1921	-	-	-	-	-	-	25	45.96	25	27.92	50	26.12
1931	-	-	-	-	-	-	25	46.48	25	28.16	50	25.36
1941	-	-	-	-	25	41	-	-	25	24.96	50	23.04
1951	-	-	-	-	16.67	52.98	16.67	17.20	33.33	16.16	33.33	13.66
1961	-	-	-	-	33.34	68.57	33.33	19.18	33.33	12.25	-	-
1971	-	-	25	70.64	-	-	25	13.18	50	16.18	-	-
1981	16.67	65.03	-	-	-	-	66.67	29.95	16.66	5.02	-	-
1991	11.11	59.11	-	-	11.11	7.60	66.67	30.26	11.11	3.03	-	-

Source: Census of India, 1981. Census of India 1991a.

Bhilwara bestows it with the status of primate city in the district. The extreme concentration of urban population in a single city indicates that the process of industrialisation and modernisation, which paves the way for rapid urbanisation, has not spread in the district in a significant manner. Therefore, the conditions required for attaining a higher level of urbanisation have largely been confined in and around Bhilwara city only. This is the reason why the level of urbanisation in Bhilwara district has remained very low – 14.40 per cent compared to the state average of 21 per cent.

Table 3.3 indicates that Bhilwara has been witnessing a varied population growth pattern since 1901. Whereas the 1901-1911 decade was marked by a negative growth rate, with 88.87 per cent 1961-71 experienced the highest decadal growth rate during the entire period of 1901-1991. However, it came down to 49.26 per cent during 1971-81, and only marginally increased to 49.88 per cent during 1981-91. Nevertheless Table 3.3 also shows that the unprecedented urban population growth in 1961-71 was accompanied by a very significant and abrupt increase in the city area which was drastically reduced due to revised computation at the 1981 census (Census of India, 1981). This reduction appears to have been an important factor in a lower population growth during 1971-81.

Table 3.3
Population of Bhilwara 1901-91

Year	Status	Area (in km)	Population			Percentage decadal variation
			Persons	Male	Female	
1901			14,844	7744	7106	-
1911			13,186	6822	6364	-11.17
1921			13,655	7062	6593	+3.56
1931			15,350	7955	7395	+12.41
1941			20,701	10,788	9823	+34.86
1951			35,761	18,867	16,894	+72.75
1961	M	51.18	43,499	23,617	19,882	+21.64
1971	M	119.11	82,155	44,330	37,825	+88.87
1981	MC	69.93	122,625	64,948	57,677	+49.26
1991	MC	N A.	183,791	98,061	85,730	+49.88

Note: NA = Not Available.
Source: Census of India, 1981; Census of India, 1991 a.

Notwithstanding the emerging decadal population growth rates, particularly since Independence, there has been a continuous rapid increase in the absolute number of the city dwellers in Bhilwara. This is mainly attributed to the phase of industrial development in the city which appears to have attracted a large number of immigrants from rural as well as urban areas. The ongoing process of population increase, in turn, is exerting tremendous pressure on existing resources and infrastructural facilities and has affected the delivery system of basic services like drainage, water supply, toilets and lighting to the city inhabitants.

Work Force Structure

The work force structure in Bhilwara characterises the typical features of a predominantly urban economy which is largely identical to those found in the urban areas at the district and the state levels. As Table 3.4 shows, although 31.22 per cent of the city's population is worker, its overwhelming majority is male (Census of India, 1991). Nevertheless, for both the sexes the proportion of working population in Bhilwara is higher than the state and the district averages. Similarly, the per cent point decadal increase in the city's working population during 1981-91 has also been higher than the above mentioned two averages. Significantly, despite the fact that the proportion of females in the work force in the city is still merely 8 per cent against 51.62 per cent for men, their decadal per cent point increase between 1981 and 1991 has been slightly higher than males (Table 3.4). However, the impact of this increase is confined to the primary sector as the proportion of female cultivators in the city during this period increased from 31.10 per cent to 36.12 per cent, while in other sectors there was a proportional decline. Obviously, the process of economic development in the city has not been able to translate its work force into an altered occupational structure so as to absorb the female workers in other than primary sector.

As a whole the dominant economic activities of the city workers, both males and females, are in the industrial and tertiary sectors which constitute the category of 'other workers' in Table 3.4. In recent years the industrial development in Bhilwara has resulted in a very high and ever increasing proportion of workers in factories and other industrial establishments. This phenomenon accompanied by flourishing trade and commerce coming under the tertiary sector now

Table 3.4
Proportion of Main Workers and their Distribution in Workforce Categories: Rajasthan, Bhilwara District and City 1981-1991

	Percentage of Workers			Cultivators		Agricultural labourers		Household industry workers		Other workers	
	Persons	Male	Female	Male	Female	Male	Female	Male	Female	Male	Female
Rajasthan											
1981 U	26.54	45.93	4.44	9.54	17.19	2.33	7.04	5.18	10.23	82.94	65.54
1991 U	27.12	46.11	5.57	7.96	18.22	3.34	8.24	5.39	9.70	83.31	63.83
Bhilwara district											
1981 U	28.67	48.70	6.56	19.34	44.13	2.49	10.01	5.0	6.08	73.18	39.78
1991 U	30.83	50.48	8.92	14.84	42.43	3.06	13.36	3.84	5.33	78.26	38.87
Bhilwara City											
1981 U	28.80	49.77	5.20	12.43	31.10	1.82	8.92	3.82	5.18	81.93	54.80
1991 U	31.22	51.62	7.89	8.47	36.12	1.90	8.89	3.70	5.19	85.93	49.80

Note: U = Urban.
Source: Census of India, 1981.
Census of India, 1991b.

covers a substantial proportion of the work force in the city. As a result, the percentage of workers in the household industry remains very low.

Socio-Cultural Set Up

Although Bhilwara is inhabited by people of different religions and faiths, the majority are Hindus, while Muslims are the second largest religious group. The prevalence of strong socio-cultural syneretic traditions in the city has engendered an ethos of incalculable communal harmony and people live with the spirit of brotherhood and cooperation. The peaceful environment has been an important element in the city's overall socio-economic development and prosperity.

The Scheduled Castes (SCs) constitute over 14 per cent of the city's total population (Census of India, 1991c). Compared to the state as well as district level proportion of the SC population in urban areas, their proportion in Bhilwara is low, although the gap is more remarkable between the district and the city (Table 3.5). The ST proportion in Bhilwara is fairly low. At the state level their proportion in the urban population is 2.53 per cent and at the district level 3.57 per cent while in Bhilwara it is only 1.27 per cent, indicating that with growing population the proportion of STs has remained very limited while other castes and communities have attained a larger share in the total population.

Table 3.5
Proportion of SC/ST to the Total Urban Population, 1991

(in percentage)

State/District/City	SC	ST
	Persons	Persons
Rajasthan	14.95	2.53
Bhilwara District	17.12	3.57
Bhilwara	14.55	1.27

Source: Census of India, 1991c.

DIMENSIONS OF POVERTY

Bhilwara has experienced a very rapid population growth since Independence as it has increased from nearly 36,000 in 1951 to more than 1,83,000 in 1991 (Census of India, 1991a). This five-fold population increase is remarkable because during this period the urban population growth rate both in the district and the state was relatively less than that in Bhilwara. Even in Rajasthan, in many other important cities like Jaipur, Jodhpur and Ajmer the population has not increased with the same rapidity (Table 3.6). The city's spectacular population growth is essentially attributed to its era of industrial and economic development since the 1960s which has attracted a large number of intra and inter district immigrants towards it in search of employment. The economic and industrial development of Bhilwara has significantly contributed to the gradual increase in the employment opportunities and income of the people, and as a result, the quality of physical and social infrastructure including housing, water supply and sanitation, etc. have considerably improved. However, over time the city's ever increasing population due to the collective impact of rural immigration and the natural population increase in the face of the city's limited resources to benefit the expanding needs of the population in terms of capacity and the opportunity to earn enough for ensuring a minimum consumption level, has led to the growing incidence of poverty and subsequent slummification in the city. Therefore, associated with the deprivation of the people in terms of earnings, poverty has found its way in Bhilwara. The inability of the city's potential to provide adequate economic opportunities and a proper living environment to a substantially large number of people has compelled them to stay in the city wherever government and marginal lands are laying vacant for a long time or on unauthorised private land without *patta* from the municipal corporation. With increasing population of the poor in the city these settlements have taken shape of slums which are continuously proliferating.

Location of Slums

Locally known as *kachchi bastis* (hereafter referred to as bastis), the slums in Bhilwara suffer from tremendous pressure on existing resources, environmental degradation, deficiency of basic services and

Table 3.6
Urban Population Growth in Rajasthan, Bhilwara and Select Cities (1951-91)

State/District/Citys	Status	1951	1961	1971	1981	1991
Rajasthan	Urban	2,955,275	3,281,478	4,543,761	7,210,508	10,040,118
Bhilwara Dist.	Urban	67,505	63,433	116,306	188,563	310,949
Jaipur	UA	304,380	410,376	636,768	1,015,160	1,514,425
Jodhpur	MC	180,717	224,760	317,612	506,345	648,621
Bikaner	UA	130,293	166,772	208,894	287,712	415,355
Ajmer	MC	196,633	231,240	264,291	375,593	401,930
Udaipur	MC	39,621	111,139	161,278	232,588	307,682
Bhilwara	MC	35,761	43,499	82,155	122,625	183,791

Source: Census of India 1981; Census of India 1991a.

infrastructural facilities, affecting both human health and productivity of enterprises. Presently, there are 39 bastis in Bhilwara. Table 3.7 gives their names and the approximate number of households in these bastis.

For the present study, out of a total 39 bastis of the city, 16 were selected for the field surveys which cross-sectionally represent the socio-economic characteristics of the basti dwellers. The 400 sample households, which constitute above 4 per cent of the total 7001 households in the sample bastis, were further distributed among them during the household survey so as to adequately represent various socio-cultural resident groups.

The sample bastis are scattered across the city, covering both its core and the periphery. However, those bastis situated in the core of the city are relatively small with flimsy and congested houses in which the families are crowded. Surrounded by densely packed affluent residential areas and the central business district, these bastis indicate the socio-economic dichotomy between the rich and poor who although live in the close proximity to each other, are yet clearly segregated. This glaring contrast is seen in the cases of basti like Gul Ali Nagari and Gul Mandi in the city.

The origin and growth of bastis on the city's peripheries have largely been associated with three factors. First, owing to inclusion of rural areas into the municipal boundary; second, by converting agricultural land into residential plots. In fact, due to easy acquisition of agricultural land on the peripheries by the urban poor for the construction of houses, in recent years the growth of bastis in these areas has been very rapid. Nevertheless, in the long run this characteristic also seems to have been helpful in controlling the undesirable flow of the poor from penetrating into the central and already crowded part of the city. Thirdly, by constructing the bastis closer to the factories and other industrial units. Except the third category where the place of work and the place of residence are in the same area, in the remaining two types of bastis, the poor residents have to travel farthest to gain access to the city's various social and economic facilities.

Table 3.7
UBS Bastis in Bhilwara

Sl. No.	Name of Basti	No. of households
1.	Pur (Part)	678
2.	Bilia Khurd	180
3.	Luxmipura	48
4.	Kumaria Khera	42
5.	Jaton Ka Khera	33
6.	Malan	294
7.	Islam Colony (Gandhi Nagar)	236
8.	Jodhamandal Ka Khera	46
9.	Gadri Khera	229
10.	Harijan Basti (Panch Mukhi)	48
11.	Azad Nagar	483
12.	Islam Colony (Shastri Nagar)	227
13.	Dadabari	167
14.	Bari Harni	108
15.	Sanganer	767
16.	Gul Ali Nagri	570
17.	Kuwara	38
18.	Odon Ka Khera	89
19.	Malikhera (Mahila Ashram)	71
20.	Kava Khera	318
21.	Labour Colony	523
22.	Mangalpura	112
23.	Kharolia Khera	48
24.	Malikhera (Pur)	27
25.	Balia Khera	27
26.	Sanjay Colony	407
27.	Kishnawaton Ki Kheri	212
28.	Deva Khera	61
29.	Mokhampura	46
30.	Harijan Basti (Shastri Nagar)	190
31.	Dhandholai	1185
32.	Shankar Colony	60
33.	Gulmandi	253
34.	Salara	92
35.	Jawaharnagar	972
36.	Choti Harni	46
37.	Kir Khera	46
38.	IV Grade Employees Colony	27
39.	Bhopalpur	43

Source: Bhilwara Municipal Council, 1990.

Table 3.8
Names of UBS Bastis in Bhilwara Selected for Household Survey

Sl. No.	Name of Basti	Total no. of of household	Sample no. of household
1.	Pur (Part)	678	39
2.	Sanganer	767	44
3.	Dhandholai	1185	68
4.	Harijan Basti (Shastri Nagar)	190	11
5.	Labour Colony	523	30
6.	Gul Ali Nagri	570	33
7.	Kishnawaton Ki Kheri	212	12
8.	Jawaharnagar	972	55
9.	Islam Colony (Gandhi Nagar)	236	13
10.	Gadri Khera	229	13
11.	Kava Khera	318	18
12.	Malan	294	17
13.	Bilia Khurd	180	10
14.	Gulmandi	253	14
15.	Islam Colony (Shastri Nagar)	227	13
16.	Dadabari	167	10
Total		7001	400

Depending upon the factors of origin and growth the appearances of the bastis on the peripheries varies a great deal. For example, some bastis like Kawa Khera and Kishnawaton Ki Kheri retain their traditional rural appearance since most of the houses are exact replicas of those found in the rural areas, while the labour colony is like any other urban low-income housing area owing to its proximity to many industrial units. Pur and Sanganer, on the other hand, have been included in the urban areas because of expansion of municipal limits and present a mixture of rural and urban settlements. In fact, some of their pockets are like the walled areas of an old city. However the peripheral bastis are relatively more deprived of urban civic amenities, although there is no real overcrowding and houses, in spite of being made from poor quality construction materials, are much more spacious than those in the core part of the city.

Characteristics of Poverty

Although in a wider perspective urban poverty is regarded as a multidimensional concept that includes the environment, access to services and psychological support (National Commission on

Urbanisation, 1988), deeply associated with the employment pattern and income levels, poverty in Bhilwara is essentially an economic problem and its origin lies in the low earning, low productive capacity of the people and indicates that the city's overall development has not been sufficient to cause a trickle down effect on the poor. Reflecting these features the sample bastis of the city indicate the prevalence of overwhelming poverty which in accordance with a definition of the slums consist of people earning low wages, suffering from chronic unemployment and underemployment and incapable of saving, reducing the possibility of effective participation in the growing economic system. The work force participation rate (WFPR) in the bastis is considerably low compared to that of the city as a whole. In the bastis WFPR is only 24 per cent, while for the entire city it is 31 per cent. Moreover, irrespective of males or females, most of the workers are engaged in low status and low income occupations (Table 3.9).

It is clear from the table 3.9 that the workers from the basti households are virtually found in all types of occupations which are largely restricted to the poor. The further distribution of workers in self-employed, regular and irregular job categories shows the engagement of half of the total slum work force in the lowest paid job category of unskilled or semiskilled irregular jobs, although the industrial development in the city has also led to a considerable proportion of regular job holders (28%). The proportion of self-employed persons is noticeably low who are basically pursuing petty trade and commercial activities which have little economic value. Mostly located near the bastis, the enterprises are subject to severe constraints which make it difficult, if not impossible, to expand into viable units capable of competing successfully with other formal sector enterprises. The average income and earnings of the participants in this sector thus tend to be slow as compared to the rest of the labour force in the formal sector.

A basti-wise study of the employment structure in the three job categories reveals that depending upon their location and other socio-economic considerations the workers' proportional distribution varies to a great extent.

Table 3.9
Distribution of Type of Jobs by Head of Household

Adult Male						Adult Female					
Self-Employed		Regular Job		Irregular job		Self-Employed		Regular Job		Irregular Job	
Type	No	Type	No	Type	No.	Type	No.	Type	No.	Type	No.
Carpenter	7	Accountant	1	Artisan	6	Bangle work	1	Mechanic	1	Brick-making	1
Cattle rearing	2	Clerk	10	Brick-making	11	Cultivation	6	Peon	5	Peon	1
Contractor	2	Compounder	1	Bus driver	10	Dairying	1	Sweeper	1	Sewing	1
Cultivator	20	Driver	3	Bus mechanic	7	House rent	1	Worker	4	Worker	23
Iron work	4	Govt. job	22	Cleaner	2	Shop	4				
Mechanic	6	Mason	8	Electrician	1	Washer-women	2				
Manufacturing	6	Mechanic	4	Fishing	7						
Painter	3	Peon	8	Mason	17						
Rag picker	3	Sweeper	8	Mechanic	2						
Rickshaw puller	6	Teacher	2	Painter	2						
Shop	18	Watchman	2	Peon	5						
Small business	8	Worker	79	Plumber	5						
Tailor	5			Shoe maker	8						
Tea stall	2			Tailor	6						
Theologian	1			Watchman	4						
Vendor	8			Worker	152						
Washerman	4			Miscellaneous	19						
	105		148		264		15		11		26

Source: Field Survey, Bhilwara, ISS, 1992.

Table 3.10
Types of Employment

Basti	Per cent distribution of type of employment		
	Self-employed	Regular job	Irregular job
Bilia Khurd	11	39	50
Dadabari	29	14	57
Dhandholai	19	12	69
Gadri Khera	56	44	0
Gul Ali Nagri	28	26	46
Gulmandi	44	17	39
Harijan Basti (Shastri Nagar)	6	88	6
Islam Colony (Gandhi Nagar)	22	33	44
Islam Colony (Shastri Nagar)	44	6	50
Jawaharnagar	10	31	59
Kava Khera	39	11	50
Kishnawaton Ki Khedi	6	31	63
Labour Colony	9	28	64
Malan	50	41	9
Pur (Part)	4	42	53
Sanganer	20	23	57
All Bastis	21	28	51

Source: Field Survey, Bhilwara, ISS, 1992.

However the massive concentration of workers in the irregular job category in nearly half of the sample slums is a typical feature of the employment structure of the bastis. Therefore, the low income levels of irregular workers are proliferating the poor and helping the perpetuation of poverty among the basti dwellers as a variety of jobs fall under the irregular work which include primary, secondary as well as tertiary sectors. The variation in this regard is mainly related to the location of the basti. Those bastis located in the core area of the city have more irregular in secondary and tertiary sectors pertaining to commercial activities. As one moves towards the peripherial areas, the proportion of workers in the primary sector starts increasing.

Incidence of Poverty

After identification of the incidence of poverty in Bhilwara, this section attempts to gauge the degree of poverty in the bastis of the city by applying different quantitative measures. It is clear from the preceding discussion that poverty is, in fact, a relative concept whereby some people are regarded as poor if they suffer from relative deprivation in terms of economic inequality. This makes poverty a complex phenomenon which cannot be reduced to a single definition and has to be defined in relation to basic economic indicators. Therefore, in identifying the poor there may be two alternative methods: First, the direct method, which does not involve the use of any income notion, in particular not that poverty-line income and is simply to check the set of people whose actual consumption baskets happen to leave some basic needs unsatisfied (Sen, 1986). Second is called the income method which is based on the calculation of the minimum income level and the identification of those below the poverty line and the income expenditure correlates of the poor. However, considering the fact that the income of a person is not merely a rough aid to predicting a person's actual consumption but also captures his ability to meet his minimum needs. Therefore, on the basis of income indicators this section deals with the measurements of poverty in Bhilwara. It takes into consideration two specific types of analyses for such measurements:

i. Differentials in income-expenditure
ii. Persons below and above poverty line

Differentials in Household Income–Expenditure: That the Bhilwara bastis show the typical characteristics of poverty and deprivation is manifested in the average household income of Rs. 1080 (Table 3.11) with on an average six-member family size in the surveyed bastis. Although the economic activities of the heads of the sampled households are clearly classified into self-employment, regular and irregular jobs which cover a wide range of occupations (Table 3.9), there is no significant variation in the average household incomes among the bastis since the coefficient of variation (CV) is only 20. In fact, owing to the prevalence of a higher degree of unemployment among the basti dwellers, a big household has not necessarily been in a position to earn more money and, therefore, there appears to be no significant positive correlation between average family size of the bastis and their average monthly household income. Moreover, when household income and expenditure levels in these localities are analysed together in most of the bastis income and expenditure are very close to each other without any significant variation. Obviously, a low proportion of those in employment and low income-high expenditure pattern is helping perpetuate poverty and destitution in these areas.

Table 3.11
Income and Level of Poverty

(*in rupees*)

Bastis	Average household monthly Income	Average household monthly Expenditure	Per capita monthly income	Persons below poverty line	Above poverty line
Bilia Khurd	1201	1163	185	6 (60.0%)	4 (40.0%)
Dadabari	1263	810	188	8 (80.0%)	2 (20.0%)
Dhandholai	870	678	169	48 (70.6%)	20 (29.4%)
Gadri Khera	1366	1145	179	11 (84.6%)	22 (15.4%)
Gul Ali Nagri	963	700	156	28 (84.8%)	5 (15.2%)
Gulmandi	1018	688	172	12 (85.7%)	2 (14.3%)
Harijan Basti (Shastri Nagar)	1319	619	230	9 (81.8%)	2 18.2%)
Islam Colony (Gandhi Nagar)	1135	1202	146	10 (76.9%)	3 (23.1%)
Islam Colony (Shastri Nagar)	1087	639	181	11 (84.6%)	2 (15.4%)
Jawaharnagar	954	850	152	42 (76.4%)	13 (23.6%)
Kava Khera	896	587	212	11 (61.1%)	7 (38.9%)
Kishnawaton ki Khedi	886	617	180	10 (83.3%)	2 (16.1%)
Labour Colony	1296	858	213	24 (80.0%)	6 (20.0%)
Malan	1442	1074	183	15 (88.2%)	2 (11.8%)
Pur (Part)	933	645	168	28 (71.8%)	11 (28.2%)
Sanganer	645	781	103	38 (86.4%)	6 (13.6%)
All Bastis	1080	817	166	311 (77.8%)	89 (22.2%)

Source: Field Survey, Bhilwara, ISS, 1992.

Persons below and above Poverty Line: The twin factors of low average household income and relatively large family size have also affected the monthly per capita income which on an average, is merely Rs. 166. The amount is certainly not sufficient for meeting the basic necessities required for maintaining the physical health and working capacity of an individual and generate such conditions that a majority of people in the bastis to pass their lives below the poverty line. By adopting recently updated criterion of the Eighth Five-Year Plan declaring Rs. 209 (1990-91 prices) monthly per capita expenditure as the urban poverty line (Economic Times, 1992), Table 3.11 indicates that 77.8 per cent households had per capita expenditure levels below Rs. 209 while only 23.3 per cent households spent more than this amount.

It is, therefore, clear from the preceding analysis that poverty is the hallmark of Bhilwara bastis. Both the measurements applied in the discussion to highlight the degree of poverty drive home the point that widespread unemployment, deprivation from well paid and better jobs, and a very low and insignificant participation of women in the workforce have resulted in the extremely bad economic condition of the basti dwellers. This feature has not only contributed in their emergence as a separate community in the entire setting of the city but also calls for immediate steps aiming at the upliftment of their living conditions and alleviation of poverty among them.

DEMOGRAPHIC, SOCIAL AND ECONOMIC CHARACTERISTICS

Demographic Characteristics

Population Structure: The 400 sampled households in the 16 surveyed bastis in Bhilwara have a total population of 2397.
It is evident from Table 3.11 that the population size of bastis shows a lot of variation depending upon different socio-economic and geographical factors which play a crucial role in determining the viability of living in these localities and, therefore, a more advantageous location in this regard has a bigger basti with a large population size.

As a general trend, while the bastis in the outskirts of the city are big and accommodate a large number of people, owing to lack of open and vacant spaces in the central parts the bastis are smaller and the population of those residing there is relatively small. However, irrespective of variation in the number of persons in the bastis, the family size is very large as each family on an average has six persons. This is against the five-person average family size in the country. In the bastis like Bilia Khurd, Dadabari, Gadri Khera, Islam Colony (Gandhinagar) and Malan the average family size is further higher up to eight. Although in some households the practice of joint family has also encouraged this characteristic, the high birth rate among the basti dwellers is the most significant factor in this regard. Considering the inverse interrelationship between fertility and some important variables of the social aggregate system like literacy, educational attainment, participation in economic activities of the couple and the income of the family, the prevalence of poverty accompanied by illiteracy, dirt and ignorance in Bhilwara bastis has resulted in high fertility rates which have consequently contributed to a large family size.

Table 3.12
Distribution of Population

Basti	Sample households	Population		
		P	M	F
Bilia Khurd	10	65	28	37
Dadabari	10	67	31	36
Dhandholai	68	349	181	168
Gadri Khera	13	99	50	49
Gul Ali Nagri	33	203	111	92
Gulmandi	14	83	41	42
Harijan Basti (Shastri Nagar)	11	63	31	32
Islam Colony (Gandhi Nagar)	13	101	47	54
Islam Colony (Shastri Nagar)	13	78	37	41
Jawaharnagar	55	345	181	164
Kava Khera	18	76	39	37
Kishnawaton ki Khedi	12	59	26	33
Labour Colony	30	183	103	80
Malan	17	134	63	71
Pur (Part)	39	216	105	111
Sanganer	40	276	138	138
All Bastis	400	2397	1212	1185

Note: NA = Not Available.
Source: Field Survey, Bhilwara, ISS, 1992.

An important question in this regard is about the desired family size of the households in these bastis. Unfortunately, there is no wholly satisfactory way to measure the number of children wanted by married women who have already embarked on their child bearing careers (Cho, 1978). It has been noted by others that when asked how many children they would want if they 'could choose the numbers', couples tend to rationalise the children already born and living with them (Ryder and Westoff, 1971). Nevertheless, the use of family planning methods by nearly one-fourth married women in the reproductive age group in the bastis indicates that despite such rationalisation there is a growing awareness among them for fewer children than are living presently.

Migrants and Non-Migrants: Besides the non-migrant households the Bhilwara bastis have a substantial proportion of immigrants. On an average immigrant households constitute 27 per cent of the total surveyed basti households, although Jawaharnagar and Kawa Khera have as high as 71 per cent and 56 per cent immigrant households respectively. The on-going process of economic development in the city has been a major pull factor for immigrants since all the heads of immigrant households have reported the search for job as the main reason for their coming to Bhilwara.

Particularly in recent years the bastis have received a continuous flow of migrants since nearly half of the migrant households are staying here for less than ten years. Intra-district migration, mainly from rural areas, is the predominant stream followed by inter-district migration within the state, while inter state migration is almost negligible. In fact, the concentration of immigrants in the bastis is to a greater extent based on a network of primary affinity of dialect, region, village, caste or kin, etc. It has particularly enabled the rural migrants coming from small village communities to become socialised and accultured in the complex and diversified environment of the city. However, unlike other bigger cities and metropolises the Bhilwara bastis are not inhabited on the basis of regional affiliations since non-migrants and migrants are mostly from the same region and inherit similar cultural values.

Table 3.13
Average Family Size and Percentage Migrants

Basti	Average size of house-hold	Per cent migrant house-holds	Per cent above 10 years migrancy length	Per cent majority migrancy reason (job)
Bilia Khurd	7	30	100	100
Dadabari	7	0	0	NA
Dhandholai	5	28	58	100
Gadri Khera	8	23	67	100
Gul Ali Nagri	6	30	40	100
Gulmandi	6	29	50	100
Harijan *Basti* (Shastri Nagar)	6	9	0	100
Islam Colony (Gandhi Nagar)	8	15	50	100
Islam Colony (Shastri Nagar)	6	46	33	100
Jawaharnagar	6	71	64	100
Kava Khera	4	56	20	100
Kishnawaton ki Khedi	5	0	0	NA
Labour Colony	6	0	0	NA
Malan	8	18	100	100
Put (Part)	6	21	25	100
Sanganer	6	2	0	100
All Bastis	6	27	52	100

Source: Field Survey, Bhilwara, ISS, 1992.

Age-Sex Composition: The high birth rates in the bastis have also affected the age-sex composition in Bhilwara. Table 3.14 indicates that the proportion of children in the total population is considerably high who constitute 43.40 per cent of the total population of the bastis, though among males their proportion is 46.53 per cent and among the females it is 40.17 per cent.

Sex-wise, while among the children the proportion of males is higher than females, among adults the situation is contrary, resulting in the sex ratio being in favour of females in as many as nine bastis. But on an average in line with the all India trend the sex-ratio is favourable to males which reflects more adverse mortality conditions for females compared to males, particularly during childhood. For, in spite of an overall improvement in the health conditions, owing to inherent sex bias, women still get differentiated from men when it comes to providing medical care to them (Premi *et al.* 1983). A subsequent section of this chapter would show that in the surveyed bastis the

Table 3.14
Age-Sex Composition

Basti	Total no. of persons	Adults		Children		Percentage of Total Adult		Percentage of Total Children		% of Males		% of Females		Sex Ratio
		Male	Female	Male	Female	Male	Female	Male	Female	Adult	Child	Adult	Child	
Bilia Khurd	65	18	24	10	13	27.70	36.92	15.38	20.0	64.29	35.71	64.86	35.14	1321
Dadabari	67	24	24	7	12	35.82	35.82	10.44	17.91	77.42	22.58	66.67	33.33	1161
Dhandholai	349	91	98	90	70	26.07	28.09	25.79	20.05	50.27	49.73	58.33	41.67	928
Gadri Khera	99	28	32	22	17	28.28	32.32	22.22	17.17	56.9	44.0	65.30	34.7	980
Gul Ali Nagar	203	61	53	50	39	30.05	26.11	24.63	19.21	54.95	45.05	57.60	42.4	828
Gulmandi	83	21	29	20	13	25.30	34.94	24.10	15.66	51.22	48.78	69.04	30.96	1024
Harijan Basti (Shastri Nagar)	63	15	22	16	10	23.81	34.92	25.40	15.87	48.39	51.61	68.75	31.25	1032
Islam Colony (Gandhi Nagar)	101	21	24	26	30	20.8	23.76	25.74	29.70	44.68	55.32	44.44	55.56	1149
Islam Colony (Shastri Nagar)	78	19	25	18	16	24.36	32.05	23.07	20.51	51.35	48.65	49.01	50.99	1108
Jawaharnagar	345	99	94	82	70	28.70	27.25	23.77	20.28	54.70	45.3	53.41	46.59	906
Kava Khera	76	19	20	20	17	25.0	26.32	26.32	22.36	48.71	51.29	54.05	45.95	948
Kishnawaton ki Kheri	59	15	21	11	12	25.42	35.60	18.64	20.34	57.70	42.3	63.63	36.37	1269
Labour Colony	183	60	55	43	25	32.79	30.05	23.50	13.66	58.25	41.75	68.75	31.25	776
Malan	134	35	43	28	28	26.12	32.10	20.89	20.89	55.55	44.45	60.56	39.44	1126
Pur (Part)	216	51	60	54	51	23.61	27.78	25.0	23.61	48.57	51.43	54.95	45.05	1057
Sanganer	276	71	85	67	53	27.72	30.80	24.27	19.20	51.44	48.56	61.59	38.41	1000
All Bastis	2397	648	709	564	476	27.03	29.58	23.53	19.86	53.46	46.53	59.83	40.17	977

Source: Field Survey, Bhilwara, ISS, 1992.

medical and health care facilities for women are in a very deplorable state. This phenomenon accompanied by their socially degraded position has led to adverse sex ratio in the bastis.

Social Characteristics

Religion and Caste: Hinduism has the largest following in the Bhilwara bastis since 90 per cent of the population in the sampled households are adherents of this religion. The remaining 10 per cent of the population is shared by other religious groups, prominent among them being the Muslims. Apart from six bastis, namely, Bilia Khurd, Dadabari, Gadri Khera, Kawa Khera, Kishnawaton ki Kheri and Malan where the entire population is Hindu, and one basti, namely Islam Colony (Shastrinagar), where all the residents are Muslims, in the remaining nine bastis different religious groups co-exist and stay together in an atmosphere of harmony and amity. Nevertheless, out of these nine bastis, except Islam Colony (Gandhinagar), a Muslim dominated basti, in the remaining eight bastis the Hindus are the preponderant majority.

Table 3.15
Language, Religion and Caste (General)

Basti	Religion Hindu	Caste General
Bilia Khurd	100	80
Dadabari	100	10
Dhandholai	93	31
Gadri Khera	100	92
Gul Ali Nagri	97	91
Gulmandi	93	7
Harijan Basti (Shastri Nagar)	91	9
Islam Colony (Gandhi Nagar)	15	92
Islam Colony (Shastri Nagar)	0	100
Jawaharnagar	95	53
Kava Khera	100	11
Kishnawaton ki Kheri	100	42
Labour Colony	87	70
Malan	100	100
Pur (Part)	97	5
Sanganer	95	45
All Bastis	90	49

Source: Field Survey, Bhilwara, ISS, 1992.

As far as caste is concerned, the classification in terms of three broad categories, that is, general, Scheduled Castes and Scheduled Tribes (SCs/STs), indicate that as a whole, 49 per cent of the total population in the bastis belong to the general category and the remaining 51 per cent comprise SC/ST residents. Since SC/ST come under Hinduism, it is clear that most of the Hindus in the bastis are SCs/STs. This is the reason why in the Muslim dominated bastis of Islam Colony (Gandhinagar) and Islam Colony (Shastrinagar) the proportion of the general caste category is as high as 92 and 100 per cent respectively. Except these two bastis and Malan where the entire sample households population belong to the general caste category, SCs/STs are residing in all the remaining bastis. However, their distribution pattern among bastis shows remarkable variations. For example, in Gul Mandi and Harijan Basti (Shastrinagar) the percentages of general population are only seven and nine respectively, while in some other bastis like Gadri Khera and Gul Ali Nagari it is more than 90 per cent. A statistical analysis of this trend shows that 0.73 value of the coefficient of variation (CV) is an indication that there is considerable variation and inconsistency in the distribution of general castes as well as SCs/STs among the bastis. Obviously these bastis are not merely aggregations of shacks and huts but communities of fellow residents and therefore, the variations in the concentration of castes and tribes in a specific basti is influenced by several socio-cultural and economic factors. In fact, many of the bastis are inhabited by the people living together mainly on the basis of caste affiliations. For example Harijan Basti and Gadri Khera are occupied by the Harijans and Gadris respectively. Even in those bastis where their names are not associated with religion or caste like Jawaharnagar, Malan and Dhandholai, etc. there are separate pockets based on caste affiliations.

Mother Tongue: The surveyed bastis in Bhilwara exhibit absolute linguistic uniformity as Hindi is the mother tongue of all the residents. Although Bhilwara, like Rajasthan State, is a Hindi speaking city and its original inhabitants use it as their mother tongue, Hindi is also the mother tongue of the immigrants who form one-fourth of the total sampled households. This is mainly because of the fact that these immigrants are mostly from within Rajasthan either through inter or intra-district migration and those from outside the state, albeit negligible, also belong to Hindi speaking states who have come here in search of better employment opportunities. In spite of being a rapidly growing industrial city, Bhilwara has yet to attract people from non-Hindi speaking states. Thus, both on account of the natural increase of population and the place of origin of immigrants, Hindi is the mother tongue of basti dwellers in Bhilwara.

Literacy and Educational Attainment: Like in any other locality of the poor, in Bhilwara bastis also there is a widespread prevalence of illiteracy. Particularly among adults 65 per cent people are illiterate and out of the remaining proportion of literates the major concentration is at the primary, middle and high school levels.

Only a negligible proportion of males have obtained education above high school while no woman has pursued education at this level. In fact, except Bilia Khurd, the proportion of literate female adults is always less than males. Noticeably with increase in the level of educational attainment the difference between males and females is widening which implies that as educational level increases the drop-outs among females are more frequent. In fact, a survey of 3168 girl children conducted by the Bhilwara UBS office in the bastis aiming at analysing the reasons for their not going to school in 1990 indicated that child marriage, lack of interest, economic and social compulsions, lack of educational facility and work at home are the main reasons behind female drop-outs and their low educational attainment in these bastis (Bhilwara Municipal Council, 1990).

Table 3.17 shows that the majority of girl children are not able to attend schools owing to economic reasons, lack of interest and lack of educational facilities. Other factors are relatively less significant. However, over time the younger generation in the bastis has an increasing interest in education. Among children the percentage of those in primary classes is the highest. It is 40 per cent for males and 24 per cent for females. Although this figure itself is very low, considering the general poverty and destitution in the bastis and the existing proportion of literate adults this percentage of children in primary classes is remarkable.

To a greater extent the inadequacy of educational facilities in the bastis is contributing to the perpetuation of a low literacy level among the children and makes the task difficult for parents to send their wards to school for education. Anganwadis in the bastis run by the ICDS so far have shown only a limited impact in motivating the children for attending classes as they are only four and confined to certain pockets.

Table 3.16
Levels of Adult Education

Basti	No. of sample house-holds	Total No. of Adults		Percent Distribution of Adult								Percent illiterate Adults
				Primary Educated		Middle School		High School		Above High School		
		Male	Female	Male	Female	Male	Female	Male	Female	Male	Female	
Bilia Khurd	10	18	24	17	33	11	4	44	0	0	0	48
Dadabari	10	24	24	33	0	21	0	8	0	0	0	69
Dhandholai	68	91	98	35	11	9	1	10	0	0	0	68
Gadri Khera	13	28	32	32	9	21	0	7	0	0	0	67
Gul Ali Nagari	33	61	53	30	2	21	9	10	4	11	0	54
Gulmandi	14	21	29	33	3	19	0	0	3	0	0	74
Harijan Basti (Shastri Nagar)	11	15	22	27	14	20	0	13	0	7	0	65
Islam Colony (Gandhi Nagar)	13	21	24	19	4	29	8	5	8	5	0	62
Islam Colony (Shastri Nagar)	13	19	25	32	0	32	4	5	0	0	0	68
Jawaharnagar	55	99	94	21	3	24	0	6	0	6	0	70
Kava Khera	18	19	20	50	0	0	0	0	0	0	0	76
Kishnawaton ki Khedi	12	15	21	25	0	0	0	0	0	0	0	90
Labour Colony	30	60	55	17	96	20	0	14	2	8	0	22
Malan	17	35	43	17	9	14	23	20	2	11	0	53
Pur (Part)	39	51	60	39	3	16	0	4	0	0	0	71
Sanganer	44	71	85	1	0	10	0	3	0	1	2	92
All Bastis	400	648	709	23	13	21	3	9	1	4	0	65

Source: Field Survey, Bhilwara, ISS, 1992.

Besides, primary schools either of municipalities or other private organisations are very few in the bastis. Out of a total of 39 bastis of the city in 20 bastis there is no government primary school, while nine of them do not have them in a radius of two km. Obviously, the non-availability of primary schools in almost half of the bastis is in itself a crucial factor behind low literacy rate among the children, particularly in a situation where the parents may lack will as well as resources to send their children to schools located in distant areas of the city.

Table 3.17
Reasons for Girl Children not Attending School

Reason	No. of girl children	Percentage
Child marriage	7	0.20
Lack of interest	932	29.42
Economic reasons	1007	31.80
Social reasons	421	13.30
Lack of educational facility	614	19.38
Domestic work	187	5.90

Source: Bhilwara Municipal Council, 1990.

Economic Characteristics

As discussed earlier, the 24 per cent working population in bastis in contrast to 31 per cent for the city as a whole explains the prevalence of a higher degree of unemployment in these localities. Only one basti, Dadabari, has 31 per cent work force participation. This phenomenon accompanied by an enormous concentration of workers in the informal sector and low paid employment emphasises the typical basti development structure characterised with the general prevalence of poverty and deprivation.

However, as Table 3.19 shows there is considerable variation in the work force participation between males and females and between children and adults in bastis. Significantly, child labour in bastis is not common since out of a total 587 workers only 18 were child workers. In most of the bastis either there is no child labour or only one. Therefore in the work force structure and employment pattern in the bastis, child labour largely has an insignificant role. Besides, the female work force participation is also very low. They constitute only

Table 3.18
Child Education

Basti	No. of sample house-hold	Total no. of children		Percentage distribution of children's education							
				Primary		Balwadis		Anganwadi		Other school	
		Male	Female	Male	Female	Male	Female	Male	Female	Male	Female
Bilia Khurd	10	10	13	30	46	20	0	0	0	20	15
Dadabari	10	7	12	71	0	0	0	29	8	14	0
Dhandholai	68	90	70	39	11	0	0	2	0	13	14
Gadri Khera	13	22	17	50	41	5	0	9	0	0	0
Gul Ali Nagri	33	50	39	52	28	0	0	4	3	16	15
Gulmandi	14	20	13	35	31	0	0	0	0	25	15
Harijan Basti (Shastri Nagar)	11	16	10	50	20	0	0	0	0	38	0
Islam Colony (Gandhi Nagar)	13	26	30	35	30	0	0	4	0	0	0
Islam Colony (Shastri Nagar)	13	18	16	44	50	0	0	0	0	11	6
Jawaharnagar	55	82	70	40	33	0	0	5	4	22	10
Kava Khera	18	20	17	45	18	0	0	5	0	0	6
Kishnawaton ki Khedi	12	11	12	27	0	0	0	0	0	0	0
Labour Colony	30	43	25	47	52	0	0	0	0	40	20
Malan	17	28	28	43	25	0	0	14	7	18	11
Pur (Part)	39	54	51	39	10	0	0	2	8	7	6
Sanganer	44	67	53	25	17	0	0	0	0	18	2
All Bastis	400	564	476	40	24	1	0	3	2	16	9

Source: Field Survey, Bhilwara, ISS, 1992.

17 per cent of the total female adult population whereas in the case of adult males their proportion is 80.71 per cent. The remaining 19 per cent unemployed adults may belong to that group of people who owing to certain handicaps, physical or mental inability or lack of interest in employment, do not work. Thus, a very low overall work force participation. Although a negligible percentage of child labour in the work force is a healthy sign and may be attributed to the growing consciousness among their parents to send their children to schools rather than asking them to do petty jobs. A low female work force participation is mainly linked with a low level of literacy and limited employment opportunities particularly because of the fact that Bhilwara does not have an infrastructure of handicrafts and cottage industries which are ideal for unskilled and illiterate women and in other industrial establishments there is hardly any opportunity for them. Even for the types of work done by their menfolk in irregular, regular and self-employed job category they have only a limited participation.

The variation in the nature of job and employment status has also caused differences in the monthly household income in the bastis. Table 3.20 shows that extreme income groups at both the ends have relatively less number of households while the major concentration is in the middle income groups.

Table 3.19
Work Force Participation Rate

Basti	No. of working persons in total population	No. of Adults	Number and percentage of working adults in total adult population		
			P	M	F
Bilia Khurd	18 (28)	42	15 (35.7)	13 (72.22)	2 (8.33)
Dadabari	21 (31)	48	19 (40)	19 (79.16)	0 (0)
Dhandholai	89 (26)	189	88 (47.08)	80 (89)	8 (8.16)
Gadri Khera	25 (25)	60	24 (40)	20 (71.43)	4 (12.5)
Gul Ali Nagri	50 (25)	114	48 (42.10)	46 (75.41)	2 (3.77)
Gulmandi	18 (22)	50	17 (34)	16 (76.20)	1 (3.44)
Harijan Basti (Shastri Nagar)	16 (25)	37	16 (43.24)	12 (80)	4 (18.8)
Islam Colony (Gandhi Nagar)	18 (18)	45	18 (40)	14 (66.66)	4 (16.66)
Islam Colony (Shastri Nagar)	19 (23)	44	18 (43.18)	16 (89.47)	2 (8)
Jawaharnagar	90 (26)	193	88 (45.6)	81 (81.81)	7 (7.44)
Kava Khera	19 (24)	39	18 (48.72)	17 (94.74)	1 (5)
Kishnavaton ki Kheri	16 (27)	36	16 (44.44)	15 (100)	1 (4.76)
Labour Colony	48 (26)	115	47 (41.74)	46 (78.33)	1 (1.82)
Malan	32 (24)	78	31 (39.74)	28 (80)	3 (6.97)
Pur (Part)	46 (21)	111	45 (41.44)	42 (84.31)	3 (5)
Sanganer	62 (22)	156	61 (39.74)	52 (74.65)	9 (10.60)
All Bastis	587 (24.48)	1357	569 (41.13)	517 (80.71)	52 (7.33)

Note: Figures in parentheses are percentages.
Source: Field Survey, Bhilwara, ISS, 1992.

Table 3.20
Monthly Income Class and Number of Households

Income Class	Number of households
Rs. 101 - 250	10
Rs. 251 - 500	63
Rs. 501 - 1000	179
Rs. 1001 - 2000	115
Above Rs. 2000	33

Source: Field Survey, Bhilwara, ISS, 1992.

POVERTY ALLEVIATION AND ROLE OF UBS PROGRAMME

The preceding sections analysed the prevalence of poverty among the Bhilwara basti dwellers and their demographic as well as socio-economic characteristics. Bhilwara's rapid population growth accompanied by a consistent increase in the number of the urban poor is resulting in a mounting pressure on the city's existing resources and infrastructure. Particularly in recent years the enormous concentration of population in these bastis and its ever increasing trend have drawn the attention of policy makers for implementing any poverty alleviation programme in the city to improve the quality of living in these bastis. It is known that to ameliorate the socio-economic and environmental conditions of the slum dwellers and to make the slums more habitable, from time to time the government has implemented a number of programmes like Integrated Child Development Services (ICDS), Integrated Development of Small and Medium Towns (IDSMT), Urban Basic Services (UBS) and Nehru Rozgar Yojana (NRY), etc., with the objective of urban poverty alleviation under the framework of planned development in India. Therefore, in order to improve the infrastructure and other facilities for the first time IDSMT was launched in the city in the Sixth Five-Year Plan (1980-85). During the period of its implementation the programme played a significant role in providing basic infrastructure and facilities such as drinking water, community baths, toilets, sewerage and street lights etc. to the basti dwellers in the city. Nevertheless, it is to be realised that a sustainable strategy of poverty alleviation has to be based on increasing the productive employment opportunities in the process of economic growth itself. However, to the extent the process of growth bypasses some sections of the population, it is necessary to formulate specific poverty alleviation programmes for the generation of a certain minimum level of income for the urban poor. Taking into consideration these aspects of urban poverty when Nehru Rozgar Yojana (NRY) was introduced in the country in 1989, Bhilwara was also selected for the scheme's implementation. The NRY began in Bhilwara in 1990. However, during the short time span this programme has been able to play only a limited role. Its loans have largely been confined to micro enterprises. Till March 1992, 583 persons had applied for loans but only 163 got them, although 314 application forms were approved for the loan. Particularly in bastis the number of loan holders was negligible and loans for house upgradation were largely denied. For example, in one instance in March 1991 in response to an announcement from the municipal authorities the neighbourhood development committee in Jawaharnagar *basti* took very keen interest for encouraging people to fill the application forms for getting the loans for house upgradation under the NRY and as many as 33 people applied for the loan. But loans were not sanctioned to them even after more than one year of their applying and during the field work for the present study the applicants were seen blaming the office bearers of the neighbourhood development committee for the money they allegedly wasted in applying for the loan and that the intention of their leaders was not fair.

However, while NRY was not launched and IDSMT was still going on in Bhilwara, at the national level the problem of urban poverty was brought into a sharper focus during the Seventh Five-Year Plan with the realisation of the inadequacy of a service delivery model involving one main supplier – the government or its allied agencies. It was realised that in all these programmes, nowhere have the twin processes of integrating basic services and of community participation been treated as being central to operationalisation of these programmes. A greater emphasis on the need for local people's involvement in the provision and management of basic services for the poor was realised. This led to the launching of a new poverty alleviation programme named UBS in 1986 (National Institute of Urban Affairs, 1986). In view of the renewed recognition of the importance of decentralised planning (Rao, 1989), the philosophy of the programme insisted on the self-help and participatory mechanism amongst the local people at the beneficiary level aiming to improve their quality of life. The UBS for the first time in the urban slum intervention recognised the fundamental position of these two processes in getting a programme off the ground. The UBS in its provisions sets three criteria for the selection of the district as a planning unit for this programme. These are (i) where the urban growth ratio is disturbingly fast, (ii) where basic services are not available to a majority of the slum population, and (iii) where it would be possible to implement the programme along with other government sponsored programmes like IDSMT and EIUS. Bhilwara was one such district out of a total of 36 districts selected for the UBS implementation from across the country on the basis of the above mentioned criteria (National Institute of Urban Affairs, 1986). Although Mandal, Jahazpur and Gangapur were other urban places covered under the programme in the district, Bhilwara was the only city (population above 100,000) belonging to class A category with a slum population ranging from 30,000-60,000.

Institutional Arrangements of the UBS Programme in Bhilwara City

The UBS programme was launched in Bhilwara in 1987 along with seven other municipalities in the district. At that time activities under the IDSMT were going on in 27 bastis of Bhilwara. The UBS not only replaced the IDSMT in these settlements but also enlarged the coverage by including all the 39 bastis of the city. The rationale influencing the decision for the adoption of Bhilwara under the UBS programme was officially explained as a significant increase in the urban population of the district, the gap in the provision of basic services and amenities as compared to the rise in the urban population, nearly 40 per cent of the slum population do not have latrines in their houses and nearly 60 per cent of the urban population in the district is illiterate (Bhilwara Municipal Council, 1987).

The programme's thrust on the urban poor was a new concept since there was no precedence of any such programme in the city. Particularly in view of growing population of the poor, the aims and objectives and proposed organisational arrangements were its unique features. As per the programme's guidelines the major consideration behind the selection of the 39 bastis in the city for the UBS programme's implementation was the poor living conditions of the basti dwellers and inadequate delivery of the civic amenities, both public and private, to them.

The UBS, since its inception, has gradually strengthened its institutional set-up in Bhilwara city. The programme is headed by a district coordinator who is overall in charge of the programme at the district level. He holds this charge in addition to his responsibilities as the chief executive of the district board and is accountable to the district collector. His work relating to UBS is more advisory in character. There are four broad areas looked after by the district coordinator. These are: fund distribution, monitoring of the programme, technical guidance in UBS activities and programme guidance. At the city level the programme is headed by the project officer (PO) who is an employee of the Municipal Council, Bhilwara. His responsibilities regarding UBS are in addition to his assignment as health officer of the Municipal Council. However, he agrees that he does not have any difficulty in dealing with the UBS programme as additional work. In fact, he seems to be very happy in performing his both the duties. There are four community organisers (COs), including a woman, under the PO. The main functions of the COs are to assist the Project Officer in formulation, implementation and management of the plan of action, to implement, monitor and manage the UBS at the basti level, to catalyse collective initiative through neighbourhood groups, basti development committees for the well-being of the communities under his jurisdiction and to continuously motivate and mobilise the basti dwellers for self-action. In order to organise them to perform their duties in an effective manner the 39 UBS bastis have been distributed among all the four COs.

The official machinery of the UBS comprising district coordinator, project officer and community organisers is supported by resident community volunteers (RCVs) at the basti level. They are members of the respective basti development committees with their main functions being to create a conducive atmosphere in neighbourhoods and encourage all residents to participate actively and voluntarily in the UBS programme, and to help the COs plan, implement and monitor the UBS programme in their allotted bastis. A basti development committee with RCVs as its members works as a representative body of the local basti dwellers and attempts to enhance the community participation and the spirit of self-reliance among them. Thus, under the UBS people's participation in the delivery of basic services at the local level has been ensured through the channels of the basti development committee. To make these bodies representative and democratic in character there is a provision for the selection of one

RCV out of every 20-25 households of the basti. Such selections in Bhilwara had taken place at the beginning of the programme in 1987. It may be clarified that the services offered by the community volunteers are not on a full time basis nor do they receive any payment against such services from the UBS or any other body.

It is clear that the institutional arrangement of the UBS in Bhilwara, as per the provisions of the programme, is at two levels. The first is at the official level while the second is through some volunteers who offer their services in the programme's operations at the local level. Another aspect of this voluntary participation in UBS is the involvement of important senior residents of the city in the UBS to offer their expertise to the programme when so desired. They are called 'trainers on call' and consist of a group of 12 such persons. Except one, a journalist, all of them are retired government/ semi-government officials who had held responsible positions during their service tenure.

Implementation of UBS in Bhilwara

The UBS in Bhilwara has been implemented since the beginning of the programme's operation in 1987. In order to set out the broad framework for UBS implementation in the district, a District UBS Plan of Operation was prepared in early 1987 in accordance with the guidelines issued by the UBS programme. This document, the collective work of officials from the UBS and the UNICEF, besides elaborating the demographic and socio-economic conditions of all the towns selected for the UBS in the district, also highlighted the salient features of urban poverty in the district and explained the various problems associated with it. It attempts to emphasise the rapid population increase mainly due to the establishment of a large number of industries in the district and the consequent gap in the provisions of basic services and amenities as compared to the rise in urban population. Since the urban local authorities could not provide appropriate support for the increase in basic services, this gap continues to widen and as a result the ratio of the urban poor families deprived of or who face inadequate basic services has been increasing constantly. Nearly 40 per cent of the slum population does not have latrines in their houses and have a very high IMR. Table 3.21 summarises the prevailing scenario of certain key socio-medical indicators in Bhilwara in 1987.

Table 3.21
Bhilwara District: Summary of Problems

Indicators		Per-centage	Year of Data
Poverty	% Urban population living below the poverty line	37.0*	1986
Employment	% of unemployed (urban)	51.77	1981
	% marginally employed (urban)	13.96	1981
Health (State level)	Infant mortality rate (Urban)	52.8	1985
	% of children (3-1 years) not immunised	44.0	1985
	% Urban Child Deaths due to:		
	Water related diseases	24.5	1985
	EPI diseases	4.9	1985
Education	% Not enrolled for primary education (urban)	51.0	1986-87
	Primary School Dropout rate (Urban)	15.41	1986-87
	Literate:		
	Male	58.56	1981
	Female	30.23	1981
	Total (Urban)	46.0	1981
Water and sanitation	*% Urban Population*:		
	Without access to safe water	NIL	
	Without access to sanitary latrine facilities	43.35	1983
Shelter (City level)	Living in slums and other substandard dwellings	37.0	1987

Note: * as per estimate of 1986 provided by district statistical office.
Source: Bhilwara Municipal Council, 1987.

According to the operation plan the following were the reasons for the justification behind the selection of Bhilwara district for the UBS programme:

1. Unexpected rise in urban population owing to growth of industries.
2. Spread of urban basic services is slow as compared to rise in population.
3. Increase in the slum area and its population.
4. Unhygienic living conditions because of poverty
5. No decline in the urban IMR.
6. Lack of awareness among parents with regard to child health care.
7. Convergence with other developmental programmes such as UIP and ICDS.

The plan of operation received compliments from the UNICEF, one of the three funding agencies of the UBS at that time when it stated that the plan was 'comprehensive and within the recommended guidelines and framework of the UBS strategy'. This was followed by the preparation of a mini plan of action for Bhilwara during 1987-88 which elaborated the physical and social needs of the UBS bastis. The information for the mini plan was obtained through the base line neighbourhood survey in the bastis covering the household level information on health, work force structure, water supply, toilet, housing, education and demographic characteristics. The subsequent annual plans of the programme are prepared with the involvement of the UBS district coordinator and project officer who provide the necessary input pertaining to the delivery of basic services to the basti dwellers, including the budgetary and other financial details.

Bhilwara's UBS district plan of operation for the Seventh Five-Year Plan had a fund of Rs. 90.232 lakh and for Bhilwara municipal council alone it was Rs. 21.8835 lakh, while seven other municipalities of the districts were allocated Rs. 9.16 lakh each. Obviously, in view of its large population size and related problems of basic services, a higher proportion of funds was allocated for Bhilwara municipal council. Although, in Bhilwara the UBS was launched in 1987, the budget was made available only from December 1988 and up to March 1991 the distribution of funds provided by the three agencies for the city's UBS is shown in Table 3.22.

Table 3.22
Agency-wise Expenditure for UBS

(in lakh rupees)

Agency	Amount received and expended
Centre	2.17
State	4.50
UNICEF	8.64

Source: UBS Office, Bhilwara Municipal Council.

These amounts were utilised for providing different physical and social services (Table 3.23).

Table 3.23
Performances of UBS: Physical and Social Activities

Sl. No.	Activity	Units
1.	Public awareness camps	188
2.	Sewerage construction	14572
3.	Toilets in private houses	349
4.	Sanitary complexes in primary schools	15
5.	Smokeless *chulha* in private houses	321
6.	Mason's Training	15
7.	Hand pump installation	31
8.	Mid-wife training	13
9.	Mid-wife kit distribution	13
10.	Immunisation for pregnant women and children	39 *bastis*
11.	Nutritious diets for pregnant women, children and milk feeding mothers	3 *bastis*
12.	Training to volunteers	171
13.	Training to balsevika, balwadi/anganwadi	3

Note: Besides above-mentioned activities, cultural programmes for raising public awareness on different social issues were also organised.
Source: UBS Office, Bhilwara Municipal Council.

For the year 1992-93 only Rs. 4.58 lakh were allocated for the city's UBS programme and this meagre amount could only be used for improving the water supply system in the bastis.

Thus, since its inception the total expenditure under the UBS in Bhilwara has been in the following manner (Table 3.24).

Table 3.24
Total Amount Received and Expended on the UBS

(in lakh rupees)

Period	Amount received and expended
1-4-87 to 31-3-91	15.32
1-4-91 to 31-3-92	10.47
1-4-92 to 31-3-93	4.58

Source: UBS Office, Bhilwara Municipal Council.

It is clear from the preceding table that over time there has been a declining trend in the allocation of funds for UBS programme in Bhilwara which has badly hampered its activities in the city. Particularly those meant for the welfare of women and children, a crucial component of the UBS, seem to have been the most hit and have got less attention in the programme's implementation over time. In fact, there has been a continuous decline in the expenditure on providing the services related to women and children, both in terms of absolute amounts and proportion. To a greater extent the withdrawal of UNICEF from the UBS funding bodies in 1991 appears to have affected the programme's this important thrust area.

As a whole, three services, namely, sewage construction, toilet construction and handpump installation share a major proportion of the expenditure. However, sewage and toilet construction involve heavy expenditure both on the part of the programme and household owners and, therefore, their overall influence has been limited, whereas the impact of hand pump installation on the living condition of basti dwellers is more visible. Especially during 1992-93 water supply was given utmost prominence. This is testified in the following section on the access of basic services in Bhilwara bastis.

During the past five years the UBS has covered an increasing number of bastis. Today, the programme is being implemented in all the 39 bastis scattered all over the city with a total approximate population of 46,258. Since the general prevalence of poverty and shortage of basic services available to a majority of the inhabitants are the essential features of these bastis, the programme has generated a lot of hope regarding the improvement in the living conditions of the basti dwellers, particularly towards the enhancement of the survival and development of their children and women.

Right from the initial stages, the programme has received the active support from both the central and state governments. The programme also had support and guidance from the UNICEF which was an important financing body of the programme with 40 per cent financial support till 1991. Since then it has been providing funds for the programme's training sessions. The experts as well as other officials of the UN organisation offered regular guidance and supervision, besides making frequent field visits to give a good footing to the programme implementation during 1987-91. The UBS local officials concede that the withdrawal of the UNICEF from the financing and supervision of the programme in 1991 was a setback to the UBS since the programme lost the able guidance, expertise and monitoring system of the UNICEF. Presently, the planning and implementation of the programme is mostly guided by official considerations.

In the process of programme implementation the distribution of work between the district coordinator and project officer has been done in such a manner that since April 1991 all the construction plans are being implemented by the former, whereas non-construction plans are looked after by the latter. Particularly in the spheres of financial allocations, monitoring of programme and technical assistance in activities of programme, the role of the district coordinator is vital. Therefore, despite the fact that the district coordinator has no direct official control over the project officer since the latter works under the municipal commissioner, Bhilwara, nor does he directly deal with the day-to-day matters of the UBS in the city, yet in the exercise of his powers mentioned above he has been playing a crucial role on the issues relating to the delivery of basic services to the basti dwellers.

Although the project officer often visits the bastis to monitor the programme, at the basti level the community organisers' role in the implementation of the programme is the most important. All four COs have been assigned the task of visiting their respective bastis to assess the people's needs regarding basic services and to see how these facilities can be improved. However, it seems that their contact with the basti dwellers has been very limited as a significant percentage of surveyed households (72%) state that they were not aware of any programme like the UBS going on in their area. In fact, the interaction of COs has largely been confined to the upper and relatively prosperous and influential class of the basti. A majority of those living below the poverty line have remained outside their contact.

The poor, downtrodden class, living on the periphery of the basti, in most cases, has been found untouched by the CO. This is so despite the fact that these neglected people are the most needy in terms of the delivery of the basic services. The percolation of the concept of UBS has yet to take place in most of the bastis. The emphasis on providing basic services must be in respect of the poorest of the poor as these are the most neglected and vulnerable classes. Since these classes are already cut off from the main part of the bastis, the existing facilities availed of by those staying in the core areas are also not available to them.

Nevertheless, the COs cannot be solely blamed for these shortcomings. It should be acknowledged that the number of bastis under each CO is considerably large. It is indeed a difficult task for him to implement, monitor and manage the UBS programme in the bastis under his charge efficiently. The total of 39 bastis of the city are distributed among four COs as 10, 9, 11 and 9. Taken as a whole, they have to deal with more than 2000 basti households. Although they have been provided with two wheelers, they can use only seven litres of petrol per month which in many cases, may not be sufficient for them. Since the bastis in the city cover a large area, the COs in charge of far-off bastis particularly face problems in making regular contacts with the people living there.

Characteristics of Community Participation under the UBS

The UBS in its planning and implementation procedure provides for the community participation in a basti through the formulation of neighbourhood groups comprising the volunteers residing in the same locality. In Bhilwara also, the volunteers work in their respective bastis in varying numbers by constituting neighbourhood groups which in turn, make up the basti development committees. In 1987, when the UBS programme started in the city, they were selected by the residents on the basis of one volunteer for every 20-25 households. Although the programme has an inbuilt preference for women as volunteers, in a majority of cases only males hold this post. This is largely because of the fact that while the basti women are themselves illiterate and unaware of their rights and privileges, their menfolk have also not encouraged them to share responsibilities and to involve them in different activities relating to the implementation, monitoring and evolution of the programme. However, that women do the work of UBS volunteers efficiently and with dedication if the opportunity is given, is visible from the fact that in Pur a woman heads the basti committee with total competence. Her contact with the basti households, particularly with women, is more frequent and she is a familiar figure for them. Moreover, she tries to involve the basti dwellers in the activities of the UBS, who accept her as their representative and leader.

The UBS basti development committees in some bastis like Sanganer, Jawaharnagar and Dhandhloi are working in a very organised manner. Particularly in Jawaharnagar and Dhandhloi they maintain detailed records of their activities and correspondence and prepare minutes of their meetings. Besides, they also issues press releases to local and regional newspapers on the problems of their bastis. They make regular contacts with local officials of the UBS and other departments concerned with the basti affairs, in particular with those relating to basic services. But in many other bastis the committees are relatively less active and there is no fixed schedule for their meetings. Personal contacts among the volunteers themselves and with the people are very limited. Therefore, in such bastis the residents do not have much experience with the concepts of self-help and community participation and they are not effectively involved in the planning and implementation of the programme. This situation has adversely affected the organisation and mobilisation of the people in their efforts to cope with the problem of basic services through the UBS.

The basic difficulty with the UBS basti committees and the volunteers is that, after nearly five years of the programme's implementation they have not been able to have an active association of the common basti residents in the programme as a driving force to promote the case of the community development in the bastis. The volunteers are generally the affluent persons of the basti who do not consider it necessary to consult and associate with others out of their own groups in matters regarding the improvement of the basic services. These volunteers may belong to groups constituted on the basis of caste, profession, political affiliations or friendship. This attitude has caused a certain degree of damage to the fundamental principle of grass-roots participation of people in the programme.

That the idea of community participation, the essential theme of the UBS, has not adequately been represented among the common basti dwellers is clear from the fact that during the field survey a very low proportion of respondents knew the volunteers of their bastis (Table 3.25). The study reveals that as a whole only 19 per cent basti

Table 3.25
Community Awareness of UBS

(percent household)

Basti	No. of sample households	Aware of UBS	RCV known	discuss problems with RCV
Bilia Khurd	10	0	0	0
Dadabari	10	0	0	0
Dhandholai	68	21	13	9
Gadri Khera	13	46	15	15
Gul Ali Nagri	33	21	3	3
Gulmandi	14	43	0	0
Harijan Basti (Shastri Nagar)	11	27	0	0
Islam Colony (Gandhi Nagar)	13	100	0	0
Islam Colony (Shastri Nagar)	13	38	15	8
Jawaharnagar	55	33	24	22
Kava Khera	18	17	0	0
Kishnawaton ki Kheri	12	67	75	75
Labour Colony	30	23	47	23
Malan	17	35	0	0
Pur (Part)	39	13	21	8
Sanganer	44	27	41	18
All Basti	400	28	19	12

Source: Field Survey, Bhilwara, ISS, 1992.

dwellers are aware of the UBS volunteers. Exceptionally, in Kishnawaton ki Kheri 75 per cent, the highest percentage of persons, are familiar with their volunteers. Similarly, in Labour Colony and Sanganer 47 and 41 per cent people know their volunteers. This characteristic is noticeable because located in the peripheral parts of the city, although these bastis occupy a very low position in terms of socio-economic indicators, a relatively higher degree of awareness of UBS and its volunteers proves the dwellers' consciousness and concern regarding governmental schemes meant for their benefit and upliftment. The credit to this effect may also be attributed to the effective interaction of community organisers and UBS volunteers with people in these bastis. Therefore, in spite of a general dismal scenario regarding people knowing their UBS volunteers in the bastis, these instances set models to be followed in other such localities in this connection.

The underlying principle of community participation enshrined in the UBS emphasises the regular involvement of the community at all stages of the project including vital decision making right from the pre-planning and planning stages through all plans of implementation, monitoring and evaluation. However, general lack of awareness about the UBS and its volunteers prevailing among the basti dwellers makes the idea of their involvement in the programme futile. Moreover, even those who know the volunteers have only limited contact with them. In fact, the proportion of persons having discussion with the volunteers is extremely low in the bastis including those where the proportion of persons knowing the volunteers is relatively high. Obviously, the interaction between UBS volunteers and the basti dwellers and their knowledge about UBS needs effective channelisation for encouraging the process by which the community, that is, the user sector is enabled to participate in planning, implementing, monitoring and evaluating the programme, particularly those relating to the delivery of basic services for child and mother care. Only then will the chances of the programme's continuity be enhanced because then the programme would meet the needs of the people as they see them.

ACCESS TO BASIC SERVICES IN BHILWARA BASTIS

As discussed before, Bhilwara bastis are characterised by widespread poverty, socio-economic deprivation and destitution. In order to improve the living conditions of the poor basti dwellers, particularly women and children, and to provide them with minimum basic amenities the Urban Basic Services (UBS) programme was launched in Bhilwara in 1987. The previous section has dealt with the programme's salient features, the process of its inception and implementation, organisational arrangement and the performance of the UBS in the context of Bhilwara. Against this backdrop the present section attemps to analyse the access and delivery of urban basic services to the basti dwellers of the city by dividing these services into two categories; first, physical services such as housing, provision of water supply, sewerage and garbage disposal and toilet facilities. Second, social services such as medical and health facilities and child and mother care.

Housing Conditions

Compared to the slums of many bigger cities and metropolises, in Bhilwara bastis the housing conditions seem to be better. Owing to easy availability of land and space here the basti dwellers do not have merely shelters but live in acceptable housing conditions. Although in most of the bastis the houses are located in an unplanned and haphazard manner, unlike typical slums they do not suffer from the poor housing environment where people stay in sub-standard living conditions. Therefore, the common features of slums like lack of privacy, exposure of contagious diseases, malnutrition, fights and quarrels, high crime rates, drug addiction, etc., do not characterise these bastis.

Table 3.26
Shelter Conditions

Basti	Type of housing (percentage distribution			Average no. of rooms per person	Average monthly rent (Rs)
	Pucca	Semi-*pucca*	*Kachcha*		
Bilia Khurd	70	30	0	3	150
Dadabari	100	0	0	3	0
Dhandholai	63	19	18	2	136
Gadri Khera	85	15	0	3	115
Gul Ali Nagri	88	9	3	2	149
Gulmandi	64	29	7	1	74
Harijan Basti (Shastri Nagar)	45	18	36	2	0
Islam Colony (Gandhi Nagar)	100	0	0	2	121
Islam Colony (Shastri Nagar)	100	0	0	2	0
Jawaharnagar	71	16	13	3	0
Kava Khera	72	0	28	2	0
Kishnawaton ki Kheri	0	25	75	1	0
Labour Colony	90	7	3	2	0
Malan	94	6	0	3	233
Pur (Part)	69	26	5	2	72
Sanganer	23	52	25	2	99
All Bastis	71	16	13	2	122

Source: Field Survey, Bhilwara, ISS, 1992.

Given the low income levels of the basti dwellers, in many cases the design and materials of their houses are not of good quality, although by using locally available building materials like stones, mortar and bricks seventy-one per cent of the surveyed houses are made *pucca* whereas only 16 and 13 per cent houses are *semi-kachcha* and *kachcha* respectively (Table 3.26). In fact, in some bastis such as Dadabari, Islam Colony (Gandhinagar) and Islam Colony (Shastrinagar) all the houses are *pucca*, while in as many as eight bastis, namely, Dadabari, Gadri Khera, Gul Ali Nagar, Islam Colony (Gandhinagar), Islam Colony (Shastrinagar), Kawa Khera, Labour Colony and Malan the proportion of *pucca* houses is more than the overall basti average 71 per cent. Among all the 16 surveyed bastis Kishnawaton ki Kheri is the lone exception where 75 per cent houses, the highest, are kachcha. This is mainly because this basti is not only cut off from the main parts of the city but also inhabited by people mostly engaged in agriculture and other allied activities. Therefore, it is this characteristic combined with the fact of its having the fourth lowest average monthly household income that is reflected in the general prevalence of *kachcha* houses in Kishnawaton ki Kheri.

In terms of house ownership, 86 per cent sample households have their own houses, while 13 per cent live as tenants. Only one per cent people stay in the houses where the status of their ownership is not clear. On an average Rs. 122 is being paid as monthly rent, although depending upon the locality and size of the house, the rental amount shows considerable variations. Significantly, housing on encroached lands is not common in the bastis and most of the houses are either inherited or on the purchased land. Field enquiry has revealed that in many cases the municipal council has not issued *patta*, granting legal status to basti houses in the urban territory and, therefore, such houses continue to be officially considered as unauthorised.

Public housing has so far made no significant contribution in improving the housing condition of the basti dwellers. Although the Nehru Rozgar Yojana (NRY) has been operating in the city since 1990, the scheme's provisions to assist the economically weaker sections in urban areas in housing and shelter upgradation through loan and government subsidy are not being implemented by its implementing authority, the city's municipal council.

However, the real housing problem in Bhilwara bastis is in terms of availability of rooms per house since on an average six-member households stay in two-room houses, which are not only crowded but also put tremendous pressures on the daily living facilities.

Water Supply

Bhilwara bastis, as a whole, appear to face water shortage since as high as 25 per cent of the surveyed households do not have enough water supply to meet their requirements although in some bastis almost all the surveyed households have adequate water supply. A relatively better water supply in certain localities may be mainly attributed to the efforts on the part of the UBS programme for improving water supply in the bastis through installation of hand pumps and pipelines. As discussed in the previous section, despite fund cuts and other limitations, expenditure on water supply has been a regular head of the UBS budget which, in due course, has shown its impact in the efficient availability of water in the bastis. Besides, distant source of water is a major constraint of the basti dwellers. Their difficulty in obtaining water may be gauged from the fact that only 18 per cent of the total basti dwellers have water supply closer to their houses. In as many as nine bastis people do not have any water source in close proximity to their houses. These bastis are Gadri Khera, Gul Ali Nagar, Harijan Basti (Shastri Nagar), Kawa Khera, Kishnawaton ki Kheri and Malan. Only 25 per cent households have water source inside the house, while only 23 per cent households have an independently installed water source. In fact, the water source inside the household is mostly independent and this is why the percentage of sample households with water supply inside the house is very close to that with independent water sources. Therefore, a vast majority of the basti population depends upon common water sources outside the house which includes community taps mainly provided by the UBS. As Table 3.27 reveals, in nine bastis the percentage of households depending upon a common water source outside the house was more than the overall basti average of 74 per cent.

Field observations indicate that there exists a certain degree of bias in favour of relatively higher income groups among the basti dwellers so far as independent delivery of water inside the house is concerned. People in higher income groups have independent sources such as tap or hand pump inside their premises where community water source from the municipal council is not adequately available and their expenditure on this account is also very significant. For example, while in the monthly household income class of Rs. 101 - 250 and Rs. 251 - 500 only 10 per cent households have a water source inside the house, in higher income classes of Rs. 501 - 1000, Rs. 1001 - 2000 and Rs. 2000 and above the percentage of households with water source inside the house is 22, 33 and 48 respectively (Table 3.28). Therefore, despite the traditional poor non-poor divide in the delivery of certain basic services (Kundu, 1993), even among the poor variation in income levels has shown its impact on their delivery. The case from Bhilwara testified that water supply is one such important head of basic services.

Table 3.27
Water Supply

(Per cent household)

Basti	Water supply source		Type of source distributions				Availability		Near water supply source	Water supply adequate
	Independent	Common	Piped	Shallow HP	Mark II HP	Well	Inside	Outside		
Bilia Khurd	30	70	50	10	30	10	30	70	10	80
Dadabari	10	90	0	10	90	0	10	90	20	80
Dhandholai	13	87	18	3	74	6	15	85	12	79
Gadri Khera	92	8	92	0	8	0	92	8	0	62
Gul Ali Nagar	6	94	12	3	70	15	12	88	0	94
Gulmandi	7	93	21	0	79	0	0	93	0	93
Harijan Basti (Shastri Nagar)	0	100	0	0	100	0	0	100	0	91
Islam Colony (Gandhi Nagar)	31	69	85	0	15	0	46	54	15	62
Islam Colony (Shastri Nagar)	23	77	23	0	46	31	31	69	15	100
Jawaharnagar	49	51	56	2	20	20	53	45	18	64
Kave Khera	0	100	0	0	94	6	0	100	0	100
Kishnawaton ki Kheri	0	100	0	0	100	0	0	100	0	100
Labour Colony	33	67	83	3	13	0	33	63	13	17
Malan	41	59	35	0	47	18	41	59	0	88
Pur (Part)	18	82	82	0	15	3	21	77	15	46
Sanganer	11	89	89	2	0	7	16	84	82	95
All Bastis	23	77	46	2	44	8	25	51	18	75

Source: Field Survey, Bhilwara, ISS, 1992.

Table 3.28
Income Class-wise Availability of Water Inside the House

Monthly household income class (Rs)	Availability of water inside the house
101 - 250	10
251 - 500	10
501 - 1000	22
1001 - 2000	33
2000 >	48

Source: Field Survey, Bhilwara, ISS, 1992

Taps and Mark II handpumps are two major water sources in the bastis, which together account for 90 per cent of the water supply. The former covers 46 per cent of the total households whereas the latter covers 44 per cent. Therefore, the piped water, the easiest and most straightforward source is available to only a limited section of the basti population. These sources are being provided in collaboration with UBS and the municipal council with the assistance of the State Water Works department. In terms of location, generally the water sources inside the houses are mostly water taps, whereas the Mark II hand pumps are the common water sources outside. The remaining 10 per cent water supply is shared by shallow hand pumps and wells, which are not the major sources of water supply in the bastis because shallow water pumps are not considered as clean water sources and the physiographic conditions as well as high costs discourage the digging of wells on a big scale.

Toilet Facility

The toilet facility for the basti dwellers presents a very dismal scene since 77 per cent of the sampled households have no toilet and an overwhelming majority of residents go out either to some open space or to the nearby fields. There are no common toilets; nor have governmental or voluntary organisations taken any initiative in this regard. The much acclaimed organisation, Sulabh International which constructs and runs public toilets and bathrooms all over the country, has yet to make its debut in these bastis.

Although the near absence of dry bucket type latrines in the bastis is an indication that the social evil of night soil carried by human beings is not prevalent in these areas, this system has not been

Table 3.29
Toilet Facility

(Per cent household)

Basti	Toilet facility			Types of toilet facility			Average installation expenditure (Rs)
	Independent	Common	No provision	Flush	Basket	Other	
Bilia Khurd	10	0	90	10	0	90	11000
Dadabari	0	50	50	50	0	50	6800
Dhandholai	13	4	75	22	0	66	8667
Gadri Khera	31	0	69	31	0	69	11250
Gul Ali Nagari	18	3	79	18	0	82	8333
Gulmandi	0	0	100	0	0	100	0
Harijan Basti (Shastri Nagar)	9	0	91	9	0	91	8000
Islam Colony (Gandhi Nagar)	38	15	46	54	0	46	7000
Islam Colony (Shastri Nahar)	38	0	62	38	0	62	8400
Jawaharnagar	33	0	67	33	0	65	6222
Kava Khera	0	6	94	0	6	94	0
Kishnawaton ki Khedi	17	0	83	17	0	83	3000
Labour Colony	23	0	77	23	0	77	5233
Malan	59	0	41	59	0	41	10600
Pur (Part)	8	0	92	8	0	92	5967
Sanganer	2	9	89	2	0	95	3000
All Bastis	18	4	77	21	0	76	7690

substituted by other modern types of toilets. As Table 3.29 shows, flush latrines are very few among the sampled households and concentrated in certain pockets. Considering this problem, although the UBS since its inception has taken various initiatives to popularise flush latrines, the impact has attained only partial success. An important reason behind people's indifferent attitude towards toilet facility is the fact that the cost for installing flush latrines is very high and in most cases it is not possible for the basti dwellers to invest, at an average, more than Rs. 7,000 for its construction. Although the city's UBS annual action plans provide for loan of Rs. 500 along with Rs. 500 as state subsidy for installing flush latrines, the remaining amount is still too high for them to contribute. Moreover, for the last six years there has been no increase in the subsidy amount. Besides, there also appears to be a lack of motivation among the basti dwellers to go in for cleaner toilets and a disinclination to understand the advantages that a toilet inside the house or a clean common toilet closer to their houses can offer.

Drainage and Garbage Disposal

Drainage and garbage disposal problems in Bhilwara bastis seem insurmountable. Forty-four per cent of the sample houses have no provision for drainage, while only 18 per cent houses have underground drainage systems. Taking all the sampled households together we find that 80 per cent houses have either open drainage or no provision at all. This indicates the lack of awareness that prevails and the absence of motivation among the basti dwellers in the adoption of a proper drainage system in their houses. Besides, across bastis, there is a high degree of variation in the distribution of households among the categories of open, underground and no drainage provision. For example, in Bilia Khurd 100 per cent houses had open drainage but in Dadabari it was only 10 per cent.

This is mainly because the nature of house construction - whether kachcha or pucca - does not show any clear relationship with the drainage system. Therefore, open drainage or its absence altogether was not confined to *kachcha* houses alone. In fact, field observations have shown that pucca houses also lack proper drainage systems and it is not uncommon to see pucca houses without any drainage at all.

The garbage disposal in the surveyed bastis in Bhilwara is very dismal. Only 6 per cent sample households give their garbage to the sweeper, while 36 per cent throw it out on the streets, while 56 per cent

Table 3.30
Drainage/Sewage Availability

(Per cent households)

Basti	Source of drainage			Open drainage/ sewage type		Garbage disposal mode			
	Open	Under-ground	No pro-vision	Kachcha	Pucca	Bin	On the Street	Outside house	Sweeper
Bilia Khurd	100	0	0	60	40	0	100	0	0
Dadabari	10	80	10	0	10	0	100	0	0
Dhandholai	23	11	66	22	15	1	49	47	3
Gadri Khera	34	16	50	8	46	31	62	8	0
Gul Ali Nagri	54	46	0	21	3	0	27	70	70
Gulmandi	21	18	61	0	27	0	64	36	0
Harijan Basti (Shastri Nagar)	43	14	43	0	18	0	0	100	0
Islam Colony (Gandhi Nagar)	77	23	0	31	46	0	46	46	8
Islam Colony (Shastri Nagar)	38	15	46	31	8	0	0	100	0
Jawaharnagar	49	11	33	35	18	2	27	33	4
Kava Khera	33	0	61	39	0	0	28	72	0
Kishnawaton ki Khedi	33	0	67	0	25	0	33	67	0
Labour Colony	13	7	80	10	3	0	0	100	0
Malan	88	12	0	29	59	18	65	18	0
Pur (Part)	28	13	59	8	21	0	51	46	3
Sanganer	11	39	41	11	0	0	5	93	2
All Bastis	36	18	44	20	17	2	36	56	6

Source: Field Survey, Bhilwara, ISS, 1992.

dispose of it just outside the house. Although initially the UBS programme had installed 115 bins for garbage collection in the bastis, they are not seen now in the surveyed bastis. As a result the whole system of garbage disposal in these localities is very inefficient and unhygienic. Obviously, the authorities have shown less concern about the installation and maintenance of the bins. In fact, in the UBS action plan 1991-92 the allocation of funds for bin installation in the bastis was refused by the state local self-government directorate.

Medical and Health Facilities

Lack of adequate basic services has made the Bhilwara urban poor more disease prone. The provision of medical and health care facilities at an accessible distance is therefore very important for them. However, the survey results indicate that in the sample bastis these facilities are barely available. Although allopathy is the most common mode of treatment among the basti dwellers, in many instances they do not have any allopathic dispensary or private clinic in their bastis.

As Table 3.31 indicates only 18 per cent of the total sample households have access to medical and health care facilities from the primary health centres (PHCs). Seventy per cent of the basti dwellers depend upon government hospitals in the city, while only 12 per cent of them consult private doctors. In fact, consulting a private doctor is common only in Bilia Khurd, Gadri Khera and Islam Colony (Gandhi Nagar) bastis. The two factors of high prescription fee and the lack of clinics with qualified doctors in the bastis have put the proportion of basti households consulting private doctors at such a low ebb. Therefore, an overwhelming proportion of basti dwellers depend upon government hospitals for medical facilities which is mainly attributed to the minimal expenses for treatment and non-availability of PHCs and other dispensaries in reasonable proximity to most of the bastis. Due to these reasons the residents of the bastis located in the peripheral areas, have to commute long distances to the city for treatment, which obviously causes a lot of inconvenience to them, particularly in emergency cases.

Table 3.31
Availability of Health Care Facility

(Per cent Household)

Basti	No. of households	Health services available		
		PHCs	Government hospital	Private doctor
Bilia Khurd	10	0	10	90
Dadabari	10	50	50	0
Dhandholai	68	10	82	7
Gadri Khera	13	0	15	85
Gul Ali Nagri	33	3	94	3
Gulmandi	14	0	93	7
Harijan Basti (Shastri Nagar)	11	0	100	0
Islam Colony (Gandhi Nagar)	13	0	38	62
Islam Colony (Shastri Nagar)	13	0	100	0
Jawaharnagar	55	33	49	18
Kava Khera	18	0	100	0
Kishnawaton ki Khedi	12	0	100	0
Labour Colony	30	0	100	0
Malan	17	0	94	6
Pur (Part)	39	0	100	0
Sanganer	44	98	0	2
All Bastis	400	18	70	12

Source: Field Survey, Bhilwara, ISS, 1992.

Mother and Child Care

Mother and child care includes emphasis on preventive health care for children, immunisation, improved infant feeding practices, child growth monitoring and pre- and post-natal care for women. In Bhilwara child and mother care is one of the important components of the UBS programme and over time it has tried to provide the necessary facilities required for this purpose in the bastis. Immunisation, midwife training, provision of nutritious diets are the major activities presently being undertaken by the programme. Child immunisation in particular, is given special emphasis and along with UBS other agencies are also working for immunising the basti children with UNICEF being a major supplier of vaccines.

However, in spite of the measures the Bhilwara basti dwellers are not fully motivated to immunise their children as only 37 per cent of the infants in the surveyed bastis are immunised. In the case of the remainder their parents are either not aware that certain vaccines have to be given to the children below one year of age or perhaps consider them too young for immunisation if they are even one or two months old.

Similarly, the consciousness among the basti dwellers regarding the need for prenatal care for the pregnant women has yet to be developed sufficiently. Only 43 per cent women go for prenatal check-ups in hospitals, where only 10 per cent child deliveries take place. More than 80 per cent births take place at home with the help of untrained *dais*, although the services of trained *dais* are also being obtained in noticeable proportion (25%).

A Comparative Assessment of Basic Services in the Bastis

The preceding discussion shows clearly that a significant proportion of the basti population lacks access to adequate basic services. Even the most crucial services like water supply, toilet and drainage are not properly made available to a vast majority of basti dwellers. A comparative assessment of the provision of these services can be made by studying the proportion of households availing themselves of the ideal basic services (IBS) which are essentially the quality indicators of the basic services. These ideal services may be identified as independent water supply, independent toilets, underground drainage and pucca houses. Table 3.32 reveals that barring *pucca* houses, all the other ideal basic services are very inefficiently delivered to the basti dwellers. Only 23 per cent of the total sample households have independent water supply in the bastis while independent toilets and underground drainage are found in 18 per cent households. In fact, a substantial and the highest proportion is occupied by *pucca* houses defined as shelters with floor and walls made of brick and roof made of cement/concrete, although if one goes by the quality of construction material and design, the situation will not be always found to be satisfactory since most of these houses are in pathetic state and lack the provision of other ideal basic services, besides suffering from shortage of space.

Table 3.32 also shows that there is not only the shortage of the ideal basic services but also a lot of variation in their availability among the bastis. The pattern of the variation may be seen by applying the Location Quotient (LQ), defined as the ratio of the percentage of households having the ideal basic services in each basti to the average percentage of the same set of services in all the bastis as a whole

Table 3.32
Proportion of Ideal Basic Services

(Per cent household)

Basti	Independent water supply	Independent toilet	Underground drainage	Pucca house
Bilia Khurs	30	10	-	70
Dadabari	10	-	80	100
Dhandholai	13	13	11	63
Gadri Khera	92	31	16	85
Gul Ali Nagri	6	18	46	88
Gulmandi	7	-	18	64
Harijan Basti (Shastri Nagar)	-	9	14	45
Islam Colony (Gandhi Nagar)	31	38	23	100
Islam Colony (Shastri Nagar)	23	38	15	100
Jawaharnagar	49	33	11	71
Kava Khera	-	-	-	72
Kishnawaton ki Khedi	-	17	-	-
Labour Colony	33	23	7	90
Malan	41	59	12	94
Pur (Part)	18	8	13	69
Sanganer	11	2	39	23
All Bastis	23	18	18	71

Source: Field Survey, Bhilwara, ISS, 1992.

(Table 3.33). Since in the case of *pucca* house, the LQ is >1 in nine bastis, it indicates a greater degree of dispersion in the prevalence of *pucca* houses in the bastis. Regarding independent water supply and independent toilet facilities, in seven bastis each the LQ is >1 while underground drainage shows the highest degree of concentration as only five bastis have LQ >1. Obviously, in most of the bastis the ideal basic services are not only inadequately available but are also concentrated to a great degree in a few bastis.

In order to assess the rank of the bastis on the basis of the availability of the ideal basic services, a composite index (CI) has been prepared in accordance with the percentage of households having these facilities at the basti level in ascending order by using Kendall's method (Table.3.34). That is, the basti with the highest percentage of any particular service among all the 16 bastis was ranked first and in case it did not have any service, it was ranked as 16. Thus, the sum of the score of all the four ideal services determined the rank of a basti which is referred to here as composite index (CI).

Table 3.33
Location Quotient of Ideal Basic Services

Basti	Independent water supply	Independent toilet	Underground drainage	Pucca house
Bilia Khurd	1.30	.55	0	.98
Dadabari	.43	0	4.44	1.40
Dhandholai	.56	.72	.61	.88
Gadri Khera	4.0	1.72	.88	1.19
Gul Ali Nagri	.26	1.0	2.55	1.23
Gulmandi	.30	0	1.0	.90
Harijan Basti (Shastri Nagar)	0	.5	.77	.63
Islam Colony (Gandhi Nagar)	1.34	2.11	1.27	1.40
Islam Colony (Shastri Nagar)	1.0	2.11	.83	1.40
Jawaharnagar	2.13	1.83	.61	1.0
Kava Khera	0	0	0	1.01
Kishnawaton ki Kheri	0	.94	0	0
Labour Colony	1.43	1.27	.38	1.26
Malan	1.78	3.28	.66	1.32
Pur (Part)	.78	.44	.72	.97
Sanganer	.48	.11	2.16	.32

Source: Field Survey, Bhilwara, ISS, 1992.

Table 3.34
Composite Index (CI) of Ideal Basic Services (IBS)

Basti	Independent water supply	Independent toilet	Underground drainage	Pucca house	Composite index
Bilia Khurd	6	10	15	10	41
Dadabari	11	15	1	2	29
Dhandholai	9	9	11.5	13	42.5
Gadri Khera	1	5	6	7	19
Gul Ali Nagri	13	7	2	6	28
Gulmandi	12	15	5	12	44
Harijan Basti (Shastri Nagar)	15	11	8	14	48
Islam Colony (Gandhi Nagar)	5	2.5	4	2	13.5
Islam Colony (Shastri Nagar)	7	2.5	7	2	18.5
Jawaharnagar	2	4	11.5	9	26.5
Kava Khera	15	15	15	8	53
Kishnawaton ki Kheri	15	8	15	16	54
Labour Colony	4	6	13	5	28
Malan	3	1	10	4	18
Pur (Part)	8	12	9	11	40
Sanganer	10	13	3	15	41

Source: Field Survey, Bhilwara, ISS, 1992.

The rank of the various bastis in accordance with the values of the composite index indicate that Islam Colony (Gandhi Nagar) having the lowest score, tops the list while Kawa Khera with the highest score occupies the lowest position.

The general ranking pattern depicts a core-periphery differential in the composite index of the ideal basic services where peripheral bastis, particularly those which have been transformed from rural to urban owing to inclusion of rural areas into Bhilwara's municipal limits, face the most serious problems with the provision of these services, while those bastis in the core of the city have a better position in this regard.

To a great extent the provision of ideal basic services in the bastis is closely associated with the income level of the household. By taking the rank of the average household income in the bastis as an independent variable and the rank of the composite index as a dependent variable, the coefficient of correlation indicates a high degree of positive interrelationship between these two variables since the r value is 0.52. However, it is clear from this value that despite a close interrelationship between the two variables, other socio-economic factors such as residents' ignorance and lack of awareness about hygienic and civic amenities have also influenced the provision of ideal basic services in the bastis. Therefore, while enhancement of income continues to be a significant component of all the urban poverty alleviation strategies, there still remains a need for a more concerted effort to make Bhilwara basti dwellers civic conscious, particularly regarding the ideal basic services. This is to be in addition to governmental and non-governmental measures to deliver better basic services and provide infrastructural facilities thereof pertaining to the bastis in Bhilwara.

REFERENCES

Bardhan, P. K. (1973), Quoted in ML Dantwala, *Poverty in India: Then and Now*, Macmillan, New Delhi.

Bhattacharya, A. N, and Lodha, R. M. (1969), *Smarika*, MLV Government College, Bhilwara.

Bhilwara Municipal Council (1987), 'UBS District Plan of Action', unpublished document, Bhilwara.

Bhilwara Municipal Council (1990), 'Report of the Girl Child Educational Survey, unbpublished report, Bhilwara.

Census of India (1981), *General Population Tables-Rajasthan*.

Census of India (1991a), *Provisional Population Totals: Rural-Urban Distribution.*

Census of India (1991b), *Provisional Population Totals: Workers and their Distribution.*

Census of India (1991c), *Final Population Totals.*

Cho, Lee-Jay (1978) 'Fertility Preferences in Five Asian Countries', *International Family Planning Perspectives and Digest*, Vol. 4, No. 1.

Dandekar, V. M., and Rath, N. (1971), 'Poverty in India: Dimensions and Trends,' *Economic and Political Weekly*, January 2.

Economic Times, 'Panel Updates Poverty Line,' July 30, 1992.

Erskine, K. D (1908), *Rajputana Gazetteers* Vol.II, Mewar Presidency.

Government of India, (1991), *Report on the Task Force on Urban Poverty Alleviation in the Eighth Five-Year Plan*, Ministry of Urban Development, New Delhi.

Imperial Gazetteer of India, (undated reprint), *Volume VIII*, Today & Tomorrow's printers and publishers, New Delhi.

Kamble, N. D. (1979), *Poverty within Poverty*, Sterling Publishers, New Delhi.

Kundu, Amitabh (1993), *In the Name of the Urban Poor*, Sage Publications, New Delhi.

Minhas, B. S. et al, (1991) 'Declining Incidence of Poverty in the 1980s' *Economic and Political Weekly*, Vol. 26, Nos. 27 & 28.

National Comission on Urbanisation (1988), *Report*, Vol II, NCU, New Delhi.

National Institute of Urban Affairs (1986), *Urban Basic Services Programme — A Reference Manual*, NIUA, New Delhi.

———— (1989), *Urban Local Bodies*, NIUA, New Delhi.

Premi, M. K., et al (1983) *An Introduction to Social Demography*, Vikas Publishing Company, New Delhi.

Rao, C. H. Hanumantha (1989). 'Decentralised Planning, *Economic and Political Weekly*, Vol. 24, No. 8.

Sehgal, K. K. (1975), *Rajasthan District Gazetteer* — Bhilwara, Directorate of District Gazetteers, Jaipur.

Sen, Amartya (1986) *Poverty and Famines*, Oxford University Press, New Delhi.

Singh, R. L. (1971), *India — A Regional Geography*, National Geographical Society of India, Varanasi.

Tod, James (1957), *Annals and Antiquities of Rajasthan*, Routledge and Kegan Paul, London.

Chapter IV

SAMBALPUR

INTRODUCTION

The present chapter is an evaluation study of the development programmes in the slums of Sambalpur with special reference to the Urban Basic Services (UBS) Programme. It evaluates the problems of poverty in slums, the effect of the government-sponsored community-based programmes on the slum households in terms of access to selected basic amenities, and the extent and nature of community participation in these programmes. The scope of the study, though emphasising on UBS programmes also includes the access of income generating programmes like Nehru Rozgar Yojana (NRY) to the slums in the context of the economic background of the surveyed households and extent of poverty.

The study is based on analysis of data gathered from the survey conducted in the slums in Sambalpur in May 1992. The survey was coordinated among 400 households selected at random from 12 out of 46 slums in Sambalpur city. Sample selection was done by the stratified sampling method. First the 12 slums were chosen and then from each slum a specified number of households was selected for a questionnaire survey. The 400 households constituted nearly 20 per cent of the total households in 12 slums taken togeter. While selecting the slums special care was taken that they were representative of the city in terms of geographical location. Also only those slums had been selected where the UBS programme has been initiated from its very inception that is March 1986.

Out of a total of 400 households the number to be covered in each slum was decided according to its share in the total households of the 12 slums taken together.

Households for canvassing the schedule in a particular slum were selected at equal intervals. Usually the schedule has been put to the head of a household and some sensitive questions like family planning, pre-natal, post-natal care and so on have been asked of the women members.

The distribution of total population and number of households of the selected slums is given in Table 4.1.

Table 4.1
Distribution of Sample Households Over Slums

Sl. No.	Slums	Total population	No. of households	No. of sample households
1.	Taunla Para	1053	211	41
2.	Manik Munda	496	99	19
3.	Danipati	815	163	32
4.	Durgapali	960	192	37
5.	Pension Para	550	110	21
6.	Budharaja	1693	339	66
7.	Kanji House Dalai Para	1084	217	41
8.	Madhabandh	713	143	28
9.	Laxmi Dungripara	610	122	24
10.	Sahoo Colony	1016	203	40
11.	Samlaipadar	838	168	31
12.	Bahidarbandh	461	92	20
	All Slums	10289	2059	400

Data were obtained during the surveys on the basis of a three-part questionnaire. The first part related to the data on socio-economic background of the slum households focusing on aspects of income-poverty and social status like caste, religion and resident status and so forth. The second part consisted of questions on five basic services namely education, housing, water supply, sanitation and health. The third part included questions on community awareness and participation and also on income generation programmes. This was done with the intention of evaluating the spread of the Nehru Rozgar Yojana which has been initiated as part of the urban poverty alleviation programmes from 1990.

In addition to the questionnaire survey, information was collected through discussions with (i) senior officials of the state government at the secretariat and the state urban development authority in Bhubaneswar, the district collector and additional district collector (development) and other concerned personnel in government in Sambalpur, (ii) the municipal chairman, executive officer, all departmental heads, the UBS functionaries such as project officer, community organisers at the municipal level; and (iii) secretaries and presidents of neighbourhood committees of the surveyed slums and the common people living in the slums.

Besides the above, various published and unpublished reports by different agencies, studies by NGOs, municipal records, and so on were also consulted extensively while writing the report.

We have examined the surveyed data regarding the availability of basic services at two levels: at the slum level to highlight inter-slum differences and at the income-class level to find out whether income class variations have any bearing on the status of the basic services. Four hundred sample households in our survey fall into 6 classes when stratified according to their monthly household income (Table 4.2).

Table 4.2
Distribution of Sample Households Over Income-Class

Sl. No.	Income classes (Monthly household income Rs.)	Number of households	Total number of households
1.	Below 100	0	0
2.	100-250	2	6
3.	250-500	47	215
4.	500-1000	184	960
5.	1000-2000	129	789
6.	Above 2000	38	308
	All classes	400	2278

Note: In the analyses the income classes have been referred to by numbers 1, 2, 3 etc.

CITY PROFILE

Demographic Characteristics

Sambalpur municipal town, the headquarters of Sambalpur district and the most important part of the Sambalpur Urban Agglomeration (SUA) is one of the principal urban centres of the state and one among the seven class I cities in Orissa. Considering the low urbanisation level of the state (only 13.43 per cent population living in urban areas in 1991), Sambalpur town as part of the Sambalpur Urban Agglomeration (SUA) contributes a large share in the state's urban growth. The SUA includes, besides Sambalpur municipal town, the two notified area committees of Hirakud and Bolangir. With a total population of 192,917 the SUA constitutes nearly 42 per cent of the total urban population of the district. Although SUA has an area of only 89.5 sq. km or 0.51 per cent of the total area of the district, its density was 2166 in 1991 as against 153 for the whole district. Within the SUA Sambalpur municipal area contributes nearly 68 per cent to the total population. The municipal town which at present has an area of 36.93 sq. km and had a population of only 17,079 in 1941 experienced a more than seven-fold increase during the last five decades. The trend in the population growth of Sambalpur municipal area can be gauged from Table 4.3.

Table 4.3
Population Growth Trend in Sambalpur Municipal Area (SMA) and Sambalpur Urban Agglomeration (SUA)

Year	SMA total population	Decadal growth rate (per cent)	SUA total population	Decadal growth rate (per cent)
1941	17,079	--	--	--
1951	23,525	65.42	--	--
1961	38,915	65.42	57,738	--
1971	64,675	66.20	105,085	82.00
1981	110,283	70.52	162,214	54.36
1991	130,766	18.57	192,917	18.93

Source: Censuses of India.

Decadal growth rates have been enormous during the four decades preceding 1981-91 both for SUA and SMA as the above figures indicate. The town which was merely a small urban centre till 1971, acquired the status of a class I city in 1981.

Besides natural growth, migration from neighbouring districts has greatly contributed towards this exceptional population growth of the town. Sambalpur municipal town, being the most important administrative and commercial centre in north-west Orissa and being considered as the most important growth centre of the state from the point of view of its linkages with other parts of the state has been the vital link with the hinterland for collection and distribution of agricultural, mineral and petroleum products. The two National Highways (Nos. 6 and 42) running through the city have also improved its position promoting a flourishing transport sector and also a vibrant service sector. Because of these economic and locational advantages even without a significant industrial base Sambalpur has attracted people from rural areas of the same district and relatively backward neighbouring districts like Kalahandi, Bolangir and Koraput.

But interestingly the urban growth has gone down to a very significant extent during the last decade both for SUA and SMA. The slowing down of industrial activity in the district has possibly reduced the city-ward migration. The number of reported registered factories has declined from 171 in 1983-84 to 147 in 1987-88. The number of new small scale industrial units has gone down from 218 in 1985-86 to 140 in 1989-90. The percentage increase in workers engaged in these small industries has only been 19.3 per cent during this period (*District Statistical Handbook*, 1990-91).

Housing and Basic Services in the City

Sambalpur being an old urban centre faces problems similar to those in any other old town in India. The abnormal urban growth during the last few decades has resulted in overall degradation in all the basic facilities in the city including water supply, sanitation, health, roads, transport and so forth for all sections of the people. Though the city is located on the banks of the river Mahanadi and just on the downstream of Hirakud dam, the water supply situation in the city is critical. The present supply of a mere 3 mgd (million gallons per day) covers only about 30 per cent of the population in the city. The solid waste and night soil disposal system is also precarious. Out of 8000 cubic feet of wastes produced by the city in a day, one-half is dumped in the backyard of houses or on roads. Even though the programme of converting dry latrines into pour flush latrines has been continuing for a long time, bucket latrines are still prevalent in the town and the present municipal facilities are totally inadequate to cater to the needs of the growing urban population. The plan of the city was completed without a drainage system. Therefore there is no proper drainage network. Waterlogging during the monsoon season is a common phenomenon. Moreover, the excessive influx of poor people in to the city has caused a tremendous pressure on the shelter condition and has led to overcrowding of existing slums and the proliferation of new slums. It is surprising that Sambalpur district though ranking fifth in terms of urban population among the 13 districts of the state, also has the highest percentage of population living in slums (42.48) and Sambalpur city contributes nearly one-third to the total slum population while the rest is accommodated in 9 other towns in the district (Table 4.4).

Table 4.4
District-wise Urban and Slum Population in Orissa, 1981

Sl. No.	Districts	Urban Population	Slum Population (Per cent)
1.	Sundargarh	397,244	26.11
2.	Sambalpur	353,433	42.48
3.	Puri	446,980	28.05
4.	Ganjam	380,389	9.69
5.	Keonjhar	111,997	29.05
6.	Koraput	254,295	16.92
7.	Cuttack	500,065	27.94
8.	Bolangir	153,225	31.15
9.	Balasore	188,857	8.22
10.	Dhenkanol	95,611	17.31
11.	Kalahandi	80,541	15.92
12.	Mayurbhanj	90,538	9.13
13.	Phulbani	37,761	14.90
	Orissa	3,070,936	23.83

Both the number of slums and population therein have increased at an alarming rate, especially during the last decade, in Sambalpur. While there were 26 slum pockets in the municipal list with a total population of 24,142 in 1981-82, now the number of slums has increased to 48 and the population has reached the figure of 50,000 which is more than double the earlier figure. In addition, there are 10 or 12 unidentified slum pockets. If the population of these pockets is also taken into account, the total slum population will probably contribute more than half to the total city population. This enormous increase in the slum population in spite of a significantly low rate of decadal growth in total population of the city during the last decade can be attributed to the identification of those slums in the municipal list in the eighties which so far were unrecognised by the municipality.

The slums are scattered all over the city, but those in core city areas are more congested. The bulk of the slum population or 61 per cent of them belonging to scheduled castes and scheduled tribes, are living in extremely deprived conditions with insufficient physical amenities like water supply, sanitation, sewerage, drainage, health care and education. As most of these slums are situated on encroached land belonging to public agencies, the city master plan does not provide permanent infrastructural facilities in these areas. Consequently, whatever minimum services that exist in the slums have been provided entirely on an ad hoc basis.

However it must be mentioned here that unlike in metropolitan cities or in other higher order class I cities, the slums in Sambalpur have different characteristics so far as standards of shelter are concerned. Except in some vulnerable localities like along the railway tracks or river beds, the slums in other areas have mud houses with tiled roofs. However because of lack of basic facilities and poverty, these areas have been earmarked as slums.

Development Programme in Slums: Role of UBS

The enormous growth in the slum settlements during the eighties in Sambalpur has compelled policy makers to adopt some important steps for the improvement of slums through structured programmes. Sambalpur was one of the towns of the state initially covered under the Integrated Urban Development Programme (IUDP). A sum of Rs. 89.76 lakhs were proposed to be spent for various schemes during the period of 1980-83 which included sites and services, housing and slum clearance, infrastructure and communication, trade and commerce and development of utility services like water supply garbage disposal, drainage etc. (Mohanty and Mohanty 1989). The Small and Medium Town Development Programme launched in 1982 (now merged with UBS) was the second attempt in this regard with financial assistance from UNICEF. An assistance of nearly Rs. 20 lakhs was made available for three years, to cover 26 identified slums for providing physical infrastructure like potable water, sanitation facilities, roads, drains, street lights and social infrastructure like pre-primary schools, functional literacy centres, community centres etc.

During the latter part of the Seventh Plan more concerted efforts were made through the adoption of four important schemes, namely, Environmental Improvement of Urban Slums (EIUS), Urban Basic Services or UBS Programme, Low Cost Sanitation (LCS) Programme and Nehru Rozgar Yojana (NRY). While NRY aims at improving the economic conditions of the poor by facilitating income generation activities on a loan-cum-grant basis, the other three programmes specifically cater to the needs of the poor through the provision of basic amenities in the slum localities. Under the Eighth

Plan policy guidelines, a more integrated approach is being advocated through a compact service delivery system.

The employment programme or NRY has been introduced recently as part of an integrated approach. The NRY comprises three components, namely, (i) setting up of micro enterprises and training and infrastructure support, (ii) wage employment through public assets creation, and (iii) a scheme of employment through housing and shelter upgradation. It is expected that these three components together will create conditions which will lead to increased investment by houeholds towards shelter improvement and simultaneous increase in income generation through home based activities. The first scheme is being implemented at present in Sambalpur only. However action plans have been prepared for the implementation of the other two components in the current year. For setting up of micro-enterprises, under 18 schemes identified by the municipality, beneficiaries (with household incomes not exceeding Rs. 7,200 per year) are given a 25 per cent subsidy with a ceiling of Rs. 5,000 for SC/ST and women beneficiaries, and Rs. 4,000 for others. The remaining 75 per cent of the unit cost is covered by loans from scheduled banks. The subsidy amount is supposed to be borne by the centre, state and the municipality in the ratio of 50:32:18 (Government of Orissa, 1990).

The NRY programme, though introduced in 1989, has not made much progress till 1991 because of certain administrative difficulties. Out of 824 applicants sponsored by the municipality only 342 received loans under this programme till 1991-92 (for detail see Appendix 4.1).

Of all the development programmes currently being implemented in the slums of Sambalpur by the local government the UBS is the most important one. Sambalpur was one of the first few towns where the programme was launched from its very inception in 1986. The UBS is both a strategy and a vehicle for providing amenities and services to poor communities. The approach is to provide certain basic physical and social facilities to the community with the involvement of the community. Through its various schemes the UBS provides basic amenities like water supply and sanitation facilities, primary health care and nutrition facilities, non-formal education etc. It also facilitates income generating activities among women through the provision of small loans.

Under the above programmes especially the UBS the municipality has provided some facilities, which could improve the quality of life in Sambalpur slums to a certain extent. According to municipal records

47 balwadis, 27 adult literacy centres, 12 sewing centres and 3 creches have been provided under the UBS programme since 1986. Eighteen community centres have been constructed. Seventeen tube-wells, 100 dustbins, 12 community bathrooms have also been provided in addition to 1026 individual latrines. The effects of programmes like EIUS and LCS however have been very insignificant (for details see Appendices 4.2 to 4.5).

Organisational Set up of UBS and Grassroots Level Participation

In keeping with the policies of decentralisation and empowering local people especially women the planning, implementation and management of the programmes especially the UBS are expected to be achieved through active community involvement. In essence, the programmes are to be finalised through the 'bottom up' approach by involving the community and establishing inter and intra-organisational communication (Government of Orissa, 1990).

According to the UBS organisational set-up the goal of community involvement is achieved through the setting up of Neighbourhood Committees (NHC) or Basti Development Committees in every slum locality. In effect, there are 47 NHCs in Sambalpur for 46 slum localities. The action plans proposed by all 47 NHCs converge with the municipal action plan and at the district level with the District Development Plan.

The community organisers in the municipality maintain constant contact with the slum localities. The NHC comprising women resident volunteers, each representing 15 to 20 houses within the neighbourhood, communicate with the UBS officials through their monthly meetings. They also choose teachers for adult literacy centres, balwadis, creches, sewing centres etc. Each NHC also operates a revolving fund of Rs. 5,000 provided by the UBS for maintaining the services provided by the authorities and providing financial support to the local people, especially in the event of exigencies, small loans at a very low rates of yearly interest (5 per cent). Provision has also been made to provide additional funds of Rs. 5,000 for active NHCs. The account is jointly maintained by the CO and the President of the NHC.

The municipal council is the nodal agency for implementing the programme of UBS along with the other concurrently running programmes. The UBS cell in the municipality through its team consisting of a project officer and four community organisers acts as the link between the community at the grassroots level and the municipal administration involving different specialised departments, to execute the work at the field level.

The Chairman of the municipality directly elected by the people is involved with the UBS cell as overall in-charge of the Poverty Alleviation Programmes. In addition, 28 municipal councillors from different caste and religious backgrounds, though not associated with programme implementation, look after the interests of the people of the respective wards by representing their problem in the regular council meetings of the municipality.

The institutional framework for providing infrastructure development includes multiple agencies like the municipal council, public health engineering department, Sambalpur Regional Improvement Trust, Special Planning Authorities and so on, besides different departments of the municipal council. The local NHCs also cooperate by providing labour or a part of the cost. Because of the existence of multiple authorities lack of coordination among them is a permanent feature. The state government recently initiated steps for setting up a District Urban Development Authority (DUDA) for monitoring and synchronising the activities of all agencies working in the district.

The decentralised monitoring set-up has been strengthened under the revised programmes of Urban Basic Services for the Poor (UBSP). Orissa is one among the few states where a new structure has been adopted since 1990 for monitoring and management of the UBSP programme in the new towns and also old UBS project areas. Figure I gives the organisational set up for monitoring the new UBSP programme in the state and in Sambalpur city. Like other districts of the state, in Sambalpur monitoring of the programme starts at the bottom level, that is, at the basti level, the project management committee at the town level, district coordination committee at the District Urban Development Authority (DUDA), and the programme review committee at the State Urban Development Authority (SUDA) are the other hierarchical authorities in the state which conduct the monitoring at the town, district and state level. At the grassroots level programme implementation and monitoring are done simultaneously by the people, the neighbourhood volunteers and the UBS staff.

Figure 1
Organisational Structure and Functionaries for Monitoring of UBS/UBSP in Orissa State and Sambalpur City

Agency *Functionaries*

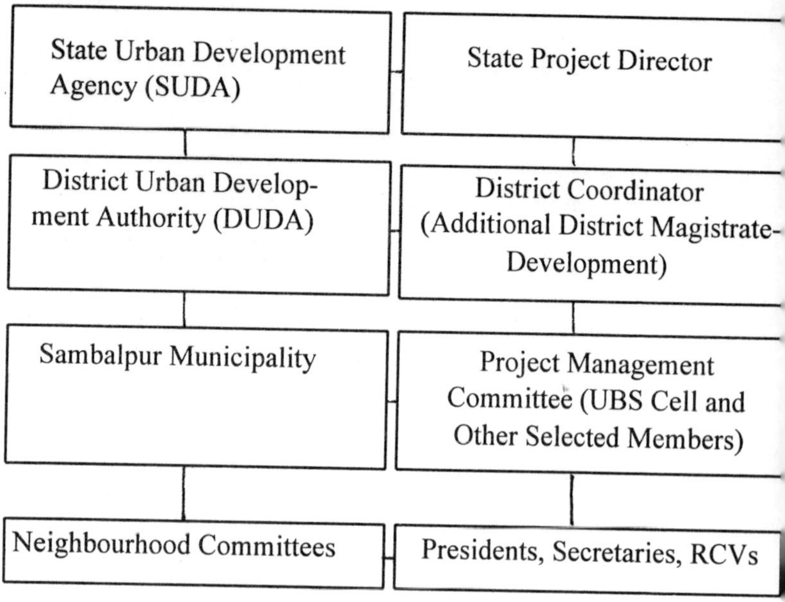

Financing of Basic Services Programmes and Role of Sambalpur Municipal Council

The Sambalpur municipal council is one of the oldest local bodies of the state and is formed by directly elected representatives. It is mainly responsible for the development work in the city. In addition, it is entrusted with the task of formulation, implementation and coordination of different state and centre sponsored development programmes especially for the poor.

Financial inadequacies of Sambalpur municipality as in case of many other class I cities in India, have contributed to a large extent to the inadequate delivery of basic services in the city. The income of the municipality from tax and non-tax sources has not increased at all during the last few years. In fact, besides collection from octroi, there has been a substantial fall in the collection from other taxes in 1990-91 from the 1989-90 level. The amount of grant from the state government has also been reduced to a great extent (Table 4.5) and the municipality had to opt for more and more loans as a result.

Table 4.5
Income Statement of Sambalpur Municipality: 1988-89, 1989-90 and 1990-91

Revenue Account	1988-89	Percentage	1989-90	Percentage	1990-91	Percentage
Tax Revenue	8,853,408	28.00	10,684,226	26.00	11,455,955	39.00
Non-Tax Revenue	10,174,613	32.00	15,409,470	38.00	5,595,881	19.00
Grants	8,193,699	26.00	7,572,922	18.00	5,725,453	20.00
Loans	4,409,000	14.00	7,226,000	18.00	6,549,455	22.00
Total	31,628,641		40,892,618		29,326,744	100.00

Source: (1) Sambalpur Municipal Council; (2) District Statistical Handbook, 1990-91.

The expenditure profile of the municipality on the other hand shows that there has been a substantial increase in the expenditure on general administration and except in conservancy there has not been any significant increase in the other fields of development expenditure during the reported period (Table 4.6).

Table 4.6
Expenditure Statement of Sambalpur Municipality for the Years 1988-89, 1989-90 and 1990-91

Item (Expenditure)	1988-89 (Rs)	Percentage	1989-90 (Rs)	Percentage	1990-91 (Rs)	Percentage
General Administration	2,921,516.13	11.03	2,534,245.17	7.16	3,116,627.37	14.06
Public Safety	376,372.20	1.42	294,245.00	0.83	166,544.00	0.75
Public Health	1,063,623.22	4.03	1,432,126.27	4.05	1,129,299.26	5.09
Drainage	84,215.56	0.3	196,447.36	0.55	158,245.43	0.71
Water Supply	1,093,461.00	4.13	192,927.36	0.54	841,984.60	3.70
Conservancy	4,498,691.00	16.90	4,716,345.95	13.33	5,482,883.00	24.73
Medical	449,998.41	1.70	679,155.00	1.92	499,783.00	2.25
Public convenience	83,486.00	0.3	105,549.00	0.30	112,279.00	0.51
Public works	2,995,021.51	11.31	3,129,314.23	8.84	2,290,262.05	10.33
Public instruction	5,537,851.95	20.91	7,288,867.31	20.60	3,441,255.30	15.52
Miscellaneous	7,374,968.00	27.85	14,812,507.68	41.86	4,927,248.94	22.23
Total	26,479,204.98		35,381,730.33 +33.62		22,166,411.95 -37.35	100.00

Source: Same as Table 4.5

Financial inadequacy of the local government is an important reason for the not-so satisfactory results of the poverty alleviation programmes which emerges from our field survey data in the following sections. The Sambalpur municipal council has the partial responsibility of financing all the programmes especially the UBS and NRY where the municipality has to bear one-fourth of the programme allocation. Environmental Improvement of Urban Slums is the only exception which is totally funded by the state government. However, it is evident from Table 4.7 that except in 1991-92 the municipal council could not contribute its share to the financial allocation of the programmes.

Table 4.7
Funding Pattern of UBS and NRY from 1989-90 to 1991-92

	Year	Central share (Rs)	State share (Rs)	Municipality share (Rs)	Total (Rs)
UBS					
	1989-90	1,83,000	1,60,000	--	3,43,000
	1990-91	94,450	1,25,000	--	2,19,450
	1991-92	1,59,000	1,25,000	1,25,000	4,09,000
NRY					
	1989-90	2,99,800	1,91,872	--	4,91,672
	1990-91	64,000	40,960	--	1,04,960
	1991-92	--	1,21,600	1,21,600	

Source: Sambalpur Municipal Council, 1992.

The total allocation for all the programmes during the last three years for the city was Rs. 29,288,82 is shown in table 4.8. A rough calculation of average per capita allocation works out to only Rs. 58.57. Considering the fact that the yearly allocation for the programmes from Central, State and Local Governments under different programmes are the major source of fund for providing basic services to the 50,000 slum population of Sambalpur, the total allocation of funds and per capita expenditure during the last three years on this account has been utterly inadequate.

Table 4.8
Funds allocated under Different Poverty Alleviation Programmes: 1989-90 to 1991-92

(in Rupees)

Year	NRY (Subsidy)	Programmes			Total (All programmes) (1989-92)
		UBS	EIUS	LCS	
1989-90	4,91,972	2,19,450	1,20,000	8,55,700	--
1990-91	1,04,960	2,00,000	1,44,000	--	--
1991-92	1,21,600	4,09,000	2,62,500	--	--
Total	7,18,232	8,28,450	5,26,500	8,55,700	29,288,82

Source: Sambalpur Municipal Council, 1992.

SURVEY FINDINGS

Social and Demographic Profile of Slum Households

The social profile as evident from the field-survey data (Table 4.9) indicates that in contrast to the general trend, the slums in Sambalpur are relatively homogeneous in terms of religion and language. Eighty-nine per cent of the sample households speak the majority language, Oriya, and 96 per cent are Hindus. Christians and Muslims form a minor proportion of the slum households. Fifty-eight per cent of the slum population belong to castes of general category. Scheduled Castes and Scheduled Tribes constitute the remaining 42 per cent. But there are concentration of SC/ST population in some slums. In our survey in 5 out of 13 slums, the SC/ST population is much above the average and ranges between 51 and 98 per cent. These slums are Danipali, Kanjihouse Dalaipara, Laxmi Dungri Para, Samlaipadar and Pensionpara. The average family size of the households is six, varying between five and seven which is no doubt larger than the normal size of a family which is five at the all India level.

The sex ratio in surveyed slums is 921 which is, though less than that of the Sambalpur district average of 967, much higher than the city-average of 884. This may signify that there are more family migration from the interior of the districts to the city slums. This may also imply that there is not significant gender variations in the infant and child mortality rates in the slums of the city.

Table 4.9
Socio-Demographic Background of Sample Households

Slums	No. of sample house-holds	Total No. of persons	Average size of house-hold	Per cent majority language (Oriya) spoken	Per cent majority religion (Hindu)	Per cent majority caste (General)	Per cent migrancy	Average migrancy duration in years	Per cent majority migrancy reason (job)	Sex ratio
Tanula Para	41	235	6	94	100	77	42	8	81	991
Manikmunda	19	111	6	85	100	95	100	10	98	850
Danipali	32	182	6	98	100	40	20	10	100	1022
Durgapali	37	267	7	79	100	58	2	10	100	921
Pension Para	21	144	7	67	67	49	33	10	100	1057
Budharaja	66	318	5	98	100	74	55	8	99	957
Kanjihouse - Dalai Para	41	223	5	100	100	2	15	8	100	858
Madhab Bandh	28	181	6	94	100	70	14	8	67	866
Laxmi Dungri Para	24	108	5	100	100	25	40	8	87	862
Sahoo Colony	40	216	5	77	100	85	75	10	43	946
Samlaipadar	31	170	5	100	88	49	49	8	87	727
Bahidarbadh	20	123	7	77	93	70	63	10	100	922
All Slums	400	2278	6	89	96	58	42	9	86	921

Source: Field Survey, Sambalpur, ISS, 1992.

In conformity with the characteristics of slums in any other town, Sambalpur slums also have a large percentage of migrant population (42 per cent). But in four out of twelve slums the migrant households are much above the average and constitute 55 to 100 per cent of total households. Bengalees from the adjacent state of West Bengal and from the neighbouring country of Bangladesh, and also Biharis constitute a sizeable section of the migrant population. Most of these migrants have settled here for a long time as the average migrancy period is 9 years and many of them have even come here more than ten years ago. The reason for migration as revealed by the respondents indicated that more than factors like education, family movement etc, the search for employment or economic reason was the singlemost important factor which had pushed them to the city. Nearly 86 per cent migrant households specified employment prospects as the sole reason for coming to the city. Given the backwardness of the neighbouring districts of Kalahandi and Koraput, the relatively developed city of Sambalpur with its burgeoining service sector served as an important pull centre.

Educational Background of Households

The percentage of school-going children is not very high in Sambalpur slums. The number of parents reporting high expenditure as reason for not sending their children to school was substantial. Out of 521 male and 478 female children in the sample households 53 per cent male and 46 per cent female children attend some type of school (Table 4.10). The number of children going to primary schools was the highest for both male and female children.

The percentage of girls going to school as compared to boys is less at every level except at the lowest that is the balwadi. The percentage of school going female children decreases at higher levels of education and is the lowest at the above high school level.

As regards the literacy level of the elder members of the households, only 43 per cent of them have any type of formal education. The percentage of literate people is much higher among males (54.51 per cent) as compared to females (only 26 per cent). It is also noted that the educational level of the majority of these people is up to the primary level and only 6 per cent males and 2.3 per cent females are educated above high school level.

Table 4.10
Percentage Distribution of Persons over Education Status

			Male	Female
1.	**Children**			
	a.	Balwadi school	8	10
	b.	Children going to primary school	32	26
	c.	Other schools (Middle & High)	13	10
		Total children going to school	53	46
2.	**Adult**			
	a.	Educated up to primary level	19.4	14.1
	b.	Middle school	15.2	5.4
	c.	High school	18.9	4.1
	d.	Above high school	8.0	2.3
		Total adult with formal education	59.5	25.9

Source: Field Survey, Sambalpur, ISS, 1992.

Employment Status

The employment status of the sample households reveals characteristics that usually prevail in slums in such cities. Unlike in metropolitan cities where a substantial portion of slum dwellers are engaged in formal sector employment in Sambalpur slums a greater percentage of workers are engaged in some type of informal sector activity or work as daily labourers, rarely engaged in jobs on a regular basis (Table 4.11). Work force participation is 29 per cent which is near equal to that of the town as a whole (29.8 per cent). In the total work force adults contributed nearly 98 per cent. In the sample slums nearly 1389 persons or 61 per cent of a total of 2278 persons were adults and 47.88 per cent of them (or 665 in number) were workers. Incidence of child labour is thus not transparent in the slum localities in Sambalpur. However, it is common to see children, especially girls, working with their parents in shops, or helping mothers in bidi making, paper-bag making etc.

Table 4.11
Distribution of Employed Persons (Male and Female) over Nature of Employment

Slums in Sambalpur	No. of sample house-hold	Total no. of persons	Total No. of adults		Total no. of working persons	Per cent adult Working		Percent Self-employed (adults)		Per cent regular employee		Per cent irregular employee	
			Male	Female		Male	Female	Male	Female	Male	Female	Male	Female
Tanulapara	41	235	68	61	68	87	12	44	50	34	38	10	13
Manikmunda	19	111	35	30	30	97	0	66	0	31	0	7	0
Danipali	32	182	43	44	57	70	23	28	54	28	0	48	38
Durgapali	37	267	76	70	61	93	7	54	50	19	25	26	25
Pension Para	21	144	32	34	35	74	22	34	12	50	50	15	37
Budharaja	66	318	98	107	127	68	29	41	40	8	2	51	56
Kanjihouse Dalai - Para	42	223	58	47	50	88	12	52	66	38	16	9	16
Madhab Bandh	28	181	55	46	56	78	17	40	60	29	10	27	30
Laxmi Dungri Para	24	108	36	36	48	62	37	13	5	20	16	70	61
Sahoo Colony	40	216	65	60	46	93	6	58	100	20	33	18	0
Samlaipadar	31	170	53	46	59	69	28	7	58	21	5	68	29
Bahidarbadh	20	123	46	34	28	92	7	19	0	46	0	34	100
All Slums	400	2278	665	615	665	79	18	39	43	26	12	32	42

Source: Field Survey, Sambalpur, ISS, 1992.

Women participation in economic activities among the surveyed households is no doubt low as compared to men. Out of the total of 665 workers only 126 (19 per cent) are women which is 11.54 per cent of the total female population. But at the same time it is important to note that the workforce participation rate among women is much higher in Sambalpur slums which is 11.5 per cent, than in the urban agglomeration as a whole which is 9.29 per cent according to 1991 census data. This substantiates the view that women in poorer households have to take part in some kind of economic activities at very low wages to supplement their family income. The share of the women workers, however, is not high in every locality. It is nil in one slum and as high as 38 per cent in another, thus displaying a wide variation. It is noted that the share of women workers is high in those slums where the proportion of SC/ST population is either very high or constitutes a big segment.

The employment status of the working population ascertained from the survey shows that a major portion of both working men and women is self-employed or hold irregular jobs more men than women have access to regular jobs. The type of activities the people are engaged in Sambalpur slum can be viewed from Table 4.12. Only one-fourth of the total working population in the sample slums is engaged in the formal sectors in government/semi government or private offices, schools, colleges. They are employed as peons, drivers etc. Twenty-five per cent of them are engaged in skilled or semi-skilled jobs and work as plumbers, painters, mechanics or are specialised in traditional crafts like making of bamboo baskets, paper plates etc. Daily labourers constitute a major portion of the workforce (22.58 per cent). They work either on agricultural farms in peripheral areas or at construction sites, or are engaged in loading and unloading jobs at railway station.

Economic deprivation is strongly related with social backwardness. More households in the SC/ST category belong to low income categories in our survey and in three out of the five slums where the majority population belong to SC/ST, a substantial proportion of their workers are engaged as daily labourers (25 to 65 per cent) without a regular source of income. The distribution of employed adults over income classes reveals interesting results. While the share of employed adults increase with income, reverse is the case with women workers. Fewer women are working in higher-income classes. The share of regular job holders also increases with increase in income (Table 4.13).

Table 4.12
Distribution of Working Persons over Types of Jobs

Slums in Sambalpur	No. of sample house-holds	Total no. of persons	No. of working members	No. of persons responded	No. in Govt./ semi Govt. offices	Private and others	Petty trade	Skilled/ semi-skilled jobs	Daily labourer	Rick-shaw puller	Farming
Tanula Para	41	235	68	45	7	8	16	11	1	2	0
Manikmunda	19	111	30	30	6	3	4	17	0	0	0
Danipali	32	182	57	50	5	7	3	20	12	3	0
Durgapali	37	267	61	58	1	14	0	25	14	0	0
Pension Para	21	144	35	34	13	8	0	12	1	0	4
Budharaja	66	318	127	124	3	5	30	15	48	23	0
Kanjihouse Dalai Para	42	223	50	50	18	6	16	1	2	7	0
Madhab Bandh	28	181	52	52	4	6	9	27	4	1	0
Laxmi Dungri Para	24	108	43	43	1	3	3	3	28	3	1
Sahoo Colony	39	216	43	43	5	8	25	3	2	0	2
Samlaipadar	33	170	58	58	8	2	1	23	19	1	0
Bahidarbandh	18	123	24	24	4	5	1	6	7	1	4
All Slums	400	2278	664	611 (91.73)	75 (12.27)	75 (12.27)	108 (17.67)	163 (16.68)	138 (22.58)	41 (6.72)	11 (1.6)

Note: Figures in parentheses are percentages.
Source: Field Survey, Sambalpur, ISS, 1992.

Table 4.13

Distribution of Adult Workers (Income Class Wise)

Income classes (Rs)	No. of sample house-holds	Total no. of persons	Total no. of adults		Total adults working		Self-employed		Regular employed		Irregular employed	
			Male	Female	Male (Per cent)	Female (Per cent)	Male (Per cent)	Female (Per cent)	Male (Per cent)	Female (Per cent)	Male (Per cent)	Female (Per cent)
101 - 250	2	6	2	2	50.0	50.0	100.0	0.0	0.0	0.0	0.0	100.0
251 - 500	47	215	48	58	70.49	29.51	23.3	38.9	2.3	16.7	76.7	44.4
501 - 1000	184	960	259	261	78.15	21.85	40.6	41.9	20.8	11.3	38.6	46.8
1001 - 2000	129	789	255	202	84.5	15.5	45.5	45.7	29.3	2.9	25.1	51.4
Above 2000	38	308	101	92	86.0	13.8	35.0	38.5	48.8	61.5	15.0	0.0
All Income Classes	400	2278	665	615	80.7	19.3	39.9	42.8	26.23	12.7	32.9	44.4

Source: Field Survey, Sambalpur, ISS, 1992.

Income-Expenditure Profile and Incidence of Poverty

Because of their employment background the average monthly income of the sample slum households is low as Rs. 1065 and in per capita terms it is only Rs. 187 per month (Table 4.14). Around 58 per cent of the households have a monthly average income below Rs. 1,000 and among them nearly 79 per cent have monthly average incomes ranging from Rs. 500-1000 and the rest have a monthly household income below Rs. 500. It is also important to highlight that in three out of five slums where the majority population belongs to the SC/ST category, the per capita income is much below the average and it is in these slums only that the majority population work as daily labourers as noted above. The fact that these slums with family sizes smaller than the average (5 members) and workforce participation above average for both men and women still have a lower average per capita income than the other slums, further helps establish the close relationship between economic backwardness and social background.

More than 57 per cent of surveyed households fall below the poverty line of Rs. 209 (1990-91 prices) in terms of the recently updated Planning Commission criterion for the Eighth Plan and not a single slum had less than 40 per cent population below the poverty line. Only two slums have a per capita monthly average expenditure above the poverty level. Four out of 12 slums are very poor where monthly per capita income ranges between Rs. 150 and Rs. 170 and in five slums the monthly per capita income is slightly higher than the previous category but falls much below the average.

It is also to be noted that the monthly average expenditure on selected urban services is very high in all the slums. Out of an average household income of Rs. 1,065 a substantial amount is spent on education, rent or house-tax, electricity, health, loan repayment and so on (Table 4.15). Water supply is the only service for which no household reported paying anything on a regular basis. However, households with independent water sources had to incur a one-time expenditure for the installation of a hand-pump, digging of a well or a municipal water pipe connection. But the number of such households is very few. The average expenditure is the highest for health which is more than 25 per cent of the entire expenditure on these accounts. Although all the households do not have to pay for all the services, a substantial number of households usually pay for health and children's

Table 4.14
Income and Expenditure Profile and Incidence of Poverty

Slums in Sambalpur	No. of sample house-holds	Total no. of persons	Average household		Percapita monthly		Per cent house-holds below poverty line	Monthly household expenditure on select services for reporting households (Rs)
			Income (Rs)	Expenditure (Rs)	Income (Rs)	Expenditure (Rs)		
Tanulapara	41	235	1296	1317	226	230	41.5	584.5
Manikmunda	19	111	1115	1099	191	188	47.4	839.6
Danipali	32	182	969	934	170	164	71.9	374.0
Durgapali	37	267	1105	1044	153	145	73.0	886.0
Pension Para	21	144	1369	1292	200	188	47.6	826.8
Budharaja	66	318	800	779	166	162	63.6	390.2
Kanjihouse Dalai Para	42	223	1155	1111	218	209	47.6	620.0
Madhab Bandh	28	181	1183	1170	183	181	64.3	541.1
Laxmi Dungri Para	24	108	820	820	182	182	58.3	218.4
Sahoo Colony	40	216	1135	1054	210	195	57.5	330.4
Samlaipadar	32	170	860	899	162	169	54.4	308.6
Bahidarbadh	18	123	1334	1312	195	192	44.4	311.5
Total	400	2278	1065	1039	187	182	57.5	542.3

Source: Field Survey, Sambalpur, ISS, 1992.

education. It is, therefore, inappropriate to argue that slum people do not spend much for civic and other services and facilities and that a major portion of their income is spent on food items. Even if we believe that the reported expenditures on the selected services was exaggerated, the survey data reveal that the proportion of non-food expenditure of slum households is often very high. But this does not necessarily imply that their economic condition permits them to spend a substantial portion of their income for availing themselves of these facilities. Very often they cannot meet their monthly expenditure from their own incomes and have to resort to borrowing from different informal sources and thus remain in perennial debt.

Table 4.15
Average Monthly Expenditures on Selected Services

	Service	No. of Households Reported Paying	Average Monthly Expenditure
a.	Education:		
	Fees	147	38.7
	Uniform	116	24.4
	Books	197	26.4
b.	Monthly Rent	52	56.0
c.	House Tax	161	3.0
d.	Electricity Charges	167	40.2
e.	Water Supply	0	0.0
f.	Sanitation	55	51.0
g.	Health	344	164.3
h.	Repayment of loans	41	138.3

Source: Field Survey, Sambalpur, ISS, 1992

It is further interesting to note that the expenditure on certain basic amenities rises with rising income. More households in the higher income class spend more on education, housing, health facilities rather than on water supply and sanitation like drainage and garbage disposal as these are usually community services (Table 4.16). However people in higher income classes do spend for capital expenditure on installation of their own tubewell or own toilets which do not form the part of monthly expenditure.

Table 4.16
Monthly Expenditure on Selected Basic Services over Income-Class

(in Rupees)

Income Class (Rs)	Total expen-diture	Educa-tion	Housing	Elect-tricity	Water	Toilet	Health
101 - 250	37	27	0	0	0	0	100
251 - 500	368	48	54	41	0	67	72
501 - 1000	581	108	56	47	0	114	153
1001 - 2000	617	113	89	41	0	76	191
Above 2000	1083	154	136	41	0	150	225
All Classes	441	90	59	40	0	51	164

Source: Field Survey, Sambalpur, ISS, 1992.

Effect of Nehru Rozgar Yojana

Against the background of this economic profile of the slum households it is worthwhile to note the effect of the Nehru Rozgar Yojana in the slums. The Nehru Rozgar Yojana one of the most important components of the poverty alleviation programmes through employment generation, was introduced in the city in the year 1989. However it has not gathered momentum yet. The survey data reveal that only 47 persons or 12 per cent of 400 housholds have received some kind of assistance through loan-cum-subsidy for setting up micro enterprises. Also the number and percentage of households that have received loans and the average loan amounts are seen to be higher in the highest income class. (Table 4.17)

Further investigation revealed that another 105 out of 400 households applied for the loan but did not receive any assistance. In most cases the reason for not receiving loans is stated as rejection of the application by banks on various grounds.

The municipal council which is the implementing authority of NRY for identifying employment generating activities in the town through urban wage employment and shelter upgradation schemes has not yet started such activities. Therefore the scope for creation of additional job prospects for poor households through these schemes is yet to take off.

Table 4.17
Income-wise Accessibility of IGP

Income class (Rs)	No. of sample house-holds	Per cent household aware of IGP	House-holds rece-ived loans	Average loan amount (Rs)	Per cent got sub-subsidy from Bank	Sub-sidy amount	Per cent women received loans
101 - 250	2	50	0	0	0	0	0
251 - 500	47	45	23	3438	4	850	4
501 - 1000	184	70	5	3413	3	850	2
1001 - 2000	129	78	10	6582	3	1663	1
Above 2000	38	95	34	13100	8	4058	3
All Classes	400	72	12	6633	5	1855	2

Source: Field Survey, Sambalpur, ISS, 1992.

It is interesting to note the responses of the remaining 248 households who did not seek loans. While 72 of them responded that they did not need a loan, 116 said that they did not know the procedure, 44 replied that they did not know anything about the programme. The remaining 20 replied that they would not be able to repay the loan. These responses indicate that there is greater need for making people aware about the procedure. Beneficiary selection should be more according to needs so that those who apply and are recommended by the municipality get the loan.

Shelter and Other Physical Amenities

Housing

Deprivation in terms of shelter is evident from the housing structures of the slum households. Only 22 (5.4 per cent) households have pucca houses in the sample slum areas. The rest of them live either in kachcha (70.8 per cent) or in semi-pucca (23.8 per cent) houses (Table 4.18).

Table 4.18
Housing Situations

Slums in Sambalpur	No. of sample house-holds	Percentage distribution of households over					Average No. of Rooms	Per cent electrified	Per cent answered 'Expensive' for not taking electricity
		Type of House			Ownership status				
		Pucca	Semi-pucca	Kachcha	Owner	Tenant			
Taunla Para	41	0.0	14.6	85.4	56	45	2	71	26.8
Manikmunda	19	5.3	26.3	68.4	32	5	2	74	15.8
Danipali	32	3.1	12.5	84.4	89	11	2	38	100.0
Durgapali	37	5.4	5.4	89.2	96	4	3	27	100.0
Pension Para	21	23.8	38.1	38.1	96	4	2	90	100.0
Budharaja	66	0.0	6.1	93.9	84	16	2	27	100.0
Kanjihouse Dalai Para	42	0.0	40.5	59.5	100	0	2	62	100.0
Madhab Bandh	28	7.1	21.4	71.4	98	2	3	54	100.0
Laxmi Dungri Para	24	0.0	12.5	87.5	79	22	2	13	100.0
Sahoo Colony	40	0.0	50.0	50.0	100	0	2	38	100.0
Samlaipadar	32	3.1	25.0	71.9	75	25	3	50	100.0
Bahidarbadh	18	16.7	33.3	50.0	83	17	2	56	100.0
All Slums	400	5.4	23.8	70.8	82	13	2.3	50	86.9

Source: Field Survey, Sambalpur, ISS, 1992.

Table 4.19
Housing Situation: Income Class-wise

Income class (Rs)	No. of sample households	Type of houses (Per cent household)			Ownership status (Per cent Household)		Per cent electrified	Average No. of rooms per household	Per cent answered 'Expensive" for not taking electricity
		Pucca	Semi-Pucca	Kachcha	Owner	Tenant			
101 - 250	2	0.0	0.0	100.0	50	0	50	2.5	100.0
251 - 500	47	0.0	11.0	89.0	83	17	17	1.7	100.0
501 - 1000	184	2.2	18.5	79.3	77	19	37	2.1	82.8
1001 - 2000	129	3.9	28.7	67.4	82	13	62	2.6	85.5
Above 2000	38	18.4	36.8	44.8	92	5	76	3.0	65.6
All Classes	400	5.4	23.8	70.8	77	11	50	2.3	86.9

Source: Field Survey, ISS, Sambalpur, 1992.

The slums display typical characteristics in terms of congestion and overcrowding. The average number of rooms per household with 6 members is only 2.3. In other words 3 persons live in one room. While 82 per cent of the households own their huts, only 13 per cent live as tenants. However, ownership of huts does not imply tenural rights to land. Most of these slums are on encroached areas which belong to different state and central government agencies. In every locality a majority of the households do not have any land *pattas* even after having resided there for a long time.

Though there are not much inter-slum differences in the access to housing facilities, there are significant differences across income classes. In all aspects of housing the higher income categories enjoy better facilities. It is significant to note that while 89 per cent households in income class 3 have kachcha houses, in income class 6 it is only 17 per cent (Table 4.19). The average number of rooms also increases with the increase in income, while in income class 3 it is 1.7 for income class 6 it is 3.

In income class 3 only 10.6 per cent of the households could afford to have electricity in their houses, in income class 6 it was as high as 68.4 per cent. Eighty-seven per cent of those who do not have connections felt it was 'too expensive'. The average initial expenditure of Rs. 2,000 as reported by the households is too high for them to spend on an electricity connection. Moreover the average expenditure of Rs. 40 per month for electricity consumption is also a deterrent. It is no wonder that 80 to 100 per cent households in lower income classes (3 and 4) stated that getting an electricity connection was 'expensive' while the percentage was 65 in the case of income class 6.

Water Supply

One of the most critical problems in the slum areas is lack of proper water supply facilities. Community water supply sources like public standpost, mark II hand pump, well are predominant in all slums. Nearly 95 per cent households depend on a community source and in most of the slums the number of such sources is very inadequate (Table 4.20). Only 56 per cent sample households have access to municipal piped water supply but the supply is irregular and cannot be depended upon. In four of the 12 sample slums there is no source of piped water supply at all. Though more than one type of source is available in every locality, water is either of indifferent good quality

Table 4.20
Water Supply Situation

Slums in Sambalpur	No. of sample house-holds	Water supply source (per cent household)			Availability (per cent household)			
		Independent	Common	Piped	Inside premise	Source near	Fit for drinking	Supply adequate
Taunla Para	41	2.4	97.6	98	19.5	90.2	100.0	100.0
Manikmunda*	19	0.0	100.0	84	0.0	73.7	79.0	89.5
Danipali	32	9.4	90.6	0	9.4	18.8	93.8	65.6
Durgapali	37	2.7	97.3	0	2.7	35.1	100.0	100.0
Pension Para	21	4.8	95.2	100	33.3	52.4	100.0	38.1
Budharaja	66	0.0	100.0	42	1.5	21.2	87.9	6.1
Kanjihouse Dalai Para	42	0.0	100.0	98	0.0	92.9	100.0	100.0
Madhab Bandh	28	10.7	89.3	82	10.7	60.7	92.9	60.7
Laxmi Dungri Para	24	0.0	100.0	0	0.0	--	41.7	12.5
Sahoo Colony	40	0.0	100.0	95	0.0	62.5	100.0	0.0
Samlaipadar	32	12.5	87.5	0	12.5	43.8	100.0	31.3
Bahidarbadh	18	22.2	77.8	89	22.2	52.6	100.0	83.3
All Slums	400	5.4	94.6	56	9.3	52.6	91.3	57.3

Source: Field Survey, Sambalpur, ISS, 1992.

or is insufficient to meet the needs of the people. Mark II hand-pumps have been provided under the UBS programme in most of these slums. But the number is not adequate and the water is also not always fit for drinking. Only 57 per cent households reported that the water was fit for drinking. An important feature noticed during the survey is that a majority of the slums in Sambalpur have grown surrounding a tank or a pond which was initially a major source of water. However, lack of regular cleaning of these ponds have made them unusable and many of them have dried completely. The municipality does not take up the responsibility of cleaning these water sources because of financial constraints. If properly maintained, these may provide alternative sources of water at least for purposes other than drinking.

Sanitation

Sanitation facilities which include toilet, drainage and garbage disposal facilities are far more inadequate in Sambalpur slums. So far as toilet facilities are concerned nearly 77 per cent of the 400 households reported that they had no provision at all for any type of facility and in some localities the percentage of such households was nearly 100 per cent (Table 4.21). Even among those who had some kind of facility of their own, (23 per cent of households), more than 90 per cent had the basket type. It is only in these slums however that a considerable proportion of households have independent toilets.

The scheme to provide independent latrines and for converting dry latrines into sanitary ones under the UBS and low cost sanitation programmes does not appear to have had much effect. The UBS progress reports shows that nearly 1026 *Barpali* latrines (locally made pit latrines) were supplied since the beginning of the programme in 1986. If five persons use a latrine on an average, the whole slum population in Sambalpur should have had access to latrine facilities. However this has not been the case as our survey results show. The reason for not availing themselves of independent latrines as reported by the households was mainly unaffordability. Even though there are heavy subsidies it is difficult for slum residents to arrange even the minimum amounts that they need to pay for installing independent latrines. The second reason as reported by them was the lack of space in their premises for setting up such facilities. It was observed during the survey that the latrine materials provided by the municipality were lying in the corner of some huts.

Table 4.21
Toilet, Drainage and Garbage Disposal Facilities

(per cent household)

Slums in Sambalpur	No. of sample house-holds	Toilet facility		Type of facility		Drainage/sewerage facility		Mode of garbage disposal
		Indepen-dent	No pro-vision	Flush	Basket	Open	No Provision	
Taunla Para	41	7.3	92.7	33.3	66.6	2.4	97.6	0
Manikmunda	19	89.5	10.5	0.0	100.0	0.0	100.0	0
Danipali	32	9.4	90.6	0.0	100.0	37.5	62.5	0
Durgapali	37	10.8	88.9	75.5	24.3	27.0	73.0	0
Pension Para	21	38.1	61.9	9.5	90.5	90.5	9.5	0
Budharaja	66	1.5	98.5	0.0	100.0	33.3	66.7	7.6
Kanjihouse Dalai Para	42	7.1	92.9	0.0	100.0	97.6	2.4	0
Madhab Bandh	28	17.9	82.1	20.0	80.0	3.6	96.4	0
Laxmi Dungri Para	24	4.2	95.8	9.2	90.8	0.0	100.0	0.0
Sahoo Colony	40	0.0	100.0	0.0	0.0	0.0	100.0	10.0
Samlaipadar	32	6.3	93.8	23.0	77.0	0.0	100.0	0
Bahidarbadh	18	83.3	11.1	6.3	93.8	0.0	100.0	0
All Slums	400	22.6	76.7	8.6	91.1	24.3	75.7	1.5

Source: Field Survey, ISS, Sambalpur, 1992.

Drainage and garbage disposal facilities are equally precarious in the slums. Seventy-six per cent households reported to have no drainage facility around their houses and of the small percentage of households that reported any type of drainage facility (24.2 per cent), 43 per cent reported these as being *kachcha* which were not cleaned regularly.

Garbage disposal facilities are virtually non-existent in the slum areas of Sambalpur. The municipal records show that at least 100 dustbins have been provided under the UBS programmes in different slums (Appendix II). However in the surveyed slums such dustbins were not available. Ninety-eight per cent households reported that they threw garbage out in the open and that there was no garbage bin available in their areas.

There is not much income class variation however as far as these facilities like water supply source, drainage and garbage disposal etc are concerned. Only 7 to 8 per cent households in income classes 5 and 6 reported to have an independent water source. All the other households belonging to all income classes have to depend exclusively on common sources (Table 4.22).

While in the case of community facilities like drainage and garbage disposal there is no income-class variation,. harp variations come into focus in the case of latrine facilities. While 32 per cent households in income class 6 had toilets of their own, in income class 3 the corresponding proportion was as low as 4.3 per cent.

Table 4.22
Water and Sanitation Facilities over Income Classes

(per cent household)

Income classes (Rs)	No. of sample house-holds	Water supply		Toilet facility (Indepen-dent	Drainage (Pucca)	Garbage disposal (Bin)
		Indepen-dent	Piped			
101 - 250	2	0.0	50.0	0.0	0	0
251 - 500	47	2.1	29.8	4.3	25.0	0
501 - 1000	184	5.2	51.0	13.0	26.5	0
1001 - 2000	129	12.2	68.2	17.8	10.3	1.6
Above 2000	38	11.4	68.4	31.6	33.3	0
All Classes	400	5.4	56	22.6	21.3	1.5

Source: Field Survey, Sambalpur, ISS, 1992.

Health Facilities

General Health

The health facilities existing in the city are utterly inadequate to provide services to the growing city population. As a result, despite the provision of six hospitals and dispensaries run by the municipality and the state government, a large segment of the slum households has to fall back upon private doctors. While 92.9 per cent reported government hospitals as the nearest available service point and 82 per cent households use the government hospitals, a substantial proportion could not depend exclusively on this facility and was forced to go to private doctors often (Table 4.23).

Table 4.23
Access of Health Care Facilities

Slums in Sambalpur	No. of sample households	Per cent households having acess to			Per cent taking govt. health care facility
		Govt. hospital	Private doctor	Others	
Taunla Para	41	98	39	5	90
Manikmunda	19	100	0	58	95
Danipali	32	97	81	0	59
Durgapali	37	54	81	84	81
Pension Para	21	90	62	76	90
Budharaja	66	98	64	11	80
Kanjihouse Dalai Para	42	98	38	93	100
Madhab Bandh	28	100	89	7	89
Laxmi Dungri Para	24	79	58	0	54
Sahoo Colony	40	100	53	78	90
Samlaipadar	32	100	84	0	56
Bahidarbadh	18	100	28	0	94
All Slums	400	93	56	34	82

Source: Field Survey, Sambalpur, ISS, 1992.

The two most important reasons for not going to government hospitals as reported by a majority of the households were the non-availability of medicines and the long wait in queues. The high average expenditure of Rs. 164 per month on health, primarily for fees and medicines incurred by the households as evident from their income-expenditure profile (Table 4.6) corroborates this. This average monthly expenditure varies sharply with income levels. While in income class 2 it is Rs. 10.4, for class 3 it is Rs. 72 and it was reported as Rs. 221.5 for the highest income class. It must be mentioned that the number of households spending for medical facilities is also much higher in higher income categories.

Mother and Child Care

Mother and child care are the two most important components of the UBS Programme. The immunisation programme for child care is covered by the health department in the municipality. Family welfare is covered by the chief district medical officer. The immunisation programme for the slums is undertaken in the municipality for 3 months with specific target so that all the slums can be covered annually. Even so the percentage of fully immunised children is not reported to be very high in our sample households (Table 4.24) 64 per cent of them were immunised (41 per cent wholly and 23.2 per cent partly).

It is important to note here that the slums with more than average adult education levels had higher immunisation levels also. Although no generalisation can be made from this observation, it is logical that awareness is higher among the educated parents and that they take better care of their children.

The fact that women have become more aware about ante-natal care in the slums is evident from the survey data. It is observed that nearly 75 per cent women had gone for health check-ups during pregnancy. While 63 to 65 per cent women preferred government hospitals as the place for child delivery, 31.6 per cent women still opted for home deliveries with the help of household members. Although noticeable inter-slum variations are not reflected in the data it was observed that the women in the slums have higher adult education levels, had better access to ante-natal care and opted for professional services during child delivery.

More women from higher income classes are conscious about health. The percentage of women going in for pre-natal care increases with income class and the proportion is highest in the income class 6 and more women in higher income classes avail themselves of hospital facilities for child delivery. While 84 per cent women in the higher income class 6 opted for regular health check-ups and 76 per cent for hospital deliveries, these percentages were 66 and 41 for the income class 3.

Table 4.24
Use of Maternal and Child Health Care Facilities

Slums in Sambalpur	No. of sample house-holds	Pre-natal check-up	Per cent adult women going for				Help during child delivery (per cent response)			Per cent adult utilis-ing family planning measure	Per cent children immun-sed
			Pre-natal check-up in		Child delivery in						
			Govt. hospital	Others	Govt. hospital	Others	Doctor	Trained Dai	Others		
Taunla Para	41	78	56	37	61	49	78	10	46	31	56
Manikmunda	19	95	84	0	95	5	95	0	5	37	39
Danipali	32	72	50	0	22	81	19	19	78	56	55
Durgapali	37	84	92	0	97	3	97	[illegible]	8	30	60
Pension Para	21	81	100	0	100	0	100	0	0	48	70
Budharaja	66	55	41	2	48	52	50	[illegible]	[illegible]	29	68
Kanjihouse Dalai Para	42	88	88	0	90	0	93	0	[illegible]	48	80
Madhab Bandh	28	71	32	18	61	57	64	4	[illegible]	42	80
Laxmi Dungri Para	24	29	33	0	21	54	21	4	67	55	44
Sahoo Colony	40	100	95	3	98	3	98	0	3	33	100
Samlaipadar	32	66	28	9	28	78	28	9	63	31	62
Bahidarbadh	18	78	67	6	67	33	72	0	61	50	55
All Slums	400	75	64	6	66	35	68	4	40	38	64

Source: Field Survey, ISS, 1992

Family Planning

The response of women to family planning was better than their male counterparts. Questions were asked especially to women about family planning practices and regarding the availability of such services and their attitudes towards it. More than 50 per cent women replied in the negative when asked whether any one of the couple adopted any family planning measures. Ten per cent of the women felt too shy to respond. It is interesting that out of 38.5 per cent who reported as using some measures, as high as 36.7 per cent were women and men accounted for only 1.8 per cent (Table 4.25).

The reasons given for not adopting family planning measures varied from case to case. An important reason reported by women was non-cooperation on the part of husbands. Nearly 33 per cent women reported that their husbands did not allow them to adopt any form of contraception. The lack of awareness was not an important factor as only 9 per cent women reported that they did not know about family planning practices or about the places where these facilities were available. The responses from all income classes were almost identical regarding family planning practices.

Our field survey data however shows that the level of adult education influences positively the adoption of family planning measures and confirms that education is the most widely reported variable which shows a consistent negative association with fertility (Rob, 1992). In the four out of six slums where the proportion of adult literates was observed to be higher than the average, the proportion of people who had adopted family planning measures was also relatively high (Table 4.26).

Table 4.25
Pattern of Family Planning Measures

Slums in Sambalpur	No. of sample house-holds	Utilisation of family planning measure (Per cent response)				Reason for not using family planning measures (per cent response)			
		Husband	Wife	None	No Response	Not Aware	Husband does not allow	Not required	Others
Taunla Para	41	2	29	63	6	10	12	78	0
Manikmunda	19	0	37	32	31	5	37	58	0
Danipali	32	3	53	44	0	21	21	58	0
Durgapali	37	3	27	68	2	22	32	0	5
Pension Para	21	0	48	0	52	0	82	9	9
Budharaja	66	2	27	62	9	6	9	83	2
Kanjihouse Dalai Para	42	0	48	50	2	0	69	8	23
Madhab Bandh	28	4	39	53	4	6	50	44	0
Laxmi Dungri Para	24	4	21	67	8	6	13	0	0
Sahoo Colony	40	0	33	67	0	10	27	4	31
Samlaipadar	32	3	28	63	6	5	35	60	0
Bahidarbadh	18	0	50	50	0	11	11	67	11
All Slums	400	2	37	52	10	9	33	47	11

Source: Field Survey, Sambalpur, ISS, 1992.

Table 4.26
Adult Literacy and Family Planning

Slums in Sambalpur	Total No. of adults	Per cent having formal education (Primary & Above)	Per cent utilising family planning measures
Taunla Para	129	59	29
Manikmunda	65	55.4	37
Danipali	87	39	53
Durgapali	146	34.25	27
Pension Para	66	42.43	48
Budharaja	205	32.68	27
Kanjihouse Dalai Para	105	46.67	48
Madhab Bandh	101	50.05	39
Laxmi Dungri Para	72	32.0	21
Sahoo Colony	125	49.06	33
Samlaipadar	99	30.31	28
Bahidarbadh	80	61.25	50
All Slums	1280	43.36	37

Source: Field Survey, Sambalpur, ISS, 1992.

Response of the Community Towards Basic Services Programmes

It is important to note to what extent the community is responding to the programmes by way of taking advantage of the facilities provided and how they are taking initiatives and participating in the decision making process through their involvement and interaction with the neighbourhood committee and municipal representatives for expressing their basic service needs.

It has already been noted earlier that the structured institutional framework with the NHC at the base has been a prerequisite for the UBS programme and instead of top-down, the bottom-up approach has been emphasised for involving people in the decision making. Data on community participation were collected keeping this background in mind.

Aspects of community awareness for slum households have been discussed in the light of their being aware of different facilities which are provided under different poverty alleviation programmes and awareness about the neighbourhood committee showing the RCV, COs and so forth. Participation has been analysed in the perspective of effectively utilising the facilities given under different programmes and involving themselves with the day to day activities of NHC, discussing their views and problems with Resident Community Volunteers (RCVs), COs and so on.

Table 4.27
Percentage Distribution of Households over Community Awareness and Participation

1.	**Community Awareness**		
	a.	Aware about UBSP	78
	b.	Aware about IGP	72
	c.	Know the RCVS	75
2.	**Community Participation**		
	a.	Involved as Balsevika	10
	b.	Discuss problems with volunteers	65
	c.	Sending children to Balwadi/Anganwadi	36
	d.	Utilising adult education facility	8
	e.	Utilising immunisation facility	64
	f.	Utilising family planning measures	38
	g.	Received loans	11
	h.	Received help from NHC for getting loan	12

Source: Field Survey, Sambalpur, ISS, 1992.

It is noted that awareness about both UBS and the income-generation component of NRY is quite high among the slum households (Table 4.31). Nearly 78 per cent of the sample households were aware of the UBS and 72 per cent of the IGP. Where the UBS was concerned the share of households who knew about the programme was not below 70 per cent anywhere except in two slums and in some cases 100 per cent respondents knew about this programme. At least half the slum households were aware of the IGP in each sample slum. Most of the sample slum households (75 per cent) also knew the RCV, Neighbourhood Committee President and Secretary.

However, high awareness, though associated with high participation in most cases, has not always been the same. The survey data reveal that except for discussing the problems with the RCVs and COs and utilising the immunisation facilities, the percentage of households utilising the other facilities and participating in other activities is quite low.

It is also significant that the higher income classes are more ctively participating in the NHC activities. More people in the income groups of 4 and 5 are involved as Balsevikas and they discuss their problems with the COs and RCVs more often (Table 4.32).

Table 4.28
Levels of Community Awareness and Participation in UBS Programmes
(per cent household)

ncome classes (Rs)	No. of sample house-holds	Aware of UBSP	Involved as Balsevika	Known to volunteer	Discuss problems with volunteer
101 - 250	2	100	50	100	100
251 - 500	47	53	0	53	32
501 - 1000	184	74	7	75	66
1001- 2000	129	89	14	81	74
Above 2000	38	87	16	74	68
All Classes	400	79	12	73	64

Source: Field Survey, Sambalpur, ISS, 1992.

Out of 210 families who have children in the 1-4 years age-group, only 75 families or 35.7 per cent sent their children to balwadis although in almost all the localities there are balwadis. Even though three-fourth of the sample slums have adult literacy centres only 8 per cent of the 725 adults without any formal education went to the adult literacy classes. As regards family planning measures it has already been noted that only 38 per cent availed themselves of any such device in spite of having access to the facilities provided through different programmes.

So far as the income generation programme is concerned only 11 per cent of the sample households received loans although most of them needed the loan. In spite of high awareness they did not have access to the facilities because of different reasons as mentioned earlier.

Basic Services and Relative Position of Slums

To conclude the findings from our survey this section discusses the performances of the slums in terms of different indicators. On the basis of the discussion in the previous sub-section we have ranked 12 slums in descending order from 1 to 12 in order to assess the position of slums in terms of per capita income, five components of basic services, community awareness and participation. While for per capita income ranks have been assigned according to the average per capita monthly income, scores have been computed for each of the other components and ranks have been assigned accordingly.

In order to compute rank order scores for components, selected variables have been taken for each service (see Appendix 1.3 for variables and explanation).

Rank order scores for all five components of basic services have been worked out and then a composite index for quality of life has been computed. In the same way indices for community awareness and participation have also been worked out separately.

Table 4.29 gives the ranks of slums in terms of all the selected indicators, viz. per capita average monthly income, housing, water supply, education, sanitation, women and child health, community awareness and participation.

It is observed that the slums ranking high in terms of average per capita income ranging from Rs. 200 to Rs. 226, (Taunla Para, Kanji House Dalai Para, Sahoo Colony and Pension Para) hold nearly equivalent ranks in terms of composite index for basic services, the only exception being Sahoo Colony, which though ranked third in per capita income, in terms of basic services comes in the eighth position.

On the other hand the slums at the lower rung (ranks 9 to 12) in terms of per capita income (Danipali, Budhraja, Samlaipudur and Durgapali), stand in equivalent position in terms of composite index for basic services, the only exception being Durgapali, which has a better access to services (rank 5), though in terms of per capita income it is positioned at the lowest (rank 12). It is observed therefore there is a positive association between income and composite index of basic services. As a result Spearman's coefficient of rank correlation between the two is quite high (0.63).

In terms of community awareness, it is again observed that the slums with higher monthly average per capita income are relatively better aware about the programmes and in terms of availing themselves of the facilities provided, they are in the near equivalent ranks. The only exception is Pensionpara. On the other hand all the four lower income slums stand very low, both in regard to awareness and participation. It is also observed that in general community awareness and participation together help to get a better quality of life (rank correlation 0.5).

Table 4.29

Ranks of Slums on the Basis of Select Indicators and Composite Index for Basic Services

Slums in Sambalpur	Ranks								
	A	B	C	D	E	F	G	H	I
	Average per capita income	Education	Housing	Water supply	Sanitation	Women and child health	Composite Index (B-F)	Community awareness	Community participation
Tanulapara	1	1	3	3	8	8	3	2	2
Manikmunda	6	7	2	4	5	5	4	10	11
Danipali	9	9	9	8	1	10	9	7	9
Durgapali	12	11	11	1	4	4	5	11	6
Pension Para	4	5	1	7	3	2	1	3	8
Budharaja	10	10	10	9	9	9	10	9	7
Kanjihouse Dalai Para	2	6	4	2	2	3	2	1	3
Madhab Bandh	7	2	6	5	7	7	7	6	1
Laxmi Dungri Para	8	12	12	12	12	12	12	8	10
Sahoo Colony	3	3	8	11	10	1	8	4	5
Samlaipadar	11	8	7	10	11	11	11	12	12
Bahidarbadh	5	4	5	6	6	6	6	5	4

Source: Field Survey, Sambalpur, ISS, 1992.

The above observations indicate that because of the lack of interest and apathy of the slum households towards active involvement in the community activities to express their felt needs their quality of life does not improve much. The poorer people in slums are more deprived in terms of basic amenities. Because a majority of these households are engaged as daily labourers lack of time also affects their participation in community activities or express their needs through the local neighbourhood committee meetings.

A Comparative Assessment of the Basic Services in Slums

Against the background given above of the findings from our field survey of the Sambalpur slums in terms of basic services, an attempt has been made here to present a comparative assessment of the present situation as observed in our survey (ISS) with that which prevailed at the time of the two previous surveys carried out in Sambalpur at two different points of time by two different agencies. The first survey was conducted by the Operations Research Group in 1982 to evaluate the situation in terms of basic services, assess the needs of the local people and suggest action plans for the Small and Medium Town Development Programme that was to be initiated from 1982, assisted by UNICEF. The second survey was conducted in 1987-88 by the National Institute of Urban Affairs (NIUA) as part of their all-India study on the access of basic services to the poor. While the first one covered 621 households over 26 identified slums then existing in the city, the second one covered 202 households from 12 selected slums out of a total of forty-six. Although the methodologies, sample sizes, the purpose and nature of these three surveys are different, some broad comparisons may be made in terms of common indicators of basic services which will focus on the trend in the access to basic services in slums during the last decade.

In terms of the water supply sources, Table 4.30 shows that picture has not changed at all during the last four years from 1988 to 1992. Only 5 per cent of the households had independent water sources in 1992 and the percentage was the same in 1988 as well. But in the case of type of source only 56 per cent reported having tap water supply in the 1992 survey as against 71 per cent in the 1988 survey by NIUA. The wide difference between the two figures may be due to the time of year when the second survey was carried out, that is the summer month of May. This is the time of acute water crisis. However, the percentage of households served by hand-pumps has increased to a great extent as our survey shows. Under the UBS scheme additional Mark II hand pumps have been provided which to some extent have helped improve the situation.

Table 4.30

Status of Water Supply: 1982, 1988 and 1992

(per cent household)

	ORG (1982)	NIUA (1988)	ISS (1992)
1. **Source**			
a. Independent	--	5	5.4
b. Common	--	95	
2. **Type of Source**			
a. Tap water	--	71	56
b. Shallow hand pump	--	1	1
c. Mark II hand Pump	--	26	52
d. Well	--	2	45
e. Pond	--	1	11
3. **Fit for Drinking**	--	95	91.3
4. **Supply Adequate**	44	95	57.3

Source: ORG, 1986; NIUA, 1991; Field Survey, ISS, 1992.

The sanitation facilities which showed some improvement during the time period between the first two surveys, has not changed significantly in the latter period from 1988 to 1992 (Table 4.31). The percentage of households with independent toilets was 3.2 as observed by ORG in 1982, 21 in 1988 by NIUA and it was 22.6 in 1992 during our survey. While the percentage of households reporting no provision of the facilities got reduced from 93 to 60 during the earlier period, it showed an increase in the latter period, that is in 1992. This could be due to the availabiliity of public toilets in 1988 when a large percentage of households reported using common toilets. The percentage of households using common toilets, in fact, increased from 4 to 19 during the period 1982 to 1988. But because of the recent effort to provide more independent toilets than common ones under the low cost sanitation programme, the percentage of households with independent toilets has increased while that of households with common toilets has reduced as observed in our survey.

Table 4.31
Sanitation Facilities: 1982, 1988 and 1992

(*per cent household*)

	ORG (1982)	NIUA (1988)	ISS (1992)
1. **Toilet Facility**			
a. Independent	3	21	22.6
b. No Provision	93	60	73.7
2. **Drainage Facility**			
a. Open	--	--	24.3
b. No provision	--	--	75.7
3. **Garbage disposal**			
a. Bin	--	22	1.5
b. Sweeper	--	41	--
c. Outside	54	37	98.5

Source: ORG, 1986; NIUA, 1991; Field Survey, ISS, 1992.

As regards shelter, it is observed in Table 4.32 that a higher percentage of households in the ISS survey occupied pucca houses (5 per cent) than in the NIUA survey (2 per cent) and while the percentage of households living in semi *pucca* houses has increased those with *kachcha* houses has decreased in the time gap between the latter two surveys. The percentages of households with electricity connections also increased in the two intervening periods. However, while between 1982 and 1988, it increased to a more significant extent from 25 per cent to 46 per cent, in the latter period during 1988 to 1992, such increase was only by 4 percentage points.

While in terms of the availability of general health facilities the situation has not shown any significant variation between the two latter surveys of 1988 and 1992 (NIUA and ISS), in terms of mother and child care the situation has improved considerably during both the time gaps, especially between 1982 and 1988. More women going to hospitals for prenatal health check-ups and child deliveries and seeking doctors' help during delivery are without doubt good indicators of better health care (Table 4.33).

Table 4.32
Housing Status: 1982, 1988 and 1992

(per cent household)

	ORG (1982)	NIUA (1988)	ISS (1992)
1. **Type of Housing**			
a. Pucca	--	2	5.4
b. Semi-pucca	--	11	23.8
c. Kachcha	--	87	70.8
2. **Ownership Status**			
a. Owner	--	--	84
b. Tenant	--	--	13
c. Not identified	--	--	3
3. **Houses Electrified**	25	46	50

Source: ORG, 1986; NIUA, 1991; Field Survey, ISS, 1992.

Table 4.33
Percentage Distribution of Households over Health Facilities: 1982, 1988 and 1992

	ORG (1982)	NIUA (1988)	ISS (1992)
1. **General Health**			
a. Visits to government hospitals for treatment	--	92	93
b. Private doctor	--	7	56
c. Others	--	81	34
2. **Children Immunised (1-4 years Age Group)**	--	91	64
3. **Mother Care**			
a. Going for prenatal check-up	36	91	75
b. Govt. Hospital as place of child delivery	30.6	41	66
c. Home as place of child delivery	59	29	32
d. other hospitals	10.7	30	34
e. Doctor as help during child delivery	18.4	71	68
f. Trained Dai as help	29.9	7	4
g. Household member/ neighbour as help	30.5	13	25
h. Others	20.0	9	40
4. **Family Planning**			
a. Husband using FP measure	--	--	2
b. Wife	--	--	37
c. None	--	--	52

Source: ORG, 1986; NIUA, 1991; Field Survey, ISS, 1992.

Although definite conclusions cannot be arrived at from the above comparisons, it may be suggested that there has been a trend towards better availability of certain services, especially social services like child and mother care and to a certain extent education. However, in terms of infrastructural facilities like water, drainage, housing, sanitation and so on, the change has been marginal over this ten-year period.

Another important factor is that the improvement noticed during the time interval of the first two surveys (1982-1988) was much more significant than that observed during the latter period, namely between 1988 and 1992. The first period witnessed a more noticeable change because of the launching of the UBS programme in 1986, after which many slum localities in Sambalpur experienced a rapid improvement in certain basic services, especially those which are included in the programme components. The slackening of the pace of programme implementation and the transition from UBS to UBSP in the latter period may be cited as the cause for the relatively low progress during 1988 to 1992.

CONCLUSION

The findings from our field survey data in the previous sections give a detailed picture of the access to basic amenities and the effect of development programmes on the surveyed households across slums and income classes. This concluding section highlights some of the major findings and problems and tries to suggest some tentative policy measures.

The analysis of our survey data shows that the slums in Sambalpur exhibit a high incidence of poverty (57.5 per cent sample households are below the poverty line). Socially backward sections, that is scheduled castes and scheduled tribes, are more economically deprived than the other castes even within a slum. Slum residents are mostly engaged in petty trade. A majority of them do not have any regular employment and work as daily labourers.

Even with a workforce participation rate (29 per cent) at par with that of the city as a whole (29.84 per cent) and with a comparatively high incidence of female participation rate (11.5 per cent), the average per capita income for the sample slum households is very low (Rs. 182).

Besides deprivation in terms of economic indicators people in slums face shelter and environmental problems in terms of overcrowding, water scarcity, limited sanitation facilities and general health facilities. There has not been very significant development in their economic condition and quality of life during the last decade despite the efforts for poverty alleviation through different programmes. However in terms of women and child health improvement is noticeable.

Income-class variation in availability of community services such as public water-point, drainage and garbage disposal facilities, general health facility and so forth is not significant. But sharp income-class variations are observed for quality services such as individual toilets, independent water sources, pucca houses, private medical facilities. Poorer people are more deprived in terms of quality services.

Community awareness is quite high in the sample slums in Sambalpur and the system of projecting effective demand for services through neighbourhood committees also exist and is effective. The involvement of women volunteers is also a very positive aspect of community participation in the sample slums. In spite of this the availability of certain physical services has not improved significantly, though this is not so in case of social infrastructure like *balwadis*, adult literacy centres, sewing centres, and so on.

In terms of using the facilities, the participation is quite low. The percentage of people sending children to *balwadi* schools, attending adult literacy centres is very insignificant. The preoccupation of the slum residents with income earning activities is the major reason cited for not attending adult literacy classes. Lack of job prospects is also another reason which deterred them from going to adult literacy centres.

SUGGESTED POLICY MEASURES

In view of the high incidence of poverty in the slums implementation of NRY programme should be more rapid and broad based. The whole process starting from identification of beneficiaries to disbursement of loan ny the bank takes a long time, which must be minimised. The beneficiary identified by the CO with the help of the NHC should receive the loan with minimum scrutiny from the bank. The repeated visit of the beneficiaries to the bank for loans may thus be minimised. Micro enterprises which are selected as eligible for loan should have sufficient market potential. It is necessary therefore to undertake some market assessment about a product based on which the number of loanees should be fixed in that trade and training should be imparted on these trades. Marketing facility of the products of these enterprises is also important. Loan receivers may be encouraged by the municipality to form cooperatives for marketing their products.

Employment generation through shelter upgradation programmes which serve the twin purposes have not been started on a large scale. HUDCO which is the financing organisation requires a clear *patta* for the land or guarantee from the state government certifying that the particular slum for which the programme has been chalked out will not be disturbed for the next 20 years. This makes it difficult for the municipality to ask for a loan as it is difficult for any state government to furnish such certificates. This mandatory time period may be reduced so that the local bodies can have easy access to such loans.

So far as the basic seervices are concerned the most critical areas are water and sanitation which need immediate attention. The integrated World Bank Programme for the district which has been negotiated recently includes a major water supply project. It may improve the water supply condition for the city to some extent. But it is difficult to say how far it will reach the slums which are not revenue-paying areas for the municipality. More localised solution through hand-pumps must be sought under the programmes of EIUS and UBS. However the hand-pumps must be maintained properly, and local women may be trained for this as maintenance workers in the training programme under NRY.

While providing individual latrines, care should be taken to select beneficiaries so that they are not left unused. A large number of community latrines may be constructed in slum areas. Sulabh International which is constructing and maintaining such units in some areas of the city should be involved in slum areas also on a large scale.

The spread of both non-formal education for adults and pre-primary education for children, must be through the motivation of adult female members. The timing of the classes should not clash with their day-time activities like household work or wage-earning activities.

Existing infrastructure facilities like medicines, vehicles and working staff should be strengthened for mother and child care. Awareness needs to be created among the slum dwellers and especially among mothers who should be motivated to take advantage of the prenatal and postnatal care and immunisation facilities for their children.

The people should be made more aware of the need of effective community development. The posts of functionaries of the NHCs should be on term basis so that all women in the locality can take part – not merely the more influential ones. It is necessary also that the municipality plays its role by properly integrating all the mini plans with the town plan and pooling all the resources under different programmes for effective implementation of the strategy of convergence as envisaged in the new UBSP programme.

Appendix 4.1

Information on NRY Scheme Under Sambalpur Municipality from 1989-90 to 1991-92

Sl. No.	Urban micro enterprises	1989-90 (Rs)	1990-91 (Rs.)	1991-92 (Rs.)
1.	Funds released towards subsidy	4,91,672.00	1,04,960.00	1,21,600.00
2.	Total expenditure during the year	24,947.50	2,26,463.75	1,00,525.00
3.	Balance subsidy to be utilised	4,66,724.50	(-)1,21,503.75	21,075.00
4.	Utilisation certificate submitted	Nil	Nil	3,00,136.25
5.	No. of banks located in municipal Area	20	20	20
6.	No. of applicants identified	824	Nil	899
7.	No. of applications sponsored	824	Nil	
8.	No. of cases sanctioned	40	220	82
9.	No. of applications pending with banks	784	564	
10.	Applications returned by banks			

Source: Sambalpur Municipality, 1992.

Appendix 4.2

Achievement of UBS in Sambalpur City since 1986 till 1991-92

Total NHC formed	47
Balwadi	47
Adult literacy centres	27
Sewing centres	12
Creche	3
Community centres (completed)	18
Community centres under construction	7
Latrines	1026
Ventilators	2020
TV sets equipped in community centres	10 B/W, 8 Colour
Smokeless chullah	637
Tubewell	17
Dustbins	100
Community bathrooms	12
Community urinals	4
Soak Pits (near tube wells)	30

Source: Sambalpur Municipality, 1992.

Appendix 4.3

Expenditure Pattern for UBS for 1991-92 and 1992-93 in Sambalpur Municipality

	Pattern	1991-92 (Rs)	1992-93 (Rs)
1.	Salary of core staff	1,28,120 (25.6%)	82,914 (20.92%)
2.	Honorarium for education (Balwadi, Creche, ALC Teachers etc)	1,98,400 (39.7%)	56,625 (14.29%)
3.	Urinals for ladies	24,000 (4.8%)	--
4.	Sanitation kits supplied	4,700 (.9%)	--
5.	Smokeless chullah	15,350 (3.1%)	2448 (.62%)
6.	Ventilators	7500 (1.5%)	2464 (.62%)
7.	Tree plantation programme	930 (.19%)	--
8.	Individual latrines barpali	20,000 (4%)	28,200 (7.1%)
9.	Study tour programme	15000 (3%)	2683 (6.77%)
10.	Women's library	9000 (1.8%)	--
11.	Construction of community centres (25 per cent borne by the NHC)	75,000 (15%)	98,000 (24.73%)
12.	Stationery	2000 (.4%)	1008 (.25%)
13.	Cleaning ponds	--	2000 (.5%)
14.	Additional revolving fund	--	1,20,000 (30.28%)
		5,00,000	3,96,342

Note: (1) Figures in the parentheses are percentages to total expenditure.
(2) In Sambalpur there are 45 balwadi teachers, 10 ALC teachers, 2 sewing teachers and 3 creche teachers.

Source: Sambalpur Municipality, 1992.

Appendix 4.4

Targets and Achievements of EIUS Programme in Sambalpur Municipality and Projected Expenditure

	Target (No. of Slums)	Projected Expenditure (Rs.)
1989-90		
Water Supply - Tube Wells	4	1,00,000
Electric Pole	4	20,000
Total		1,20,000
1990-91		
Drains	6	2,88,000

Note: According to municipal sources targets in both the years could not be achieved for various reasons. In the first year it was because of non-receipt of allocated instalment from the state government in time. In the second year tenders could not be passed in time as approval of action plan from the government came late. The same targets were being taken up in 1991-92.

Source: Sambalpur Municipality, 1992.

Appendix 4.5

Targets and Achievements of Low Cost Sanitation Programmes in Sambalpur Municipality

1. Conversion of services latrines to low cost pour flush water seal latrines (1988-89)

Target:

Total Number of Units - 1063

Conversion done:

by Sulabh International - 172
by the Public - 472

Balance to be done - 419

Note: Despite the fact that the municipality received the money from the government and loan sanctioned by HUDCO, the targets for LCS were not achieved for various reasons as mentioned by the municipality, which are as follows:

1. Non-receipt of loan amount from HUDCO.
2. Sulabh International stopped work from June 1990 on the demand of payment according to revised estimate of per unit cost of Rs. 2150 in place of Rs. 1610 which was being charged before.

Source: Sambalpur Municipality, 1992.

REFERENCES

nsus of India (1991): *Provisional Population Totals: Rural-Urban Distribution*, Office of the Registrar General, New Delhi.

vernment of Orissa (1991): *District Statistical Handbook, 1990-91, Sambalpur*, Directorate of Economics and Statistics, Bhubaneswar.

vernment of Orissa (1990) - *Guide Book for Implementation of Schemes Towards Integrated Development of Urban Centres*, Housing and Urban Development Department, Government of Orissa, Bhubaneswar.

hanty L N P and Mohanty S (1989): "Slum and Squatter Settlements in Class I Towns: Orissa Experience", *Journal of the Institute of Public Administration*, Vol. 4, No. 1-4.

tional Institute of Urban Affairs (1991): *Basic Services and the Urban Poor*, Report, National Institute of Urban Affairs, New Delhi.

perations Research Group (1982): *Development of Small and Medium Towns, Project Report for Sambalpur Town (Orissa)*, (unpublished), ORG, Bhubaneswar.

ob Ubaidur, A. K. (1992) "Socio-economic Determinants of Fertility: What do we know?" *Demography India*, Vol. 21, No. 1.

Chapter V

SILIGURI

INTRODUCTION

Siliguri is the most populous town of North Bengal zone. This is t least urbanised zone of the state of West Bengal. This zone administratively known as the Jalpaiguri division. It consists of fi districts, that is Koch Bihar, Jalpaiguri, Darjeeling, West Dinajpur a Malda. Together, they comprise 16 per cent of the urban area and 9 p cent of the urban population of the state.

The urbanisation process has been very slow in this zone. In the la four decades, there has been a mild increase in the share of the Nor zone in the urban population of the state – from 7 per cent in 1951 around 9 per cent in 1991.

There was no class I town in North Bengal in 1971. In 1981, ther were two such towns. In 1991, this number has been increased to fou The number of class II towns has remained almost the same (4) i three decades.

The uneven population distribution, that is the general characteristi of developing countries, is evident in this otherwise slowly urbanise region also. The number of class I towns doubled in North Benga while the growth of other towns remained relatively insignificant.

Increase in population in the urban area is generally the outcome o three factors: natural growth, migration and reclassification. The natural growth of population has been the most important componen of urban growth in the developing countries during the sixties and seventies. There is, however a tendency for the percentage of urban growth attributable to natural increase to decline over time in many parts of India.

Rural urban migration was viewed favourably in the economic development literature in classical theories of economic growth (Todaro, 1985). Internal migration was thought to be a natural process in which surplus labour was gradually withdrawn from the rural sector to provide the needed manpower for urban industrial growth. In contrast, recent experience from developing countries shows that the rate of rural urban migration continues to exceed rates of an job creation and surpasses the absorption capacity of both ustry and urban social services. Migration today is a major factor tributing to urban surplus labour, leading to increase in urban employment.

In the vast rural area of North Bengal, agricultural development has been sufficient enough to sustain the increasing growth of pulation. The existing tea gardens did not plough back enough ney for the economic development of the region. Low agricultural velopment has been associated with poor industralisation in the area. majority of the urban dwellers (nearly 70%) earn their livelihood m the tertiary sector.

The flow of migration was largely directed towards the urban ntres having important transport linkages within and outside the untry. Darjeeling district provided this linkage through the tional Highway (No. 31) and other important road connections th the industrial heartland of the state and other regions. multaneously, as an important tourist centre, it has accommodated bulk of the migrants and become the most urbanised district North Bengal during the last three decades as depicted in Table 5.1.

Table 5.1
Urban Population in the Districts of North Bengal

State/Districts	Percentage of Urban Population		
	1971	1981	1991
West Bengal	24.75	26.47	27.39
Kochbihar	6.83	6.90	7.85
Darjeeling	23.05	27.55	30.71
Jalpaiguri	9.60	14.05	16.40
West Dinajpur	9.34	11.17	13.33
Malda	4.22	4.78	7.08

ource: Census of India -- 1991, Paper - 2 of 1991, Provisional Population Total.

The percentage of urban population in this district increased faster an the state average during the last three decades. In 1991, the level f urbanisation in Darjeeling was significantly higher than the state evel.

CITY PROFILE

Siliguri accounts for the largest share of urban population among t towns of Darjeeling, accommodating more than half the total urb population of the district (Table 5.2).

Table 5.2
Percentage Distribution of Urban Population of the Towns in Darjeeling District

Years	Total urban population in the district ('000)	Per cent share of population in the municipal towns				
		Darjeeling	Kalimpong	Kurseong	Siliguri	Other Towns*
1971	180	24	13	9	54	--
1981	282	21	10	6	55	8
1991	410	17	9	6	55	13

Source: Census of India - 1991. Paper- 2 of 1991, Provisional Population Total.
* Darjeeling district has seven towns of which the four mentioned are municipal towns.

It was a tiny village of less than five thousand population even i the forties. In 1951, it was declared an urban area with a population c just over six thousand. It stands on the edge of the Terai, offering th first glimpse of the outer range of the Himalayas. It is bounded b Kurseong town (in the same district) in the North, Bihar an Bangladesh in the South, Jalpaiguri district in the East and Nepal in th West. The importance of Siliguri has gradually increased as a vita link for trade between India and Sikkim, Bhutan, Nepal and Tibet. Th Assam rail link in the 1950s, made this town a gateway to North-Eas India. The National Highway (No.31) and other road network ushered a new era in the transport horizon in the entire North-Eas India. Finally, in the wake of the National Emergency in 1962 on th eve of the Chinese war, Siliguri assumed a vital strategic importanc from the national point of view. This small town (15.5 sq.km) i surrounded by a vast rural area (250 sq.km).

An important component of this increasing share of population ha been the inflow of migration into the city. The migration durin 1961-71 was due to the influx of refugees from Assam as a result o the Indo-China border conflict, construction of military establishment and increase in communication facilities. During 1971-81, the Bangladesh war added significantly to the population influx. Afte

1981, some important state government offices have been established in Siliguri attracting employment in the tertiary sector. Moreover, as a gateway to the wonderful sights of the Himalayan peaks and ranges in Darjeeling, Siliguri offers important tourist activities stimulating the economy of the town.

Table 5.3 illustrates the population growth of the town. The population growth rate has actually declined during 1981-91, as compared to the earlier decades. But urban density has increased from a little over 4000 per sq.km to more than 14000 during 1961-91. There has been no expansion in the urban area to accommodate the growing population in Siliguri. This has created tremendous pressure on the existing land and available infrastructure. The demographic characteristics of Siliguri are illustrated in Table 5.4.

Table 5.3
Growth of population in Siliguri Municipal Area during 1961-91

	1961	1971	1981	1991
Population (000 persons)	65	97	154	227
Decadal growth rate per cent	-	48.90 (61-71)	57.36 (71-81)	46.83 (81-91)
Population density (persons per.sq.km)	-	4193	9903	14624

Source: Urban West Bengal, 1992-93.
Institute of Local Government And Urban Studies, Calcutta.

Table 5.4
Demographic Characteristics of Urban Areas in Siliguri, Darjeeling district and West Bengal

	Growth rate (%) 1981-91	Literacy Rate		Sex Ratio	Participation Rate	
		Male	Female		Male	Female
Siliguri (M)	46.8	79.7	69.3	822	54.67	8.48
Darjeeling Dist (U)	46.1	72.1	62.0	842	48.46	9.48
West Bengal (U)	28.9	72.1.	60.0	856	49.52	6.46

Source: Census of India, 1991. Paper - 3 of 1992.
Note: M = Municipality, U = Urban.

The population growth rate in Siliguri municipal area is much higher than the state level and slightly higher than the district level. This town enjoys a very high level of male as well as female literacy rate. But the female participation rate (the proportion of female worker to female population) is very low in the town representing the general characteristics of the state. The sex-ratio is lowest in the town in comparision to both the district and the state. The high female literacy rate does not have any significant effect on female employment or female health. The low sex-ratio accounts for the poor health of women, and increasing male migration, among other reasons. In Siliguri, external factors like political instability has largely accounted for increasing migration of the whole family, rather than single male migration. It seems that the low sex-ratio is largely attributed to poor utilisation of medical facilities by women in the town.

The Economic Base

The five districts of North Bengal contain 17 per cent of the total population of West Bengal but only 5.3 per cent of total industrial workers. Siliguri also has experienced a very slow pace of industrialisation. It is basically a service town. Nearly 47 per cent of the total industrial employment in Siliguri is in the household industries. The total number of industrial units actually fell from 1971 to 1985 as is evident from Table 5.5.

Table 5.5
Industrial Units and Employment in Siliguri

Year	No of Units	Employment (No.)
1971	174	8324
1974	169	7765
1975	163	8304
1985	162	8338

Source: District Census Handbook, Darjeeling, 1987.

This represents a paradox in the industrial scene as Siliguri has plenty of industrial resources. There are good prospects for the wood industry in this region. The tea industry is not prospering much as the profits generated by it are not reinvested for development of the plantations. Siliguri offers a very attractive locational advantage for industries. It has a railway junction and an airport very close to the city. A very important national highway passing through the city connects the entire north eastern region with the rest of the country. Being an important transport node, Siliguri could also provide a good location for an automobile spare parts industry. Even with all these potentials of industrial development, North Bengal accounts for only 1.2 per cent of the total fixed capital and only 3.2 per cent of the total value added in the state.

Lack of industrialisation has made Siliguri basically a market town. Since 1960 it has become an important centre for the wholesale trade. There are also a staggering number of shops. There are 3 shops per 100 population (In Delhi, the number is 0.21) - the highest among the nine major towns of North Bengal. A large number of shops operate on subsistence level generating disguised unemployment in the tertiary sector. Lack of expansion of the organised sector associated with the ever expanding informal sector has resulted in serious unbalanced economic growth. The informal sector can expand absorbing unskilled labour without any major capital expenditure. This sector has primarily absorbed poor migrants from the surrounding areas. The major occupations in the informal sector in Siliguri are the following -- street corner vendors, hawkers, rickshaw puller, road-side repair shop workers, lottery ticket sellers and suchlike. The average earning of a worker in the informal sector vary between Rs. 15 and Rs. 40 per day.

The Emergence of Slums

The process of unplanned urbanisation often results in a paradox of growth and poverty, Siliguri being no exception. The expanding economic base in the tertiary sector has encouraged the inflow of migration from within as well as from outside the state. As urban infrastructure trails behind the growth of population, slums have emerged in plenty throwing a serious challenge to the local body as well as the state government.

There are 48 recognised slums in Siliguri at present, where 21.57 per cent of the total population reside. A majority of them are migrants. Nearly half of the total slum dwellers live below the poverty line, 40 per cent are without any formal education. Around 80 per cent of the slum dwellers are migrants.

As Siliguri is becoming the fastest growing town in West Bengal, slums also growing here at an alarming pace. A majority of the slum dwellers are engaged in unskilled or low skill jobs earning meagre wages or, if self employed, are living on subsistence incomes. They are not only low skilled but also illiterate. Employment generation programmes in the informal sector are very often threatened by the lack of skill of the poor. Upgradation of skills, entrepreneurship training, provision of credit facilities and improving the literacy level are some of the crucial needs of the people here. The status of health, particularly that of mother and child is also very poor in the slums. Any programme on slum development should concentrate not only on improving the level of earning but also on improving the social and physical infrastructure simultaneously so that there is overall improvement in the quality of life which will help in pulling the slum dwellers out of the vicious circle of poverty.

Infrastructural Programmes

Assorted programmes of urban services through different organisations are in operation at present in Siliguri:

1. The Environmental Improvement of Urban Slums (EIUS), locally known as the *basti* development programme, is generally regarded as the first response (1981) to the appalling living conditions of the slum dwellers in the city. The components of the EIUs are: paving the lanes within the slum area, street lighting, supply of potable water from spot sources, low cost sanitation on a community basis and drainage improvement. The underlying objective of the EIUs is to reach out to the poor with some basic services, to bring about improvement in their immediate environment.
2. The Urban Community Development (UCD) Programme assisted by the UNICEF was first launched in Siliguri (1984) in West Bengal. Its emphasis is on basic social services such as pre-school facilities, pre-natal care for women, immunisation of children below one year, training programmes for skill formation for women and so on. This has been known as Urban Basic Services (UBS) programme since 1985-86.
3. The Integrated Child Development Scheme (ICDS) has been operating in the city since 1986-87. Its major components are: pre-primary schooling, mother and child care including supply of nutritional food, child growth monitoring and immunisation.

Siliguri has been allotted 100 ICD centres, of which around 85 have started functioning.

4. The Integrated Development of Small and Medium Towns (IDSMT) has been in operation in Siliguri since the middle of the Sixth Plan (1983). This programme contains two major components: (1) a general component and (2) a low cost sanitation component. The schemes under (1) are: municipal markets, by-pass roads, dormitories, bus terminus, industrial estates and land development. Under (2) above, the dry latrines are being converted into sanitary latrines or into the two-pit flush model.
5. The eradication of illiteracy programme is going on with the active cooperation of the Department of Mass Education of the Government of West Bengal. This programme involves both children and adults.

Income Generating Programmes

The Self Employment Programme for the Urban Poor (SEPUP) and the Self Employment Scheme for Registered Unemployed (SESRU) are directed towards generating income and employment opportunities for the urban employed. The SEPUP is specially addressed to the urban poor. Moreover, the Directorate of Small Scale Industries and the Khadi and Village Industries Commission have launched various loan schemes where those eligible can get loans for training and setting up their own projects.

The Nehru Rozgar Yojana was launched in 1989 to create employment opportunities for the urban poor. It is a package of three major components: (i) micro-enterprises (similar to SEPUP), (ii) urban wage employment for the unskilled workforce, and (iii) the creation of employment through shelter upgradation scheme. The urban wage employment component is restricted to towns with less than one lakh population and hence Siliguri is not eligible for it. The micro enterprise component provides for bank loans (up to Rs. 35,000) and a subsidy (25%) for self employment. The shelter upgradation component provides for assistance up to Rs. 4,000 per household (HUDCO loan 75 per cent, government subsidy 25 per cent). Both these components are backed up by separate financial allocation for skill training and skill upgradation arrangements. The income generation programme and the infrastructural programmes together are known as the poverty alleviation programme.

THE SURVEY

The present survey tries to illustrate the working of the poverty alleviation programme in the slums of Siliguri. The basic objective is to find out the nature of community participation in these programmes. There are 48 slums in Siliguri of which 24 have been taken up in the survey. In these slums, 400 households (consisting of 5 per cent of the total slum population) have been surveyed on the basis of individual questionnaires.

The questionnaire has been prepared in three parts: (1) General socio-economic information, (2) information regarding basic services and (3) information regarding income generating activities. The basic services observed here are of two types – physical amenities consisting of electricity, water supply, sanitation and housing and social infrastructure of education and health. The sample slums have been ranked according to different indicators of development. A list of the indicators is provided at the end. The cross-section analysis of the data is done at (1) *basti* level and (2) household level. Information at the organisational level has been obtained from personal interviews with the officials concerned.

The role of the organisation as well as the actual beneficiaries in the successful implementation of the poverty alleviation programme has been analysed with the objective of deriving policy implications.

Location of Slums

With increasing urbanisation, the urban centres have grown asymmetrically within the town, the major concentration being in the centre of the town. Slums have consequently emerged in these mushrooming urban centres. These slums can be classified into three categories depending on the land they have occupied – (1) Refugee colonies in the heart of the town, (2) squatter settlements on encroached railway land and (3) squatter settlements on river beds.

1. Refugee colonies in the centre of the city are relatively better off. The majority of the refugees are migrants from Bangladesh, settling here immediately after the Partition of 1947. They are settled on municipal land, get physical infrastructure like electricity, toilet facilities, and so on and pay house-tax. The municipality is obliged to provide physical and social infrastructure in these areas.

2. Squatter settlements on railway land create problems for the municipal administration. The local body cannot have any control over this land. Consequently they are reluctant to provide physical infrastructure in these areas. The railways are considering selling these lands to the local bodies.
3. The settlements on river beds are the poorest slums. The land is marshy and in many cases unfit for human settlement. Cheap wood is used to build shelters. Many slum dwellers in these areas cannot get electricity as housing conditions are not suitable for it.

The municipal area is divided into 30 wards within which the slums are distributed. Nearly 47 per cent of the total slum households are below the poverty line. According to the Eighth Plan estimates people whose monthly per capita expenditure is below Rs. 209 are below the poverty line.

The present survey has been conducted at two levels: (i) the organisational level, focusing on the activities and finances of the local body in implementing participatory programmes, and (2) the household level, examining the direct beneficiaries, participation in the provision and utilisation of these services. The following section takes up the organisational issues.

Administration of the Local Body

Like all other local bodies, Siliguri Municipality (established in 1949) is primarily engaged in maintaining the physical and social services in the urban area. The Municipal Board is headed by the chairman and formed by thirty elected commissioners and eleven executive staff members. The total staff strength of the municipality is 562, the number of supervisors being 24. The municipality was established under the Bengal Municipal Act. The last election held in the local body was in 1988. The next election was due in 1993, after a five year interval. Now that it has become a corporation, it will function under a nominated Board, till the election takes place. The increasing responsibility of the municipality as well as the expanding urban population of the city have been instrumental for the local body changing its status into a corporation.[1]

---

1. The local body has become a municipal corporation in 1994. The election also is over. The chairman of the erstwhile municipality has been re-elected to be the mayor of the new corpoiration.

In the early eighties the Urban Community Development (UCD) programme was launched in some districts of some states as a pilot project. This programme was sponsored by the Government of India, administratively supported by the state governments and fully financed by the UNICEF. Siliguri municipal town in Darjeeling district was selected for implementing UCD in West Bengal in 1982. The municipality was given the responsibility of implementing the UCD programme. This programme was totally different from the service delivery approach followed by the local bodies. Its emphasis was on the setting up of a field level organisation and approaching the service delivery problem in a participating manner.

In 1986, the nomenclature of the UCD was changed to urban basic services (UBS) scheme with the following changes:

(i) District, rather than the town, was selected as the unit of operation. All municipal towns in the selected district were to be covered by UBS (In West Bengal, Darjeeling district was chosen).
(ii) The Government of India, the state government and the UNICEF were to jointly finance the UBS in a 2:4:4 ratio.
(iii) Training and capacity building schemes were to be fully financed by UNICEF.
(iv) District co-ordinators for each selected district were to be appointed.
(v) Monitoring committees were to be constituted at each level of the urban unit, namely, the town, district, state and national levels.

Districts have been chosen under the UBS scheme according to certain characterstics, namely, (i) the urban growth rate is disturbingly fast, (ii) adequate basic services are not available in the slums and (iii) other government sponsored programmes like IDSMT and EIUS are in operation to be supplemented by UBS. All the towns in the selected districts are to be covered under the scheme in phases with a priority for large towns. Municipal authorities, however, had to provide sufficient supervisory and infrastructural facilities, including assigning a senior municipal officer for project implementation. All the four municipal towns in Darjeeling district were covered under UBS.

Within the towns selected the UBS had to focus on the slums where a majority of the population are poor having meagre access to basic services. All 48 slums in Siliguri have been covered under this programme. For operational purposes, these slums are divided into neighbourhood of 20-25 households, each represented by a resident volunteer (preferably woman) at the municipal level.

Siliguri Municipality has a UBS committee consisting of Executive Officer, Finance Officer, Project Officer, three Commissioners, a District Inspector of Schools, Superintendent Engineer of the PWD, District UBS coordinator and Project Officer of ICDS. This committee is headed by the chairman and it prepares the UBS plan for the town.

The UBS organisation starts at the grassroot level. Resident community volunteers, (RCVs) preferably women, are chosen in the slums, one each for 20-25 slum households. Every 20 RCVs constitute a Basti Committee. Each Basti Committee prepares a "Mini Action Plan" which are then collected at the ward level. The ward level committee reports them to the municipal level UBS committee. At present, there are 375 RCVs and 6 community organisers (trained) in the municipality. There are 49 Basti Developent Committees at present.

From 1991-92, UBS has been changed into Urban Basic Services for the Poor (UBSP). This scheme is implemented in convergence with the scheme of Environmental Improvement of Urban Slums (EIVS) in the state sector and the centrally sponsored programme of Nehru Rozgar Yojana (NRY). It is also in convergence with other schemes operated by other government departments at the centre and state levels.

The structural framework for UBSP remains more or less the same.

A State Urban Development Agency and District Urban Development Agencies for each of the districts have been constituted for implementation, supervision and monitoring of the NRY and UBSP (jointly known as Poverty Alleviation Programme). The Municipal Committee consisting of the chairman, a commissioner and the Executive Officer is responsible for the same at the local level.

The UBSP is totally financed by central and state governments. The central fund is allocated among the states/UTS on the basis of incidence of urban poverty as per the NSS 38th round. The selection of towns and slum pockets within towns is made by the state government on the basis of literacy level, infant mortality rate, magnitude of slum population and EIUS and allied schemes.

Activities of the Local Body

Various income generating programmes are in operation in the slums as discussed earlier. The slum dwellers, having titles to the huts they live in, are eligible for taking up repair work for their shelter under the shelter upgradation scheme. For this purpose, Siliguri Municipality has taken a loan of nearly Rs. 5 crores from HUDCO. During 1992-93, nearly 5000 families in the slum area have taken the house-upgradation loan of Rs. 3,000 along with the subsidy of Rs. 1,000 deposited in their account. The loan amount is repayable in 10 years with an annual interest rate of 7.25 per cent and the monthly instalment payment is Rs. 39. The municipality has taken steps for extending the facility in respect of special type of training to upgrade the skill of the unemployed and partly unemployed persons residing nearby where the shelter upgradation scheme has been undertaken. The number of beneficiaries are 1920 till now, getting a training allowance of Rs. 300 per month for a three month training period. Under this scheme, shelter upgradation means repair of walls, floors, provision of sanitary latrines and electrification.

Under the micro-enterprises scheme a loan amount up to Rs. 35,000 is sanctioned to those whose monthly income is below Rs. 500. Various small scale units like shops, leather bag manufacturing, selling lottery tickets, tailoring, *agarbatti* manufacturing, washing machine repairing, TV Antenna manufacturing and so forth, are covered by this scheme. Under this scheme, 25 per cent of the project cost is given as central subsidy. The rate of interest on loans up to Rs. 10,000 is 10 per cent and for loans beyond that, it is 11.5 per cent per annum.

The social infrastructural programme gained new momentum with the launching of the UBS scheme. As outlined in the UBS, Siliguri municipality has made elaborate arrangements for vaccination for mother and child, eradication of illiteracy and various self-employment schemes sponsored by the government in slum areas. According to municipal sources, there is at least one Adult Education Centre and one Anganwadi school in every slum. A list of various activities taken up by the local body is given here.

The activities in the UBS cell of the local body are categorised in the following way:-

1. *Child survival* - includes immunisation and Diarrhoea management.
2. *Community organisation* - various training programms for the RCVs are taken up.

3. *Pre-school education and adult education centres* - Balwadi schools and many adult literacy centres have been opened with a view to educate the women, and the children.
4. *Vocational training for women* - many skill formation centres have been opened for women.
5. *Water supply and sanitation* - Materials have been supplied to the slum dwellers for construction of low cost latrines; community latrines, garbage bins, common bathing space for women, construction of children's park, construction of well platform, small drain repairing activities are some of the programme under this head. The list of activities undertaken by the local body under UBS is given below.

Activities Undertaken by Siliguri Municipality under UBS up to 31 March 1991

Sl. No.	Activity	Achievement	Fund and Agencies involved
1	2	3	4
1.	Survey	1984: Twice done in collaboration with NIUA	UCD
		1987: Done by UBS Cell	UBS
		1991: Enumeration of population and households by RCVs.	UBS
2.	Immunisation	2,886 slum children (under 1 year age) immunised against six diseases	UBS
3.	Diarrhoea management	Awareness campaign: 40 hoardings displayed in the slums regarding diarrhoea management and ORT.	UBS
4.	Sanitation and Environment	Constructed:- (i) 350 individual household two-pit latrines	UBS and contribution from beneficiaries
		(ii) 1600 individual household two-pit latrines	LSP and contribution from beneficiaries

(Contd)

1	2	3	4
		(iii) 8 (4 seater) two-pit community latrines	UBS
		(iv) 8 (4 seater) two-pit community latrines	LSP
		(v) 10 two-pit latrines in pre-school education centres	LSP
		(vi) Smokeless chulahs (250)	UBS and contribution from beneficiaries.
		(vii) 14 garbage pits	UBS
		(viii) 14 bathing places for women	UBS
		(ix) small drains to prevent water logging	EIUS and UBS
5.	Road	Constructed bituminous or brick paved roads/ lanes in very slums	EIUS
6.	Water Supply	Installed: (i) 16 (Mark II) hand pumps	UBS and States Government
		(ii) 15 hand pumps	UBS
		(iii) 7 street taps	Municipal Fund
		Constructed:- (i) 90 ring wells	UBS
		(ii) 125 ring well platforms	UBS
		Renovation and chlorination work of ring wells being done every year with the help of NGOs.	
7.	Income Generating scheme for women	Arranged loan finance for 80 women for setting up micro enterprises	Bank (DRI scheme)

(*Contd*)

1	2	3	4
		Arranged loan finance and subsidy for 300 women for setting up micro enterprises	NRY
		Imparted vocational training to 85 women in different trades like sewing, embroidery, beautician, wool knitting etc.	UBS, NRY, Youth Service Deptt.
8.	Pre-school education	7 pre-school centres until ICDC appeared in the town	UBS
		92 pre-school centres including 7 UBS centres handed over to ICDS	ICDS
9.	Sports and games	3 children's parks constructed	UBS
		Inter-slum atheletic meet for children and women being organised annually	UBS
		Football coaching camp for slum children organised	UBS and Youth Services Deptt.
10.	Cultural activities	Inter slum music and recitation competition for children and women organised annually	UBS
11.	Adult education	100 nos. adult education centres are in operation	Mass Education Extension Deptt. of the State government

Source: Siliguri Municipality.
Note: LSP - Liberation of Scavenger Programme (a state-sponsored programme).

Finance of the Municipality

The municipal budget is presented in two major accounts – Revenue and Capital. Revenue expenditure is incurred out of the municipal revenue fund. These expenditures are recurring in nature. The size of the revenue expenditure of the municipal body is mainly determined by the size of its available financial resources. These resources are generally classified into tax-revenue, non-tax-revenue and state transfers to municipal bodies loosely termed as grants or revenue grants. In the capital account, grants, loans and advances constitute the whole of capital income, from which capital expenditure is financed.

A glance at the finances of the local body during 1986-90 reveals that the shares of both receipts and expenditure in the capital account have increased in the budget (Table 5.6). In per capita term, both revenue and expenditure in the capital account have increased from 1986 to 1990, but expenditure has been more than revenue.

Table 5.6
Finance of Siliguri Municipality: 1985-86 to 1989-90

Item	1985-86	1986-87	1987-88	1988-89	1989-90
Capital Receipts (Rs. 000)	4854	8234	3700	11478	14396
Capital Expenditure (Rs. 000)	1990	6243	6002	8282	17884
Surplus(+), Deficit(-) (Rs. 000)	2864	1991	-2302	3196	-3488
Revenue Receipt (Rs. 000)	7558	10890	11051	16789	16261
Revenue Expenditure (Rs. 000)	7288	9887	11578	14572	14087
Surplus (+), Deficit (-) (Rs. 000)	270	1003	-527	2217	2174
Capital Receipts as % of total receipts	39.10	43.05	25.08	40.06	46.95
Capital Expenditure as % of total Expenditure	21.45	38.70	34.15	36.23	55.93
Population of Siliguri (Estimated No.)	189173	197118	205397	214023	223013
Per Capita Capital Receipt (Rs)	25.65	41.77	18.01	53.62	64.55
Per Capita Revenue Receipt (Rs)	39.95	55.24	53.80	78.44	72.91
Per Capita Capital Expenditure (Rs)	10.51	31.67	29.22	38.69	80.19
Per Capita Revenue Expenditure (Rs)	38.52	50.15	56.41	68.08	63.16

Source: Budgets of the Municipality.

In the revenue account, per capita revenue has generally been higher than per capita expenditure. Revenue account has generally been stable but capital account has shown wide fluctuations. Capital receipts consist of grants for various schemes for physical infrastructure. Irregular disbursement of grants explains the wide fluctuation in the capital receipts. Per capita capital expenditures have been more than double the previous year during 1989-90. Capital expenditure consists of expenditure on developmental projects like water supply, drainage and other public works. The budgetary trend shows that the development expenditure of the local body has increased sharply in comparison to maintenance expenses in the last two years. According to the National Institute of Urban Affairs reports, the development and maintenance expenditure per capita for a class I city like Siliguri should by nearly Rs. 350 and Rs. 120 per annum respectively. This indicates the inability of the local body to improve the civic services. A detailed analysis of various components of the municipal budget helps to understand the mechanism through which the local body is coping with the spread of urbanisation. Table 5.7 describes the temporal behaviour of different compenents of revenue income. The share of tax revenue in total revenue income has declined over time. The share of non-tax revenue has remained confined between 4-7 per cent excepting in the last year when abruptly it became nearly double, because of improved collection of rent and fees. Per-capita revenue figures show some improvement over time. Per-capita grants have nearly doubled in five years while revenue from own sources has not increased to that extent. Per-capita grant increased almost at per as population growth-rate, but growth-rate of own source of income was much lower depicting the weakness in the internal finance of the local body (Table 5.8). Growing urbanisation has only resulted in making the local body more dependent on the higher authorities.

In the revenue expenditure account, maintenance of public works (public road) accounts for the largest share of revenue expenditure. Conservency is the next priority as reflected in the expenditure table. Maintenance or water supply is the lowest priority revealing nil expenditure for five consecutive years. Expenditure on medical services is also very low, accounting for less than 3 per cent of total maintenance expenses (Table 5.9).

Table 5.7
Percentage Distribution of Various Components of Revenue Income: 1985-86 to 1989-90

	1985-86	1986-87	1987-88	1988-89	1989-90
Tax Revenue	45.91	39.27	40.46	56.46	38.09
Non-tax Revenue	7.55	4.94	7.57	6.68	14.28
Grants Transfer	47.39	45.23	42.06	34.86	45.73

Source: Budgets of Siliguri Municipality.

Table 5.8
Distribution of Per capita Revenue Income: 1985-86 to 1989-90

	1985-86	1986-87	1987-88	1988-89	1989-90
Per capita Tax Revenue (Rs)	18.34	21.69	21.77	39.58	27.77
Per capita Non-tax Revenue (Rs)	3.01	2.72	4.07	5.26	10.41
Per capita Revenue Grants (Rs)	18.59	30.82	27.95	33.02	34.47

Source: Budgets of Siliguri Municipality.

Table 5.9
Percentage Distribution of Various Components of Municipal Revenue Expenditure: 1985-86 to 1989-90

	1985-86	1986-87	1987-88	1988-89	1989-90
General Administration	16.76	11.90	14.50	14.04	15.4
Public Lighting	6.94	6.90	6.84	6.74	7.96
Water Supply	0	0	0	0	0
Health Services	.746	3.96	2.55	2.07	3.14
Conservancy	22.1	27.12	24.72	19.7	37.60
Public Works	40.0	44.4	43.3	34.56	24.49
Public Institutions	.905	.95	1.26	1.00	1.72
Others	10.52	6.24	6.57	5.22	9.52

Source: Budgets of Siliguri Municipality.

In the capital expenditure account also, public works, (road construction) takes the maximum share, more than half of the total. The rest is distributed among other components such as water supply, drainage facility, public safety and others. Water supply sometimes accounts for a significant share, but expenditure on the rest is less than 10 per cent of the total on an average. Siliguri being an important transport centre, the municipality provides all the supporting expenses to maintain public roads. But other necessities receive inadequate attention as revealed by allocation of funds. Increasing urbanisation has increased the demand for basic urban services, but the local body is not financially strong enough to meet the requirements as revealed in the poor allocation structure in municipal budgets (Table 5.10)

Table 5.10
Percentage Distribution of Various Components of Municipal Capital Expenditure: 1985-86 to 1989-90

	1985-86	1986-87	1987-88	1988-89	1989-90
General administration	-	-	-	-	3.57
Public safety	-	-	-	-	.44
Water supply	41.55	3.49	1.81	31.96	2.25
Health services	.70	.28	-	-	9.96
Drainage and sewerage	3.36	3.07	13.99	9.09	1.09
Burning ghat	-	-	.24	-	22.9
Public works	54.37	93.24	83.92	66.92	63.11

Source: Budgets of Siliguri Municipality.

The municipality maintains a separate account for expenses under the UBS scheme. The fund is shared among the central government, the state government and UNICEF at the ratio of 20: 40 : 40. In addition the state government is supposed to bear the entire staff cost of the project. Staff cost generally forms 12 per cent of the project cost. The municipality received a total of Rs. 13,59,001 during 1986-91 for an estimated slum population of 51,459 (obtained from a survey by the municipality in 1984) incurring a per capita expenditure of Rs. 26.4 over a period of five years. Table 5.11 shows the distribution of the total finance for UBS by different authorities.

Table 5.11
Receipt and Expenditure of UBS Funds released to Siliguri Municipality by Different Funding Agencies during 1986-91

Funding agency	Receipt (Rs)	Expenditure (Rs)	Surplus (+) Deficit (-) (Rs)
Central Government	3,79,000 (27%)	2,40,745 (18%)	+ 1,38,255
State Government	4,76,000 (35%)	4,98,000 (38%)	(-) 22,010
UNICEF	5,04,001 (38%)	5,84,799 (44%)	(-) 79,998
Total	13,59,001 (100)	13,23,554 (100)	35,447

Source: Municipal budgets, Siliguri,
Note: Figures in parentheses are percentage to corresponding total.

According to the norms of distribution, the state government should bear the maximum share of total expenses. The expenditure pattern, however, shows that the state government did not contribute its full share. The share of the state government in the project cost, even after including the staff cost, was less than forty per cent (Table 5.11).

The disbursement of fund was not always regular. The fund was sanctioned in April 1986. The municipality, however got the first instalment only in April 1987.

It did not receive any money during 1990 excepting during the last month. Irregularity in the supply of fund has often led to discontinuity of activities.

The average annual allocation for UBS per town was fixed on the basis of the existing slum population of that area. Siliguri, with a slum population of more than 50,000, was in category A, eligible for a fund of Rs. 23 lakhs over a period of five years.

Towns were classified into four categories for allocation of funds under the UBS Scheme as shown on the next page.

Classification of Towns

Category	Slum Population (No)	Allocation of funds 1986-90 (Rs. Lakhs)
A	30,000 - 60,000	23.00
B	18,000 - 30,000	15.50
C	4000 - 18,000	13.00
D	1000 - 4,000	8.50

Source: UBS Scheme, Ministry of Urban Development, Government of India.

But actual disbursement was only Rs. 13.5 lakhs. This reduced the financial power of the local body to employ more people. During the initial years of the project, the project officer's remuneration was Rs.1,500 approximately. After a few years, the management of the UBS cell became the additional work of some senior municipal officer who received additional remuneration of less than Rs. 100 for the job. Initially the local body reported six trained community organisers working at a remuneration of Rs. 300 per month (later enhanced to Rs.500). At present, there are only two community organizers at a salary of Rs. 600 per month. Now remunerations do not make the service attractive.

The local body also is not in a position to offer more remuneration because of financial constraints. The UBS fund constitutes less than 3 per cent of the total municipal budget. There is not much financial incentive for the employees to take up an extra work load.

The municipal plan of action in Silguri during 1989-90 demanded an amount of Rs. 3.53 lakhs, but received only Rs. 1.06 lakhs instead. During the five years of the UBS scheme, the staff cost of the project has remained largely within the permissible limit of 10-12 per cent. The bulk of the expenditure has been directed towards water supply and environment sanitation. Comparatively, little has been spent on vocational training for women. Expenditure on adult and child education has been geared up in later years. Expenses on immunisation have been moderate (Table 5.12).

Table 5.12
Percentage Distribution of Various Components of Expenditure Under UBS: 1986-89 to 1990-91

Components	1986-88	1989-90	1990-91
Staff cost	11.75	12.18	10.38
Child survival	71.18	7.59	8.6
Community organization	6.12	15.78	--
Pre-school education and adult literacy centre	8.22	47.09	40.12
Vocational training for women	7.99	.18	-
Water supply and sanitation	57.22	17.17	40.20

Source: Budgets of Siliguri Municipality.

FINDINGS OF THE SURVEY

Demographic Profile of Sample Slums

In the present sample of 24 slums, consisting of 400 households, the average size of the household is very large (6) as depicted in Table 5.13. The language spoken by the majority is Bengali, the religion of the majority is Hindu. The majority of the slum dwellers are owners of the residences. Most of the slum dwellers are migrants (74 per cent). New migrants (length of migrancy 1-3 years) are found in 3 out of 24 slums. The average length of migrancy is 8-10 years for others, though many persons came much earlier. Nearly eleven per cent of the migrants came for family movement, 33 per cent reported political disturbances as the cause of migration and the remaining 49 per cent of the migrants have come in search of jobs.

Scheduled caste people have dominated in 10 out of 24 slums. In three slums, their share in the total population is above 95 per cent in the remaining seven slums, it is more than 50 per cent.

Table 5.13
Socio-economic Background of Siliguri Slum Dwellers

Slums in Siliguri	No. of house-holds	Total no. of persons	Average size of house-hold	Per cent majority language (Bengali) Spoken	Per cent majority religion (Hindu)	Per cent majority cast (General)	Percent-age of owner-ship	Per cent migrants	Average migrancy length (Years)	Migrancy reason (Per cent distribution)		
										Job	Family move-ment	Others
1	2	3	4	5	6	7	8	9	10	11	12	13
Matangini Colony	25	145	6	70	100	67	100	91	10	35	6	59
Prankrishna Colony	10	58	6	100	100	90	100	83	10	76	7	17
Harijan Majdur Colony	15	118	8	0	60	43	100	100	10	100	0	
Nutan Para	20	117	6	98	75	88	100	43	8	71	5	24
Vibekananda Colony	15	78	5	68	80	100	100	53	8	75	0	25
Jyoti Nagar Colony	15	86	6	100	100	97	100	74	8	58	0	42
Debashish Colony	25	189	8	100	100	53	83	95	10	20	80	0
Deshbandhu Colony	15	69	5	100	100	33	44	70	8	52	48	0
Swami Nagar Colony	14	52	4	6	29	97	100	100	8	94	0	6
Adarsha Nagar	12	71	6	100	100	95	100	100	10	25	0	75
Subhas Nagar	13	73	6	100	100	0	100	100	10	0	0	100
Raja Ram Mohan Colony	18	69	4	100	100	50	100	92	10	17	0	83
Chittaranjan Colony	13	63	5	100	100	13	100	100	10	0	0	100
Dash Colony	15	84	6	100	100	92	100	85	10	0	38	67

(Contd...)

1	2	3	4	5	6	7	8	9	10	11	12	13
Sramik Nagar	20	111	6	100	100	73	100	50	8	37	49	14
Prantik Palli	15	75	5	100	110	74	100	59	10	0	42	58
Durga Das Colony	20	133	7	83	110	31	98	69	10	100	0	0
Jyoti Nagar Colony I	10	60	6	100	100	67	99	100	10	90	0	10
Sraban Nagar	20	110	6	77	100	42	97	100	10	97	0	3
Udayan Colony	15	88	6	100	100	72	95	20	3	40	20	40
Fuleswari Colony	25	176	7	100	100	42	96	32	1	49	0	51
Promode Nagar	15	66	4	65	95	18	100	61	10	100	0	0
Lichu Bagan Colony	15	67	4	100	100	7	93	18	3	40	0	60
Sarbahara Colony	20	123	6	75	75	3	100	70	10	30	0	70
All Slums in Siliguri	400	2281	6	85	92	56	96	74	8	49	14	37

Source: Siliguri Survey.
Note: Others means largely political disturbances like partition, Bangladesh War etc.

A substantial portion of the new migrants are from the Scheduled Caste. The 1991 Census has reported the Scheduled Caste population being 10.20 per cent of the total city population. It appears that a majority of them live in slums.

Migration has been a major component in the demographic profile of Siliguri slum dwellers.

The highest percentage of migrants comes from Bangladesh. Inflow of population from outside the state but within India is almost the same as inflow from outside the country. Migration within the state but outside the district is also quite significant. Political disturbances have largely been responsible for migration from outside the country. But it is primarily economic pull that causes migration from within the country. The relatively poorer states of Bihar and Orissa have accounted for nearly as much migration to Siliguri as from Bangladesh (Table 5.14).

Table 5.14
State-wise Distribution of Migrants of Sample Slums

State of Last Residence	Percentage of Migrants
Nepal	5
Sikkim	3
Bhiar	18
Orissa	19
Bangladesh	38
West Bengal (Distt. other than Darjeeling)	17
	100

Source: ISS Survey, 1992.

Children form 38 per cent of the total population in the slums. Migrants have generally settled down in the town, yet they do not bring all other members from their native villages. The large family size is generally accounted for by high birth rate reflected by the high proportion of children below 14 years. Migration as well as natural increase have contributed significantly to the increasing congestion of the slum population.

Migrants from neighbouring areas have come to the town in search of relatively better economic prospects. They however have not lost touch with their native village where they still own some assets. In the town, they generally own the dwelling unit, that is, they have a right on the land holding, when the slum is recognised by the local body. Tenancy is not in practice in the slums as there is hardly any additional space to let out. These assets owned by the slum dwellers do not generate sufficient income for even moderately improving the level of living. The meagre income, however enables the slum dwellers to meet some regular expenses. In the present survey, 54 per cent of the slum dwellers (216 out of 400 households) did not report possession of any kind of assets other than their dwelling units. Among the rest, the distribution of asset holding is as follows in Table 5.15.

Table 5.15

Assets (Other than the Dwelling Unit) **owned by Slum Dwellers**

No. of households	Per cent	Rural	Urban
50	27	Land	2 goats, cycle
27	14	Land	gold and silver ornaments
82	44	Two bufalloes	Rickshaw
25	15	Two oxen	Ornaments, sewing machines
184	100		

Source: Field Survey, ISS, 1992.

The slum dwellers generally do not consider the assets as income generating resources. They are kept largely for mortage or sale in order to meet emergency expenses. Rural assets, that is, land is used for maintaining the family, generally a joint family in the rural area. There is not enough saving from urban assets to plough back into rural land. Even so, people owning land in the native village try to save something from their urban income as they wish to go back to the village when they are unable to work in the urban area. There is hardly any reverse cash-flow from rural to urban areas.

The income-expenditure pattern (Table 5.16) shows that per-capita average monthly expenditure (Rs. 171) in the sample slums is much below the poverty line demarcation in the Eighth Plan (Rs. 209). To be precise, only 5 out of 24 slums are above the poverty line. The average level of per capita expenditure is higher than the corresponding level of income indicating that the majority slum dwellers are in perpetual debt. Generally consumption is more than income for the low income group. Expenditure on food is the major expense. Even at this low level of income, there is considerable variation in income and expenditure among the slum dwellers as revealed by the coefficients of variation

(0.70 and 0.62 respectively). This variation, to some extent explains the asymmetric expenditure pattern towards social infrastructure as will be revealed later.

Table 5.16
Per capita Income and Expenditure

Slums in Siliguri	Total No. of persons	Total Household Monthly Income (Rs)	Total Household Monthly Expenditure (Rs)	Percapita Monthly Income (Rs)	Percapita Monthly Expenditure (Rs)
Matangini Colony	145	22511	22636	155	156
Prankrishna Colony	58	10255	10130	177	175
Harijan Majdur Colony	118	13382	13132	113	111
Nutan Para	117	20884	22134	178	189
Vibekananda Colony	78	13757	15507	176	199
Jyoti Nagar Colony	86	12008	15383	140	179
Debashish Colony	189	27768	31391	147	166
Deshbandhu Colony	69	17382	17882	252	259
Swami Nagar Colony	52	13257	12382	118	111
Adarsh Nagar	71	19005	18506	268	261
Subhas Nagar	73	2252	1877	173	144
Raja Ram Mohan Colony	69	6754	7504	98	109
Chittaranjan Colony	63	17506	18131	278	288
Dash Colony	84	14132	14132	168	168
Sramik Nagar	111	19384	18510	175	167
Prantik Palli	75	17256	17506	230	233
Durga Das Colony	133	22009	21509	165	162
Jyoti Nagar Colony I	60	8854	8979	148	150
Sraban Nagar	110	17260	16885	157	154
Udayan Colony	88	8232	13757	94	156
Fuleswari Colony	176	21943	26518	125	151
Promode Nagar	66	14258	14633	216	222
Lichu Bagan Colony	67	10883	12758	162	190
Sarbahara Colony	123	16885	18260	137	148
Total	2281	367811	390037	161	171
S.D.				132.21	122.47
Mean				186.47	194.76
C.V.				.70	.62

Source: Siliguri Survey.
Note : C.V. - Coefficient of Variation.

Employment Profile

In the urban area the growth rate of the labour force absorption in the organised sector is generally much lower than that of population. This leads to the inevitable growth of the informal sector. The tertiary sector has been the dominant economic base in Siliguri, which is by and large a service town. Slum dwellers have set up several small shops of their own, where all members of the family work together. This results in disguised unemployment on one hand and underestimation of female participation ratio on the other hand. Female members of such households do not report themselves as employed as they do not get any wages.

In the sample slums, 30 per cent of the slum dwellers constitute the main workforce (against a state-level figure of 29 per cent). Among them, 48 per cent are self-employed, 25 per cent are in regular jobs, and the rest are in irregular jobs (Table 5.17). Regular and irregular jobs have an almost equal share in the employment market of the slums. The break-up of male and female workers in the employment structure of the sample slums has been depicted in Table 5.18.

Table 5.17
Work-Force Structure

(*number*)

Working Status	Total	Male	Female
Self employed (%)	337 (45.4)	283 (54.1)	54 (33.0)
Regular job (%)	182 (25.5)	148 (26.1)	34 (31.0)
Irregular job (%)	176 (25.5)	136 (24.0)	40 (36.0)
Total workers	695 (100)	567 (100)	128 (100)
Total population	2281	1164	1117
Slum level participation rates (%)	29.5	49.14	9.22
State level participation rate (%)		28.94	8.03

Source: Field Survey, Siliguri, ISS, 1992.

Table 5.18
Employment Structure

Slums in Siliguri	No. of house-holds	Total No. of per-sons	Total No. of working persons	Share of working persons in total	Per cent distribution type of work		
					Self-employed	Regular jobs	Irregular jobs
Matangini Colony	25	145	37	26	65	11	24
Prankrishna Colony	10	58	17	29	59	12	29
Harijan Majdur - Colony	15	118	24	20	29	4	67
Nutan Para	20	117	34	29	41	21	38
Vibekananda Colony	15	78	21	27	42	29	29
Jyoti Nagar Colony	15	86	23	27	91	0	9
Debashish Colony	25	189	55	29	75	7	18
Deshbandhu Colony	15	69	16	23	50	6	44
Swami Nagar - Colony	14	52	29	26	100	0	0
Adarsha Nagar	12	71	26	37	46	50	4
Subhas Nagar	13	73	3	23	33	33	33
Raja Ram Mohan Colony	18	69	17	25	88	12	0
Chittaranjan Colony	13	63	15	24	87	13	0
Dash Colony	15	84	24	29	33	33	33
Sramik Nagar	20	111	34	31	59	15	26
Prantik Palli	15	75	23	31	74	26	0
Durga Das Colony	20	133	60	45	38	60	2
Jyoti Nagar Colony I	10	60	25	42	8	40	52
Sraban Nagar	20	110	47	43	38	49	13
Udayan Colony	15	88	18	20	61	39	0
Fuleswari Colony	25	176	42	24	36	14	50
Promode Nagar	15	66	21	32	48	38	14
Lichu Bagan Colony	15	67	25	37	16	68	16
Sarbahara Colony	20	123	39	32	36	5	59
All Slums	400	2281	675	30	48	26	25

Source: Field Survey, Siliguri, ISS, 1992.

Female participation is moderate in the work force structure. They are mostly occupied in irregular jobs. Their participation in self-employed jobs is the least. The female participation ratio (9.22%) in these slums is slightly higher than the state level (8.03%). The male participation ratio (49.14) is much higher than the state level (28.94%).

There is not much difference in the proportion of female workers in different categories of jobs, yet, the majority of them are accommodated in irregular jobs. Irregular jobs are very low paid, providing least security to the workers.

Employment in the informal sector offers very low wage to the unskilled slum dwellers.

Often small employment generating units are overcrowded with too many workers, keeping the wage-rate down at subsistance level. The tertiary sector in Siliguri has not been able to provide gainful employment to the slum dwellers. They look towards diversification of occupation wherever possible to reduce the risk that adverse circumstances will cause a sharp drop in income.

The census data for the last three decades however show a very low female participation rate in the town as depicted in Table 5.19.

Table 5.19
Work force Participation Rate by Sex in Siliguri Municipality

Year	Participation Rate	
	Male	Female
1961	57.9	3.0
1971	51.9	2.9
1981	52.6	4.7

Source: Census of India, Year 1981.

According to census data, the male participation in the town has declined over the years while the female participation rate has increased slightly. In the slums, however, the female participation rate is more than double the rate in the town. Women are generally casual workers, rather than regular employees. There is little mobility between these two forms of employment.

The male participation rate in slum is slightly lower (49.14) than that in the town. In the slums, the majority are self-employed who are generally less skilled than the wage earners, poverty compels the secondary workers (often women) to enter the labour force, thus increasing the participation ratio but often at low wages and in unsatisfactory working conditions. Female workers are worse off in poverty compared to their male counterparts. Their participation in the labour force and absorption in irregular jobs (which generally offer the worst working conditions) are much more than male workers. This is known as the "Feminization of Poverty" (Levy, 1985).

This analysis so far depicts that migration to Siliguri has been the result of the push factor from relatively poorer areas rather than the pull factor. As Siliguri gradually became an important centre for wholesale trade with improved communication, people from relatively poorer areas of Bihar and Orissa came to Siliguri in search of jobs. But Siliguri was not sufficiently well-off to accommodate the migrants. The migrants took shelter wherever they could, taking whatever employment they could get. Without growing and sustaining economic development, the slum dwellers of Siliguri could neither raise their level of income above the poverty line, nor improve their surroundings.

Housing and Other Physical Amenities

The housing condition in the slums is far from satisfactory (Table 5.20). The majority of the slum dwellers in the present survey live in *kachcha* houses. Tenants form a negligible portion of the households. On an average, 58 per cent of the households in these slums pay housetax (an average of Rs. 7 per quarter) which is less than one per cent of the average household income (Rs. 751 per month). The average monthly rent also is moderate (Rs. 13). Even in relatively better-off slums with higher level of average household income, the tenancy practice is not in vogue. The owners generally do not have enough space to rent out probably because of large family size. The low rent also reflects the poor quality of housing space as increasing population pressure in the slums and in the whole city indicates there is no shortage of demand for housing.

The physical amenities directly connected with the supply of housing are electricity, water supply, toilet facility and drainage facility. In the sample slums, only 23 per cent of the 400 households have access to electricity. This indicates that most of the houses in the slums are without electricity. The average monthly expenditure on electricity is rather high (around Rs. 107). The major reasons cited by the households for not having electricity are the following (1) it is very expensive, (2) it is not yet provided in the area, and (3) the main connection line is far from the house. The high average monthly expenditure on electricity shows that many people cannot bear this expenditure. Nine out of 24 slums have not been provided with domestic electricity, though there are street lights at various distances. Nearly 34 per cent of the total sample houses cannot have electric connections as housing conditions are not suitable (Table 5.21).

Table 5.20
Housing Situation

Slums in Siliguri	No. of house-holds	Type of housing (Percentage distribution)			Average no. of rooms dwelling unit	Percent owner-ship status	Average monthly house-hold income	Average monthly rent (Rs)	Percent pays house tax	Average house tax (Rs)
		Pucca	Semi *Pucca*	*Kachcha*						
1	2	3	4	5	6	7	8	9	10	11
Matangini Colony	25	4	4	92	2	100	1501	0	72	8
Prankrishna Colony	10	10	0	90	2	100	1501	0	0	0
Harijan Majdur Colony	15	0	0	100	2	100	1501	0	93	8
Nutan Para	20	10	25	65	2	100	1501	0	25	26
Vibekananda Colony	15	33	0	67	2	100	1501	0	0	0
Jyoti Nagar Colony	15	6	27	67	3	100	751	0	53	4
Debashish Colony	25	23	6	71	2	83	751	90	83	9
Deshbandhu Colony	15	40	0	60	2	44	1501	178	33	9
Swami Nagar Colony	14	8	21	71	2	100	1501	0	14	3
Adarsha Nagar	12	67	16	17	2	100	2000	0	75	5
Subhas Nagar	13	0	0	100	2	100	751	0	100	4
Raja Ram Mohan Colony	18	25	0	75	1	100	751	0	88	4
Chittaranjan Colony	13	0	100	0	2	100	1501	0	100	3
Dash Colony	15	33	7	60	2	100	1501	0	93	14
Sramik Nagar	20	10	0	90	2	100	1501	0	15	14

Contd...

1	2	3	4	5	6	7	8	9	10	11
Prantik Palli	15	53	14	33	3	100	1501	0	40	10
Durga Das Colony	20	10	25	65	3	97	1501	3	90	4
Jyoti Nagar Colony I	10	20	30	50	3	100	751	0	90	3
Sraban Nagar	20	0	5	95	2	97	1501	3	80	3
Udayan Colony	15	67	0	33	2	95	376	20	80	15
Fuleswari Colony	25	20	14	66	1	96	751	6	63	15
Promode Nagar	15	0	7	93	1	100	1501	0	0	0
Lichu Bagan Colony	15	0	20	80	1	93	751	7	0	0
Sarbahara Colony	20	0	0	100	1	100	751	0	100	15
All Slums in Siliguri	400	18	13	68	2	96	751	13	58	7

Source: Field Survey, Siliguri, ISS, 1992.

Table 5.21
Access to Electricity

Slums in Siliguri	No. of house-holds	Percentage electrified	Average monthly expenses on electrification (Rs)	Reason for not having elec-tricity (Majority Response)
Matangini Colony	25	0	0	NPM
Prankrishna Colony	10	0	0	NPM
Harijan Majdur Colony	15	13	49	NPM
Nutan Para	20	5	20	DML
Vibekananda Colony	15	17	128	DML
Jyoti Nagar Colony	15	0	0	DML
Debashish Colony	25	6	25	HCN
Deshbandhu Colony	15	13	64	HCN
Swami Nagar Colony	14	21	369	Expensive
Adarsha Nagar	12	22	1087	HCN
Subhas Nagar	13	0	0	NPM
Raja Ram Mohan Colony	18	28	93	Expensive
Chittaranjan Colony	13	0	0	NPM
Dash Colony	15	27	39	Expensive
Sramik Nagar	20	0	0	NPM
Prantik Palli	15	17	40	Expensive
Durga Das Colony	20	15	340	EXPENSIVE
Jyoti Nagar Colony I	10	20	190	EXPENSIVE
Sarban Nagar	20	0	0	NPM
Udayan Colony	15	13	66	Expensive
Fuleswari Colony	25	11	32	Expensive
Promode Nagar	15	30	28	Expensive
Lichu Bagan Colony	15	0	0	NPM
Sarbahara Colony	20	0	0	NPM
All Slums in Siliguri	400	23	107	

Source: Field Survey, Siliguri, ISS, 1992.
Note: NPM: Not provided by municipality. DML: Distant main line
HCN: Housing condition not suitable

As compared to electricity, the water supply condition is much better. Among 400 households, 49 per cent have an independent source of water, the rest have common sources. Around 91 per cent of the houses are located near the water supply sources. Eighty-seven per cent of the households think that the quality of water is fit for drinking and nearly all of them are satisfied with the duration of supply (Table 5.22).

A majority of the houses (75%) have independent toilet. Expenditure on cleaning the toilets varies from Rs. 5 to Rs. 29 per month. But private installation charges are high. Most of the toilets are built by the municipality against a deposit of Rs. 150 by the beneficiary. The local body has converted dry latrines under the 'Liberating the scavengers' scheme into two pit flush system with government subsidy and contributions from the beneficiaries.

The provision of common toilet is a unique feature of the town. The local body has constructed some community toilets that are used by 18 per cent of the sample households. In two slums, there are no independent toilets at all. These community toilets are spread over one-third (8) of the sample slums (24). In some slums, the people themselves take up the responsibility of cleaning the toilets rather than employing sweepers. In the slums, where toilet facilities are in a dismal condition, these community toilets are very necessary for cost-effective environmental sanitation, provided people accept them. The slum dwellers in Siliguri are quite keen in accepting this facility (Table 5.23).

The drainage facility and garbage disposal system present a dismal picture in the town. Among the 400 households, 60 per cent get open drainage facility which is hardly cleaned. For the rest, there is no drainage provision at all. People living in the river bed slums, use the river as an open drain. As regards garbage disposal, 93 per cent of the households dispose of the garbage outside their houses. These are often not cleaned by the municipal sweepers (though on the pay role, the number of sweepers is 216). Open unclean drains are continuous source of diseases. In such living conditions, the provision of independent toilets or adequate supply of drinking water hardly makes an impact on the surrounding environment (Table 5.24)

Social Infrastructure

Education and health facilities are two important components of the social infrastructure considered in this survey. Education has been divided into two categories – children's education and adult education.

Siliguri fares quite well in educational service. Both male and female literacy levels have been found to be very high in the town as well as in the slums. According to the 1991 census, male and female literacy rates are 79.78 and 69.39 per cent respectively in the city, much higher than the state averages (56.54 and 38.94 per cent respectively). In the slums however, male and female literacy rates (59.84 and 42.36 per cent respectively) are lower than the city level, but higher than the state average.

Table 5.22
Water Supply Situation

(Percentage household)

Slums in Siliguri	No. of households	Water supply source		Type of source distribution				Availability		Near to water supply source	Quality of water	Duration of supply
		Independent	Common	Piped	Shallow HP	Mark II HP	Well	Inside the premises	Outside the premises		response fit for drinking	response adequate
1	2	3	4	5	6	7	8	9	10	11	12	13
Matangini Colony	25	12	88	0	0	0	100	12	88	100	88	88
Prankrishna Colony	10	50	50	10	0	10	80	50	50	100	100	100
Harijan Majdur Colony	15	7	93	0	0	0	100	7	93	100	100	100
Nutan Para	20	50	55	0	25	75	30	45	60	55	100	100
Vibekananda Colony	15	47	53	0	7	47	47	47	53	60	100	100
Jyoti Nagar Colony	15	67	33	0	0	47	67	67	33	73	100	100
Debashish Colony	25	57	43	0	0	14	89	60	40	89	89	97
Deshbandhu Colony	15	67	33	0	0	0	100	87	13	100	100	100
Swami Nagar Colony	14	7	93	0	7	0	93	21	79	93	100	100
Adarsha Nagar	12	100	0	0	0	42	92	100	17	100	100	100
Subhas Nagar	13	100	0	100	0	0	100	100	0	100	100	100
Raja Ram Mohan Colony	18	100	0	100	0	0	63	100	0	100	100	100
Chittaranjan Colony	13	0	100	0	0	0	100	0	100	100	100	92
Dash Colony	15	93	7	7	0	0	100	87	13	100	100	100
Sramik Nagar	20	75	25	20	0	0	95	60	40	90	100	100

Contd...

1	2	3	4	5	6	7	8	9	10	11	12	13
Prantik Palli	15	100	0	0	0	0	100	100	0	100	100	100
Durga Das Colony	20	55	45	10	0	0	95	50	50	85	100	100
Jyoti Nagar Colony	10	40	60	0	0	0	100	50	50	100	100	100
Sraban Nagar	20	5	95	0	0	0	100	5	95	45	100	100
Udayan Colony	15	93	7	7	0	0	93	87	13	100	100	100
Fuleswari Colony	25	40	60	6	0	0	94	31	69	100	97	91
Prpmode Nagar	15	0	100	0	0	0	100	7	93	100	0	93
Lichu Bagan Colony	15	0	100	0	0	0	100	0	100	100	0	73
Sarbahara Colony	20	0	100	0	0	0	100	0	100	100	10	65
All Slums in Siliguri	400	49	51	11	2	10	89	49	51	91	87	96

Source: Field Survey, Siliguri, ISS, 1992.

Table 5.23
Toilet Facility

(Percentage distribution)

Slums in Siliguri	No. of house-holds	Toilet facility			Type of toilet facility		Basket cleaned daily	Average instal-lation Expendi-ture (Rs)	Average cleaning expendi-ture (Rs)
		Independent	Common	No Provision	Flush	Basket			
1	2	3	4	5	6	7	8	9	10
Matangini Colony	25	60	0	40	60	0	NA	217	29
Prankrishna Colony	10	90	0	10	90	0	0	150	0
Harijan Majdur Colony	15	60	0	40	60	0	0	150	0
Nutan Para	20	95	0	5	95	0	0	678	0
Vibekananda Colony	15	80	20	0	100	0	7	300	0
Jyoti Nagar Colony	15	100	0	0	100	0	0	300	0
Debashish Colony	25	77	23	0	71	29	17	122	7
Deshbandhu Colony	15	53	47	0	87	13	0	1329	6
Swami Nagar Colony	14	14	86	0	50	7	0	0	0
Adarsha Nagar	12	100	0	0	100	0	0	1921	15
Subhas Nagar	13	100	0	0	67	0	0	150	0
Raja Ram Mohan Colony	18	100	0	0	75	0	0	131	8
Chittaranjan Colony	13	100	0	0	23	77	69	150	0
Dash Colony	15	100	0	0	93	7	0	1211	10
Sramik Nagar	20	95	0	5	80	15	0	356	17

Contd...

1	2	3	4	5	6	7	8	9	10
Prantik Palli	15	100	0	0	100	0	0	150	10
Durga Das Colony	20	70	0	30	70	0	0	150	22
Jyoti Nagar Colony I	10	100	0	0	100	0	0	150	21
Sraban Nagar	20	70	0	30	65	5	0	168	11
Udayan Colony	15	100	0	0	80	13	13	141	0
Fuleswari Colony	25	86	11	0	54	34	37	150	5
Promode Nagar	15	0	100	0	100	0	13	0	16
Lichu Bagan Colony	15	60	40	0	20	80	0	101	14
Sarbahara Colony	20	0	100	0	100	0	5	0	16
All Slums in Siliguri	400	75	18	7	77	12	7	341	9

Source: Field Survey, Siliguri, ISS, 1992.

Table 5.24
Sewerage Facilities

(Per cent household)

Slums in Siliguri	No. of house-holds	Source of drainage		Open drainage/type		Garbage disposal mode			Cleaning 'No'
		Open	No Provision	*Kachcha*	*Pucca*	Bin	Outside	Sweeper	
1	2	3	4	5	6	7	8	9	10
Matangini Colony	25	44	56	56	44	0	92	8	24
Prankrishna Colony	10	100	0	0	100	0	100	0	100
Harijan Majdur Colony	15	0	100	0	0	0	100	0	93
Nutan Para	20	10	90	95	5	0	100	0	85
Vibekananda Colony	15	53	47	47	53	0	100	0	100
Jyoti Nagar Colony	15	0	100	0	0	0	100	0	100
Ddebashish Colony	25	60	40	40	60	0	100	0	97
Deshbandhu Colony	15	40	60	60	40	0	100	0	73
Swami Nagar Colony	14	100	0	0	100	0	100	0	93
Adarsha Nagar	12	100	0	92	8	8	67	25	100
Subhas Nagar	13	100	0	0	100	0	0	100	100
Raja Ram Mohan Colony	18	100	0	0	100	0	88	13	100
Chittaranjan Colony	13	100	0	0	100	0	100	0	100
Dash Colony	15	13	87	93	7	0	100	0	100
Sramik Nagar	20	5	95	0	0	0	100	0	100

Contd...

1	2	3	4	5	6	7	8	9	10
Prantik Palli	15	0	100	0	0	0	100	0	100
Durga Das Colony	20	40	60	35	65	0	100	0	100
Jyoti Nagar Colony I	10	100	0	20	80	0	100	0	100
Sraban Nagar	20	0	100	0	0	0	100	0	100
Udayan Colony	15	100	0	100	0	7	93	0	100
Fuleswari Colony	25	97	3	97	3	9	91	0	100
Promode Nagar	15	100	0	100	0	0	100	0	100
Lichu Bagan Colony	15	100	0	60	40	0	100	0	100
Sarbahara Colony	20	70	30	65	35	0	95	5	100
All Slums in Siliguri	400	60	40	64	36	1	93	6	94

Source: Field Survey, Siliguri, ISS, 1992.

In this survey, children (up to 14 years) form 38 per cent of the total sample population of 2281. The percentage of children attending primary school is quite high (68 per cent). In comparison, the percentage of children going to Balwadi/Anganwadi and other private schools is rather low, 28 and 14 respectively. The slum dwellers have shown a clear preference for primary schools. The concept of pre-school education has not gathered momentum as revealed by the poor percentage of children in the Balwadi schools. Private schools are very expensive generally. Even then, many slum dwellers find it worthwhile to spend more on these schools rather than send the children to relatively cheaper schools. Even with a high literacy rate, it is observed that nearly half of the slum children do not go to school. Many of them work in self-employed shops like tea shops, tailoring units and so on, but they are not reported as working children, as these units are generally within the family and the children do not get any cash payment.

In the sample slums, the percentage of female children (59) in primary school is higher than that of the male. There are more female children in the pre-school centres (Balwadi) as well. In other private schools, the proportion is equal (Table 5.25).

In the older age group, however the proportion of female goes down in comparison to male. Female participation is very low at higher level of education. The percentage of women at the graduation level is as low as one in the slums (Table 5.26).

The average level of adult illiteracy is as high as 40 per cent in the slums. Yet the attendance at the adult education centre is very low, (19%). There is no adult literacy centre (ALC) in seven slums. But the percentage of illiterates varies from 50 to 67 in some of them. In nine slums the facility is utilised by less than ten per cent of the illiterates. There are 100 ALCs under operation according to municipal sources. In the 24 sample (out of total 48) slums however, 17 ALCs were found to be working. Many of them have been discontinued for want of funds. (Table 5.27).

The pattern of ownership of assets influences the level of economic well-being. In the urban areas, labour is the most important asset that the slum dwellers have. Unskilled labour can hardly become a significant income generating asset. Lack of education leads to lack of skill formation obstructing the way to the economic welfare of the slum dweller. The adult literacy centres in the slums are very necessary for improving the quality of labour as well as attitude towards life.

Table 5.25
Children's Education

Slums in Siliguri	No. of sample house-holds	Total no. of children		Percentage distribution of children's education*					
		Male	Female	Primary school		Balwadis/Anganwadis		Other school	
				Male	Female	Male	Female	Male	Female
1	2	3	4	5	6	7	8	9	10
Matangini Colony	25	29	30	52	40	3	10	0	0
Prankrishna Colony	10	14	14	29	79	0	0	14	14
Harijan Majdur Colony	15	26	27	19	26	0	0	4	4
Nutan Para	20	29	22	28	27	0	0	17	32
Vibekananda Colony	15	13	7	23	43	0	0	0	0
Jyoti Nagar Colony	15	19	15	26	40	0	0	0	0
Debashish Colony	25	35	33	34	36	43	30	0	0
Deshbandhu Colony	15	20	15	35	33	0	7	0	0
Swami Nagar Colony	14	26	30	31	17	0	33	0	0
Adarsha Nagar	12	12	7	17	43	0	0	17	14
Subhas Nagar	13	4	2	75	0	0	0	25	50
Raja Ram Mohan Colony	18	16	13	13	38	38	54	6	0
Chittaranjan Colony	13	11	15	45	80	9	0	0	0
Dash Colony	15	14	8	14	38	7	50	0	38
Sramik Nagar	20	19	17	16	29	16	12	11	12

Contd...

1	2	3	4	5	6	7	8	9	10
Prantik Palli	15	9	20	56	50	22	5	22	5
Durga Das Colony	20	28	28	32	29	29	25	25	11
Jyoti Nagar Colony I	10	11	14	45	57	0	7	9	14
Sraban Nagar	20	18	27	33	19	28	22	6	0
Udayan Colony	15	12	6	67	33	0	0	50	50
Fuleswari Colony	25	33	22	48	41	6	27	0	0
Promode Nagar	15	17	16	29	31	24	19	0	13
Lichu Bagan Colony	15	11	16	27	25	9	0	0	0
Sarbahara Colony	20	27	20	19	40	19	35	0	0
All Slums in Siliguri	400	453	424	32	36	12	16	7	7

Source: Field Survey, Siliguri, ISS, 1992.

* The percentage has been calculated in the relevant age group. For attending Balwadis/Anganwadi, the age group is upto 6 years. For attending primary school the age group is 6 to 14 years. 'Other School' means other private schools up to class V standard.

Table 5.26
Level of Adult Education

Slums In Siliguri	No. of sample house-holds	Total number of adults		Percent distribution of adult							
				Primary educated		Middle school		High school		Above high school	
		Male	Female	Male	Female	Male	Female	Male	Female	Male	Female
1	2	3	4	5	6	7	8	9	10	11	12
Matangini Colony	25	45	43	13	16	7	5	4	2	2	0
Prankrishna Colony	10	17	13	18	15	15	5	0	0	0	0
Harijan Majdur Colony	15	34	30	3	3	9	0	0	0	0	0
Nutan Para	20	33	34	0	0	0	6	1	6	0	0
Vibekananda Colony	15	30	30	8	4	10	0	20	5	3	0
Jyoti Nagar Colony	15	24	28	0	7	0	0	8	11	4	0
Debashish Colony	25	65	59	3	10	15	5	15	19	13	0
Deshbandhu Colony	15	17	17	12	11	5	14	8	11	9	6
Swami Nagar Colony	14	27	29	10	7	12	3	11	0	0	0
Adarsha Bagar	12	28	23	7	0	13	8	21	5	6	4
Subhas Nagar	13	24	23	10	7	5	0	10	0	15	0
Raja Ram Mohan Colony	18	21	19	5	5	9	5	14	11	18	15
Chittaranjan Colony	13	21	16	12	8	10	6	12	6	0	0
Dash Colony	15	36	26	3	4	10	6	16	5	9	0
Sramik Nagar	20	34	41	6	12	6	0	12	12	10	5

Contd...

1	2	3	4	5	6	7	8	9	10	11	12
Prantik Palli	15	21	25	10	8	9	4	13	0	5	0
Durga Das Colony	20	37	40	24	15	22	11	0	0	0	0
Jyoti Nagar Colony I	10	22	20	23	15	15	14	5	5	4	0
Sraban Nagar	20	34	29	9	21	12	9	8	0	3	0
Udayan Colony	15	38	32	3	3	2	0	22	0	3	0
Fuleswari Colony	25	57	64	10	10	8	3	0	9	0	2
Promode Nagar	15	23	22	17	9	15	9	17	5	0	0
Lichu Bagan Colony	15	20	23	15	17	10	9	5	4	0	0
Sarbahara Colony	20	43	33	15	6	18	9	9	0	0	0
All Slums in Siliguri	400	731	699	16	12	14	10	14	8	11	1

Source: Field Survey, Siliguri, ISS, 1992.

Table 5.27
Utilisation of Adult Literacy Centres in Sample Slums

Slums in Siliguri	No. of sample house-holds	Total no. of adults		Level of Adult illiteracy		Per cent utilising adult education facility	Reason for not utilising adult education facility (per cent response)		
		Male	Female	Number	Percentage		Does not exist	No Time	No Need
1	2	3	4	5	6	7	8	9	10
Matangini Colony	25	45	43	26	29.5	0	100	-	-
Prankrishna Colony	10	17	13	5	17.3	0	100	-	-
Harijan Majdur Colony	15	34	30	41	64.0	0	100	-	-
Nutan Para	20	33	34	45	67.1	7	-	62	29
Vibekananda Colony	15	30	30	30	50.0	17	-	43	34
Jyoti Nagar Colony	15	24	28	36	39.2	15	-	40	35
Debashish Colony	25	65	59	12	9.67	2	-	57	32
Deshbandhu Colony	15	17	17	14	42.3	3	-	42	51
Swami Nagar Colony	14	27	29	32	57.3	13	-	38	39
Adarsha Nagar	12	28	23	30	40.2	0	100	-	-
Subhas Nagar	13	24	23	20	48.3	14	-	72	12
Raja Ram Mohan Colony	18	21	19	10	26.2	13	-	23	61
Chittaranjan Colony	13	21	16	10	25.2	0	100	-	-
Dash Colony	15	36	26	25	34.3	8	-	28	59
Sramik Nagar	20	34	41	32	39.4	0	100	-	-

Contd...

1	2	3	4	5	6	7	8	9	10
Prantik Palli	15	21	25	16	42.0	0	100	-	-
Durga Das Colony	20	37	40	25	39.0	8	-	47	43
Jyoti Nagar Colony I	10	22	20	12	29.0	5	-	71	32
Sraban Nagar	20	34	29	15	23.6	8	-	38	52
Udayan Colony	15	38	32	35	50.2	3	-	74	22
Fuleswari Colony	25	57	64	49	60.2	1	-	57	38
Promode Nagar	15	23	22	16	36.2	18	-	35	43
Lichu Bagan Colony	15	20	23	12	48.2	30	-	50	20
Sarbahara Colony	20	43	33	25	32.3	17	-	43	40
All Slums	400	731	699	573	40.0	19		48	37

Source: Field Survey, Siliguri, ISS, 1992.
Note: Column 7 is a percentage of column 5.

But in response to the questionnaire about the reason for not going to the ALCs, the majority cited lack of time. A good many of them also felt there was no need for joining such centres. The present bread earners, even if they do want to have no time for joining these centres. The retired older people find no need for it as there seems to be no prospect of earning money by being literate at their age. Availability and utilisation of health services in the slums have been observed from three aspects; child immunisation, maternity care and family planning.

The immunisation programme is going on for a long time in Siliguri. However, the programme has not been very effective in the slums. A significant proportion of the slum dwellers reported unawareness of such programme. In 4 out of 24 slums, they reported total unawareness. According to the municipality authorities, this programme is not a specific slum-based programme. Psychological apathy towards immunisation prevents the slum dwellers to come to the municipality. The resident community volunteers have a major role to play here in educating people. The local body can arrange for mobile health centres for the slums and offer some incentives to make the programme successful as shortage of time has been reported as the most dominant cause (44%). The ineffectiveness of this programme is revealed by the fact that, among the 877 children, only 34 per cent have been immunised so far. Long waiting period also is a very important deterrent cause (34%) for not using the immunisation facility (Table 5.28).

The slum people utilise both private and public medical facilities. Among the sample households, 23 per cent go in for private medical facilities. But for expensive treatment, generally they go to government hospitals which offer cheaper alternatives. Non-availability of medicines and hospital beds in the hospitals compels the slum dwellers to go to private doctors. By and large medical facilities provided by the public sector remain the major supporting service for the urban poor (Table 5.29).

It is encouraging to see that the slum people are sufficiently eager to avail themselves of the medical facilities. A large section (86%) of the women go in for pre-natal check up. Ninety-seven per cent of them choose government hospitals for pre-natal check-ups as well as for child delivery. But the percentage (20) of people seeking help from untrained *dais* and experienced ladies at home is also quite significant (Table 5.30).

Family planning measures, however are not quite popular. Fifty-two per cent of the sample slum dwellers do not use them. Among them, 40 per cent say that their husbands do not allow them to adopt such measures. Many people (22%) do not need such measures. In an urban centre where the average size of household is very high (6), such unwillingness towards family planning measures can prove problematic (Table 5.31).

Expansion in medical facilities contributes directly in improving the quality of the most abundant asset of the urban poor, physical labour. In the slums, low earning compels the workers to work for longer hours (either by service condition or by diversification of activities). They find it very difficult to consume the services available even if they are aware of the utility of the services. The public sector supplies these essential services at cheaper prices, but the time spent (which otherwise can be utilised for earning more) is so much that the high opportunity cost of these services reduces the effective demand for them even if people are aware of their importance.

Table 5.28
Pattern of Immunisation

Slums in Siliguri	Total No. of Children	Per cent children immunised	Reason for not Using Immunisation			
			Facility not available	Shortage of time	Long queue	Not aware
Matangini Colony	59	20	50	50	0	0
Prankrishna Colony	28	14	0	40	30	30
Harijan Majdur Colony	53	19	0	100	0	0
Nutan Para	51	14	0	25	25	50
Vibekananda Colony	20	40	0	25	35	40
Jyoti Nagar Colony	34	29	0	0	0	100
Debashish Colony	68	34	0	29	0	71
Deshbandu Colony	35	26	0	0	0	100
Swami Nagar Colony	56	21	0	42	20	38
Adarsha Nagar	19	53	0	0	100	0
Subhas Nagar	16	33	0	0	100	0
Raja Ram Mohan Colony	29	28	0	50	50	0
Chittaranjan Colony	26	50	0	70	30	0
Dash Colony	22	50	0	0	100	0
Sramik Nagar	36	47	50	50	0	0
Prantik Palli	29	48	0	40	35	25
Durga Das Colony	56	41	0	40	35	25
Jyoti Nagar Colony I	25	36	0	0	0	0
Sraban Nagar	45	27	71	0	0	29
Udayan Colony	18	44	0	0	0	100
Fuleswari Colony	55	53	0	0	0	100
Promode Nagar	33	30	0	75	0	25
Lichu Bagan Colony	27	33	0	100	0	0
Sarbahara Colony	47	30	0	50	0	50
All Slums in Siliguri	877	34	6	44	24	26

Source: Field Survey, Siliguri, ISS, 1992.

Table 5.29
Utilisation of Health Care Facility

Slums in Siliguri	No. of sample house-hold	Health Service Utilisation (Per cent distribution)		
		Government Hospital	Private sector	Others
Matangini Colony	25	60	36	4
Prankrishna Colony	10	90	10	0
Harijan Majdur Colony	15	93	7	0
Nutan Para	20	95	25	0
Vibekananda Colony	15	87	23	7
Jyoti Nagar Colony	15	100	53	0
Debashish Colony	25	54	37	3
Deshbandhu Colony	15	33	60	0
Swami Nagar Colony	14	100	7	0
Adarsha Nagar	12	100	67	0
Subhas Nagar	13	100	0	33
Raja Ram Mohan Colony	18	100	0	75
Chittaranjan Colony	13	85	0	0
Dash Colony	15	73	0	27
Sramik Nagar	20	35	40	40
Prantik Colony	15	100	13	0
Durga Das Colony	20	95	10	0
Jyoti Nagar Colony I	10	100	0	0
Sraban Nagar	20	100	5	0
Udayan Colony	15	87	0	13
Fuleswari Colony	25	91	0	9
Promode Nagar	15	67	0	20
Lichu Bagan Colony	15	7	7	47
Sarbahara Colony	20	40	0	35
All Slums in Siliguri	400	66	23	11

Note: There are many people who take all kinds of health facilities available. So the percentages do not add up to 100.
Source: Field Survey, Siliguri, ISS, 1992.

In this context, it will be interesting to have a glimpse at the overall situation in the slums during the course of operation of the UBS project. The National Institute of Urban Affairs (NIUA) undertook a major nation-wide survey of the availability of basic services in the slums in 1987 - when UBS was just launched. The present survey was taken when the project was almost over. NIUA took up 361 households in 15 slums whereas the present survey covers 400 households spread over 24 slums. Tables 5.31 and 5.32 yield a comparative picture in both physical and social services in Siliguri at two points of time.

Table 5.30
Pattern of Maternity Care and Child Delivery

Slums in Siliguri	No. of sample house-holds	Per cent going for pre-natal check up	Per cent going for pre-natal check-up in		Place of Child Delivery (Precentage)		Help during child delivery (percent response)		
			Government hospital	Others	Government hospital	Others	Doctor	Trained *Dai*	Others
1	2	3	4	5	6	7	8	9	10
Matangini Colony	25	68	94	6	76	24	76	4	20
Prankrishna Colony	10	90	100	0	100	0	100	0	0
Harijan Majdur Colony	15	93	100	0	100	0	100	0	0
Nutan Para	20	90	100	0	95	5	95	0	5
Vibekananda Colony	15	100	100	0	100	0	100	0	0
Jyoti Nagar Colony	15	93	100	0	100	0	100	0	0
Debashish Colony	25	94	100	0	94	6	26	57	17
Deshbandhu Colony	15	100	93	7	87	13	53	33	14
Swami Nagar Colony	14	71	70	30	71	29	64	0	36
Adarsha Nagar	12	100	100	0	100	0	100	0	0
Subhas Nagar	13	100	100	0	100	0	100	0	0
Raja Ram Mohan colony	18	100	80	20	100	0	50	0	50
Chittaranjan Colony	13	100	100	0	100	0	77	0	23
Dash Colony	15	100	100	0	93	7	0	80	20
Sramik Nagar	20	90	94	6	95	5	55	40	5

Contd...

1	2	3	4	5	6	7	8	9	10
Prantik Palli	15	93	100	0	100	0	40	60	0
Durga Das Colony	20	80	100	0	75	25	75	0	25
Jyoti Nagar Colony I	10	100	100	0	100	0	90	0	10
Sraban Nagar	20	60	100	0	70	30	60	0	40
Udayan Colony	15	100	100	0	93	7	100	0	0
Fuleswari Colony	25	100	100	0	100	0	100	0	0
Promode Nagar	15	60	100	0	60	40	53	0	47
Lichu Bagan Colony	15	53	80	20	47	53	40	0	60
Sarbahara Colony	20	45	100	0	40	60	35	0	65
All Slums in Siliguri	400	86	87	13	88	12	69	11	20

Source: Field Survey, Siliguri, ISS, 1992.

Table 5.31
Pattern of Family Planning Utilisation

Slums in Siliguri	No. of sample house-holds	Family planning measures used by (Percentage)			Reason for not willing to use family planning measures (per cent response)			
		Husband	Wife	None	Not aware	Husband do not allow	Not needed	Others
1	2	3	4	5	6	7	8	9
Matangini Colony	25	0	20	80	21	32	21	16
Prankrishna Colony	10	0	20	80	20	20	40	20
Harijan Majdur Colony	15	0	0	100	7	60	13	20
Nutan Para	20	0	35	65	41	47	6	6
Vibekananda Colony	15	0	40	60	0	33	0	0
Jyoti Nagar Colony	15	0	13	87	34	33	23	10
Debashish Colony	25	6	83	11	23	46	24	7
Deshbandu Colony	15	6	67	27	27	56	17	0
Swami Nagar Colony	14	0	21	79	60	20	20	0
Adarsha Nagar	12	0	33	67	26	41	33	0
Subhas Nagar	13	34	33	33	20	60	20	0
Raja Ram Mohan Colony	18	0	12	88	33	43	24	0
Chittaranjan Colony	13	0	46	54	25	48	27	3
Dash Colony	15	33	67	0	30	40	30	0
Sramik Nagar	20	40	35	25	NA	NA	NA	NA

Contd...

1	2	3	4	5	6	7	8	9
Prantik Palli	15	40	33	27	NA	NA	NA	NA
Durga Das Colony	20	55	5	40	22	67	11	0
Jyoti Nagar Colony I	10	40	0	60	15	83	2	0
Sraban Nagar	20	50	0	50	20	80	0	0
Udayan Colony	15	0	93	7	0	0	100	0
Fuleswari Colony	25	2	89	9	NA	NA	NA	NA
Promode Nagar	15	0	27	73	0	100	0	0
Lichu Bagan Colony	15	7	20	73	0	100	0	0
Sarbahara Colony	20	0	35	65	0	100	0	0
All Slums in Siliguri	400	13	35	52	30	40	22	8

Source: Field Survey, Siliguri, ISS, 1992.

Table 5.32 shows a clear improvement in housing, electricity, water supply and toilet facilities. Side by side, there has been a marked deterioration in environmental sanitation. Any improvement in housing services in such deplorable living conditions hardly makes any significant impact on community health.

Table 5.32
Comparative Assessment of Physical Services in the Sample Slums: 1987 and 1992

(Percentage)

Item		NIUA Survey (1987)	ISS Survey (1992)
Living in houses	Pucca	2	18
	Semi Pucca	6	10
	Kachcha	90	68
Houses electrified		10	23
Houses with independent water connection		49	33
Houses with independent toilet		75	68
Houses with Community Toilet		18	11
Utilising garbage bin		1	7
Throwing garbage outside the house		93	82
Houses having adequate water supply.		96	90

Note : NIUA - National Institute of Urban Affairs. ISS - Institute of Social Sciences.
Source: (1) Basic Services and the Urban Poor - NIUA (1991). (2) Field Survey, ISS, 1992.

In social infrastructure, there has been a marked improvement on the health sector. People are willing to utilise medical services even if they have to pay for them as shown by the increasing per cent of them going to private doctors (Table 5.33).

But when children's education in public sector is considered, the picture is dismal. NIUA data have been taken on the basis of enrolment while the present survey was conducted on a specific questionnaire asking the households how many of their children were going to balwadi or primary schools. The alarming drop in the percentage of children in both balwadi and primary schools over a span of five years is primarily explained by the fact that many balwadi schools have opened with fanfare but had to be closed for want of funds. In primary schools, the percentage of drop-outs has been increasing over the years. The enrolment in schools increases the literacy ratio, but an increasing number of drop outs indicates a lack of general skill formation in human capital (Table 5.33).

Table 5.33
Comparative assessment of social services in the Sample Slums: 1987 and 1992

(Percentage)

Item	NIUA Survey (1987)	ISS Survey (1992)
Children in Balwadi School	73	14
Children in primary school	84	38
People going to private doctors	7	23
Going for antinatal check-up	81	87
Child delivery:		
At home	35	20
At hospital	65	69

Note : NIUA - National Institute of Urban Affairs. ISS - Institute of Social Sciences

Community awareness and community participation have been the most important components of UBS. The major thrust of this programme is to promote community participation towards determining the demand as well as maintenance of civil services. The survey shows that almost all of the slum dwellers have been aware of UBS. They know the resident volunteers also quite well and discuss their problems with them. The income generation programme also has been given extensive coverage. The neighbourhood committees take an active role in identifying eligible persons to get loans (Table 5.34). However awareness has not been matched with utilisation of services. There are very few workers as balsevikas (teachers in balwadi schools) from the slum dwellers. A little more than a quarter of the sample households send their children to balwadi schools. There are not many utilisers of adult literacy centres. Income generating programmes in terms of housing upgradation is however very popular in the slums (Table 5.35).

Poverty alleviation programmes have two aspects-space related programmes and people-related programmes. The programmes furnishing direct financial assistance to local economic development programmes contains eligibility requirements based directly upon urban poverty, a factor connected with labour market conditions. If jobs are too few, if wages are too low, if labour force participation rates are depressed because workers have dropped out of the labour

Table 5.34
Community Awareness of Urban Basic Services Income Generation Programmes

(Per cent household)

Slums in Siliguri	No. of sample house-holds	Aware of UBS	Involved as bal-sevika	Known to volunteer	Discusses problems with the volunteer	Aware of IGP	Help to Get Loan		
							UBS official	Local NGOs	Neighbourhood committee
1	2	3	4	5	6	7	8	9	10
Matangini Colony	25	100	0	100	100	100	0	100	0
Prankrishna Colony	10	100	0	100	100	90	0	100	0
Harijan Majdur Colony	15	100	0	100	100	100	0	89	0
Nutan Para	20	100	5	100	100	100	100	0	92
Vibekananda Colony	15	100	13	100	100	100	15	0	100
Jyoti Nagar Colony	15	100	13	100	100	100	0	0	86
Debashish Colony	25	100	0	100	100	100	0	0	96
Deshbandhu Colony	15	100	0	100	100	80	0	0	20
Swami Nagar Colony	14	93	0	93	29	93	100	0	110
Adarsha Nagar	12	100	17	100	100	92	150	50	300
Subhas Nagar	13	100	0	100	100	100	50	0	50
Raja Ram Mohan Colony	18	100	0	100	100	100	71	14	114
Chittaranjan Colony	13	100	0	100	69	92	100	9	91
Dash Colony	15	100	0	100	73	100	0	0	100
Sramik Nagar	20	80	5	100	100	100	0	0	87

Contd...

1	2	3	4	5	6	7	8	9	10
Prantik Palli	15	53	0	100	100	100	0	0	100
Durga Das Colony	20	95	0	100	100	90	8	92	8
Jyoti Nagar Colony I	10	100	0	100	90	90	11	0	111
Sraban Nagar	20	100	0	100	100	100	0	0	100
Udayan Colony	15	93	27	93	67	100	0	22	89
Fuleswari Colony	25	94	46	74	63	77	0	0	100
Promode Nagar	15	100	0	100	100	100	0	22	78
Lichu Bagan Colony	15	100	0	100	100	100	0	18	82
Sarbahara Colony	20	100	0	100	100	100	0	42	58
All Slums in Siliguri	400	96	5	98	91	96	25	23	82

Source: Field Survey, Siliguri, ISS, 1992

Table 5.35
Community Participation in Urban Basic Services and Income Generation Programmes

(Per cent households)

Slums in Siliguri	No. of sample house-holds	Sending children to Balwadi/ Anganwadi	Utilising adult education facility	Utilising immunisation facility	Utilising family planning measures	Households received loans
1	2	3	4	5	6	7
Matangini Colony	25	13	NA	20	20	72
PrankrishnaColony	10	0	NA	14	20	70
Harijan Majdur Colony	15	0	NA	19	0	60
Nutan Para	20	0	7	14	35	65
Vibekananda Colony	15	0	17	40	40	87
Jyoti Nagar Colony	15	0	15	29	13	47
Debashish Colony	25	73	2	34	89	71
Deshbandhu Colony	15	7	3	26	73	33
Swami Nagar Colony	14	33	13	21	21	71
Adarsha Nagar	12	0	0	53	33	17
Subhas Nagar	13	0	14	33	67	67
Raja Ram Mohan Colony	18	91	13	28	13	88
Chittaranjan Colony	13	9	0	50	46	85
Dash Colony	15	57	8	50	100	100
Sramik Nagar	20	28	0	47	75	75

Contd...

1	2	3	4	5	6	7
Prantik Palli	15	27	0	48	73	47
Durga Das Colony	20	54	8	41	60	65
Jyoti Nagar Colony I	10	7	5	36	40	90
Sraban Nagar	20	50	8	27	50	70
Udayan Colony	15	0	3	44	93	60
Fuleswari Colony	25	33	1	53	91	63
Promode Nagar	15	42	18	30	27	60
Lichu Bagan Colony	15	9	30	33	27	73
Sarbahara Colony	20	54	17	30	35	95
All Slums	400	28	9	34	48	68

Source: Field Survey, Siliguri, ISS, 1992.

force in discouragement, if people are working part-time because full-time jobs are not available, economic development programmes that brings in jobs are obviously welcome.

Space-oriented programmes take longer time to yield benefits to the target population, but it enjoys political support. On the other hand, people-oriented programmes get weak political backing if the programmes bypass the local political structure.

People's participation in maintaining basic services may take different forms, namely, taking part in the decision making process, sharing expenditure, supplying labour and so on. The present survey offers a very good opportunity to probe into the first two. People's participation in the decision making process can be studied to the extent they are associated with the neighbourhood committees. The possibility of sharing expenditure will be clear from the behaviour of people in different income-classes towards the use of basic services.

Income Class Variation and the Utilisation of Basic Services

An analysis of the income-level disaggregation has been done taking six income-classes. It is observed that the proportion of self-employed people has increased in the higher income class. Direct financial assistance to the people can help to change the structure of the labour market by reducing the dependency on wage-labour. It can provide the welcome dent in the labour market by opening up independent employment prospects (Table 5.36).

Siliguri municipality took special efforts to adopt the "liberating the scavengers" programmes as well as building individual wells with some contributions from the beneficiaries. These were area-based programmes irrespective of income status. These programmes were participating in terms of sharing expenditure. Similarly the provision (or no provision) of sanitation facilities was equally disadvantageous to people irrespective of income class. Access to electricity however has increased in the higher income group, so has been the quality of houses. The per cent of school going female children is higher than the male ones for all income classes. A small per cent of higher income groups prefer to send their children to private schools. Health consciousness has been increased among people, a significant per cent utilises medical facilities available in government hospitals. Here too the per cent declines in higher income groups who opt for private doctors in order to save time. The immunisation facility has not been utilised by the higher income group in a significant way. The response to family planning programmes does not show much variation across the income class. There does not seem to be much variation in the household income levels to generate such consciousness towards utilisation of these services (Table 5.37 and 5.38).

Table 5.36
Income-wise Distribution of Employment

Income class	No. of sample house-holds	Percentage distribution of						
		House-holds	Self-employed		Regular job		Irregular job	
			Male	Female	Male	Female	Male	Female
Below Rs. 100	2	0.5	0	0	0	100	100	0
Rs. 101 - 250	6	1.5	50	0	25	0	25	100
Rs. 251 - 500	51	12.7	34.7	50	16.3	37.5	49.0	12.5
Rs. 501 - 1000	237	59.2	44.5	37.9	26.8	19.6	25.3	43.1
Rs. 1001 - 2000	77	19.2	55.7	33.3	27.0	66.7	17.2	11.1
Above Rs. 2000	27	6.75	47.8	25	31.9	75.0	21.7	0.0
All Income Class	400	100	49.9	42.1	26.9	26.8	23.6	31.6

Source: Field Survey, Siliguri, ISS, 1992.

Across the income levels, the percentage of females going in for pre-natal health check up is very high but in the case of child delivery, 69 per cent of the females take a doctor's help, the rest depends on experienced ladies or untrained *dais* at home. This percentage is quite significant even in higher income groups.

The majority of the slum people in the survey are aware of the UBS in the area. The local body's involvement in this programme is evident from the fact that 82 per cent of the households received loans through their help. The percentage of households receiving loans declines with an increasing level of income, signifying the egalitarian pattern in the distribution of loans.

The expenditure profile of the slum dwellers show that even the poorest has to spend 20-22 per cent of their income towards basic services. The major percentage has, been however towards loan repayment. The expenditure profile does not make clear distinction between capital expenditure and current expenditure in services like

Table 5.37
Distribution of Physical Services by Monthly Household Income Class

Item	Below Rs. 100	Rs. 101 - 250	Rs. 251 - 500	Rs. 501 - 1000	Rs. 1001 - 2000	Above Rs. 2000	All Income Class
Sample Households	2	6	51	237	77	27	400
Per cent living in kaccha house	100	83	75	78	48	44	68
Per cent electrified	0	17	12	14	43	42	23
Per cent having independent well	100	100	100	88	91	100	89
Per cent having independent toilet	100	100	73	69	.78	93	75
Per cent served by pucca drain	0	33	24	29	32	33	36
Per cent disposing garbage outside house	100	100	98	97	95	89	93
Per cent answering yes to cleaning of garbage by sweeper	0	5	8	9	7	9	6

Source: Field Survey, Siliguri, ISS, 1992.

Table 5.38
Distribution of Social Services by Monthly Household Income-Class

Item	Below Rs. 100	Rs. 101 - 250	Rs. 251 - 500	Rs. 501 - 1000	Rs. 1001 - 2000	Above Rs. 2000	All Income Class
1	2	3	4	5	6	7	8
Sample household Number	2	6	51	237	77	27	400
Total No. of Persons:							
Male	0	3	53	233	104	60	453
Female	0	4	43	227	85	65	424
Children immunised (per cent)	0	57	40	24	30	21	34
Percent children in primary School:							
Male	0	100	40	34	31	15	32
Female	0	50	41	41	40	24	36
Balawadi:							
Male	0	0	17	10	13	7	12
Female	0	0	16	24	7	2	16
*Other:							
Male	0	0	4	6	13	5	7
Female	0	0	8	4	14	2	7

Contd...

1	2	3	4	5	6	7	8
Per cent Illiterate adults	50	33	36	48	25	31	40
Per cent female going to govt. hospital for pre-natal check-up	50	67	70	74	48	48	66
Per cent female going to hospital for child delivery	0	83	65	67	74	67	69
Per cent using family planning measures	0	47	53	47	50	45	48
Per cent utilising ALC facilities	0	23	22	28	17	4	17

Source: Field Survey, Siliguri, ISS, 1992.
* Other school refers to private schools.

Table 5.39
Income-class wise Distribution of People's Awareness and Utilisation of UBS

(*Per cent*)

Income classes	No. of families	Aware of UBS	Families received loan	Families received loan through basti level committee
Below Rs. 100	2	100	100	100
Rs. 101 - 250	6	100	100	100
Rs. 251 - 500	51	98	71	100
Rs. 501 - 1000	237	95	71	80
Rs. 1001 - 2000	77	99	49	72
Above Rs. 2000	27	96	44	67
All Income classes	400	96	73	82

Source: Field Survey, Siliguri, ISS, 1992.

housing, water-supply and sanitation. Generally, people mention the capital expenditure only as current expenditure in these services are very low. It can be observed that expenditure on sanitation is the least for all income classes. Even the relatively better-off people are insensitive towards cleanliness of the surroundings. The garbage bins are hardly ever cleared and approximately 70 per cent of the city is covered by *kachcha* drains. Payments for house-tax are on the average, Rs. 14 quarterly. People in higher income groups tend to spend more on education, health and electricity. The loan repayment component in total expenditure reduces with rise in income. With increasing income, expenditure towards people-oriented services tend to increase more than space oriented services (Table 5.40).

Table 5.41 shows the ranking of all the slums according to the individual as well as composite indices (for indicators see Appendix 1.3). It is observed from the table that many slums which have the highest ranking according to per capita income, have gone down in composite ranking, while the reverse is true in the case of those slums that have the lowest ranking in per capita income. It is an encouraging development for the organisation to have a more egalitarian social scenario. It is evident that the slums with relatively high per capita income have high ranks in education and housing which involve more personal expenditure towards these services. Increase in per capita income has led to increase in expenditure towards private consumption of public goods, but not towards community consumption of public

Table 5.40
Total Expenditure and Percentage Distribution of Urban Services according to Income-Class (Monthly)

Item	Below Rs. 100	Rs. 101 - 250	Rs. 251 - 500	Rs. 501 - 1000	Rs. 1001 - 2000	Above Rs. 2000	All income class
Education	0	10	14	15	25	24	16
Housing*	18	17	4	6	7	9	8
Electricity	0	3	15	17	15	20	16
Water Supply	0	4	8	10	8	6	7
Sanitation	0	0	0	4	1	1	2
Health	14	16	14	18	20	20	18
Loan Repayment**	66	50	45	30	24	20	33
Total	100	100	100	100	100	100	100
Average Expenditure on basic services (Rs)	22	52	72	209	325	360	94

Source: Field Survey, Siliguri, ISS, 1992.
*Expenditure on house refers to payment of house-tax or rent or (and) occasional expenses for getting the land.
** Loan repayment refers to loans from the municipality.

Table 5.41
Ranks of Slums according to Individual as well as Composite Indices

Slums in Siliguri	Education	Housing	Water supply	Sanita-tion	Women and child health	Awareness	Community participation	Composite index	Per capita income
1	2	3	4	5	6	7	8	9	10
Matangini Colony	18	17	13	13	21	21	23	19	15
Prankrishna Colony	10	12	10	10	4	4	5	3	10
Harijan Majdur Colony	24	24	24	24	13	15	11	9	22
Nutan Para	5	6	8	8	10	19	18	15	8
Vibekananda Colony	2	9	1	1	12	16	16	12	6
Jyoti Nagar Colony	8	18	16	16	14	14	14	11	9
Debashish Colony	21	16	21	21	23	24	24	22	13
Deshbandhu Colony	3	4	20	20	9	9	15	13	3
Swami Nagar Colony	17	5	3	3	8	8	3	5	21
Adarsha Nagar	4	1	7	7	7	5	7	6	2
Subhas Nagar	19	20	23	23	1	1	10	8	20
Raja Ram Mohan Colony	20	23	12	12	17	2	2	14	23
Chittaranjan Colony	1	8	4	4	2	6	6	6	1
Dash Colony	12	13	22	22	16	13	9	2	11
Sramik Nagar	13	11	5	5	19	18	17	17	12

Contd..

1	2	3	4	5	6	7	8	9	10
Prantik Palli	7	2	9	9	11	7	13	16	4
Durga Das Colony	14	21	19	19	21	17	20	10	14
Jyoti Nagar Colony I	23	10	15	15	3	3	4	7	18
Sraban Nagar	15	14	6	6	20	20	19	18	16
Udayan Colony	22	22	2	2	15	10	8	23	24
Fuleswari Colony	16	15	18	18	24	23	22	21	17
Promode Nagar	9	7	11	11	6	11	1	1	5
Lichu Bagan Colony	6	3	14	14	3	12	12	4	7
Sarbahara Colony	11	17	17	17	18	21	21	24	19

Source: Field Survey, Siliguri, ISS, 1992.

goods. The residents have increased the supply of services like water supply, electricity or have improved the condition of private latrines, but have paid little attention towards cleaning of public drain or garbage bins. This inaction of the beneficiaries has been matched by lack of action from the local body as well. Community participation has not been directed sufficiently towards adequate utilisation of adult education centres or Balwadi schools. Many such centres and schools have opened with great fanfare but have closed down after some time. The organisational structure is there but motivation from both sides has not been geared up. As a result, the percentage of people utilising these two facilities is low.

Interaction with other parallel programmes may have contributed towards this lack of motivation. The teachers in balwadi schools get lower salaries than their counterparts working under state-level programmes like ICDS. As a result, many of the balwadi schools have been transferred to the ICDS.

Income generating programmes in any form are likely to be successful in the low income area. But increase in the level of income is not likely to be matched by increase in expenditure towards the services except on a limited scale. The employment aspect of UBSP needs to be stressed more in order to motivate people. The job creating potential of the service sector needs more emphasis in order to make such programmes successful.

CONCLUSION

The present survey has tried to focus on the nature of community participation from various aspects. It has examined the organisational and financial structure of the local body, surveyed the availability and utilisation of basic services by the actual beneficiaries, namely, the slum dwellers and observed the pattern of individual expenditure on basic services. This section is divided into three parts summarising the observations in these three areas.

The local body of Siliguri has been very active in the provision of basic services in the city. The supply of basic services however is not uniform. Public works take the lion's share of capital expenditure. The maintenance expenditure on public works is also the highest followed by expenditure on conservancy. However, the city profile poorly reveals the consequences of such expenditure. The enrolment of sweepers in the municipal register is quite high, but the administration fails to make them work. Maintenance expenditure on water supply and drainage is almost nil. Very low percentage of expenditure is earmarked for health services. The increasing urbanisation of the town does not have any significant effect on the pattern of expenditure of the local body. The pressure on the supply of basic services mounts, but the local body is not well equipped to meet the expenditure. The share of tax revenue as well as grants in the local body's revenue income has declined over time. However, it has been able to generate the same income from its own sources, since the share of non-tax revenue has increased. The pattern of revenue income has not responded to the changing economic profile of the town despite some increase in the local body's own source of income.

The local body is not empowered to attract technically qualified labour force as it cannot offer salaries beyond a certain level (MFC, 1982) without the state government's consent. But it has to carry out the welfare programmes announced by higher level authorities. This creates extra pressure on the existing administrative labour force, which cannot be expanded easily. Addition of responsibilities without the necessary organisational flexibility takes its toll on quality of service. UBS activities have been thrust upon the local body without its being supplied with the necessary manpower as the funds are not sufficient. Despite this limitation, Siliguri Municipality has tried to involve itself to the maximum extent possible in carrying out the programme. It has set up the necessary administrative structure, organised the meetings with the RCVs, formulated the mini plans and by and large, fulfilled the structural requirements.

1. The organisational involvement in Siliguri slums has been instrumental in increasing community awareness about the programmes. Almost all of the sample slum dwellers (96%) know about the UBS and different income generating programmes. The resident volunteers and community organisers regularly visit the areas. Nearly 82 per cent of the sample households got loans through these organisers. In Siliguri, house upgradation schemes are the most widespread among the income generation schemes. A majority of the sample households are owners of houses, having titles to the land. But housing condition, as has been revealed earlier are of a very inferior quality. This is why the municipality has very rightly emphasised house upgradation scheme. Water supply and private toilets also have been sufficiently provided by

the municipality. A majority of the households have separate wells within the premises. Two pit latrines have been constructed under the Low Cost Sanitation Programme with some contributions from the beneficiaries (Rs. 150 per house). In some slums, there are community latrines (16 in all).

2. However, supply of other infrastructural services, namely, electricity, drainage facility and garbage bins are far from adequate. Neither the municipal workers nor the inhabitants have shown any consideration towards improving the immediate surroundings. Inhabitants take care of the community latrines. Sometimes they clean the toilets themselves, sometimes they make a monthly payment (around Rs. 10-12 per month per family) to the sweepers. A survey in these areas has revealed that these latrines are quite clean but the courtyards of the houses are full of filth.

3 Immunisation and family planning programmes have been moderately successful in Siliguri. Around 48 per cent of the slum households uses family planning measures, while 34 per cent have undertaken immunisation facilities. The municipality claims almost all children in the slums have been immunised, but the sample survey does not justify this. This is specially true in the slums inhabited by the new migrants. For immunisation, they have to go to the municipality every Wednesday. Most of the new migrants are self-employed. So they do not want to waste manhours by going to the municipality. A mobile health care centre is likely to be more effective for a wider coverage of immunisation facilities.

A detailed budget analysis shows that social infrastructure forms only 25-30 per cent of the municipal budgets, physical infrastructure taking the major share of expenditure. A survey of the slum areas, however, reveal only limited achievement regarding physical infrastructure. Apart from construction of individual wells and latrines the state of physical infrastructure is not impressive. The whole slum area is covered by kuccha drains. There are 52 garbage collection points in 48 slums. They are hardly ever cleaned. There are 14984 holdings in the whole town without any privy, of which 9624 holdings arc in the slum area. There are 14 bathing space for women in 48 slums. Mark II hand pumps (16) and ordinary hand pumps (15) have been installed. But they have not covered all the slums.

In social infrastructure, the problem remains equally acute. It has been found that 48 per cent of the slum dwellers are still unaware of the immunisation facilities. The percentage of female school going children is still very low. According to municipal sources, the number of school drop-outs is increasing faster in the slums than in other parts of the city.

The idea of community participation in the basic services has not also gained momentum. Many of the balwadi schools have closed down as the teachers do not take any interest. They are low paid. The children gather in these centres only during meal time when food is distributed free of cost. In some such centres, primary schooling activity has started in order to create interest among the children. The slum dwellers understand the importance of education quite well. The schools are always full of students. Many slum dwellers are prepared to go in for more expensive education But pre-school activities have not yet been taken up on a large scale.

Three of the sample slums have no adult education centres. The participation in the rest is very poor (9%). In comparison, the medical facilities are being utilised by increasing number of the slum dwellers.

This analysis shows that despite reasonably satisfactory participation from the organisation's side, actual beneficiaries' participation in the utilisation of these services is very low. The income-expenditure profile of the beneficiaries helps to provide a glimpse of their preferences. The high incidence of poverty compels the slum dwellers to spend on those services only that will increase their economic welfare. Attendance at Adult Literacy Centres (ALCs) or balwadi schools have dropped after initial enthusiasm. A majority of the slum dwellers are workers in the informal sector, where the hourly wages are too low, that is, leisure is very expensive. This acts as a major hindrance towards utilising these facilities. The teachers in these centres are reluctant to offer their services as they are very poorly paid.

These services can be effectively supplied if some incentives are attached with their supply. The employers in the informal sector may be offered some economic gain if they help their workers to utilise these services. The slum dwellers may be offered some concessions in loan repayment if they send their women and children to these centres.

These incentives may be offered to the implementing agencies, that is, the local bodies as well. The municipalities which are more effective in carrying out these welfare programmes should have more access to finance. The introduction of performance budgeting at every level of municipal activity will be a yardstick for evaluating their progress.

People-oriented programmes are likely to be successful if more incentives for utilising these services are offered to the lower income group, as the expenditure profile shows that the higher income group tends to spend more on these services. Space-oriented programmes are likely to be successful if the implementing agencies are offered incentives in terms of financial and administrative flexibility.

The ranking of the slums depicts a conscious effort of the local body in improving the quality of life in the slums. The slums with very low per capita income have shown better position in the composite index scale. The local body has tried to spread UBS activities and the NRY to the slums which have a low ranking on the income scale. This shows very positive participation from the organisational side. But the proof of the pudding is in its eating, which till now, has not generated much enthusiasm in Siliguri.

REFERENCES

Banerjee, T. K (1989), 'Urban Poverty and Policy', paper presented in the regional seminar on 'Urban Poverty' organised by the Institute of Local Government and Urban Studies, Calcutta.

Institute of Local Government and Urban Studies (1992), *Siliguri's Development Perspective*, Seminar Report, ILGUS, Calcutta.

Jha, Gangadhar (1988), *Local Finance in Metropolitan Cities*, Mittal Publications, Delhi.

Levy, John M. (1985), *Urban and Metropolitan Economics*, Mcgraw-Hill Book Company, New Delhi.

Mills, E. S. and Charles M. Becker (ed) (1986), *Studies in Indian Urban Development*, Oxford University Press, New York.

Mishra, Girish K. and Narain, M. K. (ed) (1989), *Development Programme for Urban Poor*, Indian Institute of Public Administration, New Delhi.

Municipal Finance Commission (1982), Report, Department of Local Government and Urban Development, Government of West Bengal, Calcutta.

Siliguri-Jalpaiguri Development Authority (1988), *Outer Development Plan*, Report, SJDA, Siliguri.

Siliguri-Jalpaiguri Development Authority, *Annual Report*, 1990-91, 1991-92.

Siliguri Municipality, *Budget Reports*, 1986-92.

Todaro, Michael P (1985), *Economic Development In the Third World*, Orient Longman, New Delhi.

Chapter VI

EVALUATION AND CONCLUSION

The analysis of household survey data in four UBS project cities in the foregoing chapters evaluated the extent of poverty in slums, access of households to basic amenities and their attitude to, perception of and participation in the government sponsored programmes especially the UBS. The programmes evaluated were the same, the objectives of the survey were also similar and the questionnaire canvassed was also identical in all the four case studies. However there have been differences in the results especially in so far as the aspect of community involvement is concerned. In addition, various important observation and issues emerged beyond the specified boundary while analysing the data. These have also been highlighted in the respective case studies. This concluding chapter offers a comparative assessment of the four case studies and highlights some special features.

Background of the Case Study Centres

The profiles of the case study cities show diversity in terms of population size and socio-economic settings.

The four case study cities are growing urban centres belonging to the class I category. According to the census (1991) classification while Baroda acquired its metropolitan status and fell in to the M5 (above 1 million) category in 1991, Siliguri belongs to M2 (2-3 lakh) and Bhilwara and Sambalpur in the M1 (1-2 lakh) category.

Except for Sambalpur, all the other three cities experienced a much higher growth rate than the average decadal growth rates of their respective states during 1981-91. However in keeping with the all-India urban growth trend three cities barring Bhilwara, experienced declining growth rates during the last decade and in the case of Sambalpur the decline was quite significant (Table 6.1).

Table 6.1
Trends in Population Growth in the Surveyed Cities and Respective States

City	Decadal growth rate		State	Per cent urban population in 1991	Decadal growth of urban population	
	1971-81	1981-91			1971-81	1981-91
Baroda	57.1	39.2	Gujarat	34.4	41.4	33.60
Bhilwara	49.26	49.8	Rajasthan	22.88	58.69	39.24
Sambalpur	70.52	18.57	Orissa	13.43	68.54	36.08
Siliguri	58.36	46.83	West Bengal	27.39	31.73	28.9

Source: Census of India, 1991.

The share of city population in the total urban population of the respective state is not high with respect to all the four cities. However, except Sambalpur, each city contributes significantly to the total urban population of the district to which it belongs. Baroda city, for example, constitutes more than 77 per cent of the total urban population of the Baroda district. It is significant to note that Siliguri, despite its being the smallest city among the four, has the highest density, more than double that of Baroda which is nearly ten times bigger in area.

Table 6.2
Area and Population Density in Surveyed Cities in 1991

City	Total area in sq.km (1981)	Total population	Density (no. of persons per sq. km.	City population as per cent to urban population of rerspective	
				District	State
Baroda	150.00	1,021,084	6,784	77.59	7.2
Bhilwara	69.93	183,791	2,628	59.11	1.83
Sambalpur	36.93	130,766	3,541	52.5	1.15
Siliguri	15.54	215,382	13,860	28.30	3.1

Source: Census of India, 1991.

While in the case of Baroda, Sambalpur and Bhilwara economic factors influenced each city's primate position in the state, in the case of Siliguri certain socio-political circumstances led to its enormous population growth. An important component of the exorbitant population growth in Siliguri was the inflow of migrants in huge numbers from the erstwhile East Pakistan first after Partition in 1947 and for a second time in 1971 during the Indo-Pak War. The Indo-China war of 1962 enhanced Siliguri's strategic importance which also led to a heavy influx of people from neighbouring areas into the city during sixties.

The rapid growth of population in these cities surveyed has led to phenomenal growth in slums and squatter settlements. For example, in Baroda the number of slums increased by more than sixteen times from 20 in 1920 to 336 at present. Sambalpur town though has the lowest urban population, has also the highest percentage of population (42.48) living in slums (Table 6.3).

Table 6.3
Number of Slums and Per cent Slum Population in Surveyed Cities

City	No. of slums in 1992	Per cent slum population to total population (1991) of the city
Baroda	336	21.6
Bhilwara	39	25.00
Sambalpur	48	42.48
Siliguri	48	21.57

Source: Baroda Municipal Corporation, Siliguri, Sambalpur and Bhilwara Municipalities.

The nature and characteristics of slums, however, are not uniform in all the four cities. In terms of shelter conditions, the slums in Sambalpur and Bhilwara, have different characteristics than those in Baroda and Siliguri where the share of the migrant population is very high. Not all the slums in Bhilwara and Sambalpur are dilapidated and makeshift arrangements. Many of these slums here may be categorised as extended villages which are now flanked by newly developed residential and commercial areas. Though they have been incorporated in the city area, they still retain some of their rural characteristics and stand out as physically degraded pockets in the midst of affluent neighbourhoods. On the other hand, the slums in Siliguri and Baroda are primarily on unauthorised land inhabited mostly by migrants. Though most of the slum dwellers own their huts, the shelter situation is precarious.

All the slums in these cities however suffer from extremely inadequate basic facilities. There is heavy concentration of users as against the facilities available such as water taps, handpumps, bathrooms and other such facilities and in terms of per capita living space. They suffer in terms of basic health facilities and nutrition as well. As most of these slums are situated on encroached land belonging to public agencies, the city master plans do not provide the necessary permanent infrastructure in these areas. As a result whatever minimum services exist in the slums have been provided entirely on an ad hoc basis.

Demographic and Social Profiles

The 1600 households surveyed in our study consisted of 8,923 persons, 4,616 of them were male and 4,309 female indicating a sex-ratio of 934, which is higher than the all India average of 929. Table 4.6 shows while in Bhilwara and Siliguri it is much higher than the average, for Sambalpur it is lower at 921 and for Baroda it is a significantly low 870. However, in all the cities, except Baroda, the sex ratio in slums is much higher than the city average.

Out of a total of 1600 households 48.5 per cent are migrants and the percentage of migrant households is the maximum in Siliguri (74), in Baroda more than half of the surveyed households are migrants. It is minimal in Bhilwara (27). A majority of the migrant households came to the city mainly in search of jobs, barring Siliguri where a substantial proportion shifted to the city because of different socio-political reasons as mentioned earlier.

More than half (53.7 per cent) of the surveyed households belong to the Scheduled Castes and Tribes. In Baroda the percentage of such households is as high as 78. A majority of the households in each city speak in their respective state languages. A substantial segment (31 per cent) of households in Baroda speak in languages other than the state language Gujarati. This is due to its industrial character. People from different states have flocked there in search of employment opportunities in industrial establishments.

The educational background of the male members in the slums however, is not very poor in any city, and in Siliguri it is very high as 70 per cent of them are literate. Female literacy, however, varies significantly from one city to another though Siliguri ranks highest in this aspect also. In Bhilwara on the other hand only 17 per cent women are literate (Table 6.5).

Table 6.4
Demographic and Social Characteristics of Households

City	Number of persons			Sex ratio	Average household size	Per cent households			
	Male	Female	Total			Migrants	SC/ST	Majority religion (Hindu)	Majority language (*)
Baroda	1052	915	1967	870	5	51	78	92	69(G)
Bhilwara	1212	1185	2397	978	6	27	51	90	100(H)
Sambalpur	1186	1092	2278	921	6	42	42	96	89(O)
Siliguri	1164	1117	2281	960	6	74	44	92	85(B)
Total	4614	4309	8923	934	5.6	48.5	53.7	92.5	-

Source: Field Survey, ISS, 1992.
* G - Gujarati, H - Hindi, B - Bengali, O - Oriya.

Table 6.5
Educational Background of Adult Members

(Per cent)

Level of adult education	Baroda		Bhilwara		Sambalpur		Siliguri	
	Male	Female	Male	Female	Male	Female	Male	Female
Up to Primary School	11	5	23	13	19.4	14.0	16	12
Middle School	16	8	21	3	15.2	5.4	20	12
High School	25	4	9	1	18.9	4.1	23	12
Above High School	3	3	4	0	8.0	2.3	11	1
Total literate	55	20	57	17	59.5	25.9	70	37

Source: Field Survey, ISS, 1992.

Employment Profile and Economic Background

The relatively better educational status of the male population in the slums however has not ensured better job prospects for them. The surveyed households in the cities in our study centres reflect the typical characteristics of the urban poor who suffer from chronic unemployment and underemployment and lack of education and training to participate in the growing economic activities.

This becomes clearer from the data on participation in economic activities among the slum households as observed in Table 6.6. Except in Sambalpur, where it is marginally lower than the city average, in three other cities the work force participation rate is significantly lower than that for the entire city. It is surprising that the industrial development of the city has not ensured better job opportunities for slum households in Baroda. While the participation rate is lower than the city average in all the cities, it is the minimum in Baroda slums. The number of employed persons per family is only one in Baroda while it is 1.46 in Bhilwara, 1.69 in Siliguri and 1.66 in Sambalpur. This abnormally low level of workers in the city of Baroda may be due to a very low level of female participation rate in the workforce. The percentage of female workers is almost negligible in Baroda (2.3 per cent), while it is 9.22 per cent in the case of Siliguri, 11.54 per cent in that of Sambalpur and 7.3 per cent in Bhilwara.

Table 6.6
Distribution of Workers over Types of Employment

City	Per cent workers to city popula-tion (1991)	No. of workers in sur-veyed slums	Per cent of workers to polula-tion of surveyed slums	Percentage Distribution of Workers over Type of Employment		
				Self-employed	Regular Job	Irregular Job
Baroda	31.6	445	22.5	21	40	39
Bhilwara	31.9	582	24.0	21	28	51
Sambalpur	29.85	665	29.0	40	23	34
Siliguri	35.1	675	30.4	51	25	24

Source: Census of India, 1991b; Field Survey, ISS, 1992.

The distribution of job holders over self-employed, regular and irregular categories shows that a significant percentage of them are engaged in self-employment activities and irregular jobs and Siliguri has the highest percentage of self-employed workers.

Because of this employment status household incomes are very low and the large family size makes the per capita income further lower in all the cities. Table 6.7 shows the income-expenditure profile of the surveyed households in the four cities. Here again, despite having the maximum percentage of workers engaged in regular jobs (40) and a relatively smaller family size Baroda has the lowest monthly household income. It is much less than each of the other three cities. This suggests that a high level of industrialisation in the city has not provided adequate employment to its burgeoning population who were mostly unskilled labourers. As a result they remained unemployed or had to fall back upon petty jobs with minimum wages. In all the other three cities though people are engaged more in self-employment activities or have irregular jobs, their monthly household income is comparatively high.

The monthly income of the poor households, however, falls short of meeting the minimum monthly expenditure in most cases. While in Sambalpur and Bhilwara the income is marginally higher than the expenditure, in Baroda and Siliguri expenditure is much higher.

Table 6.7
Income-Expenditure Profile of Households

City	Average monthly household income (Rs.)	Average monthly household expenditure (Rs.)	Per capita monthly income (Rs.)	Per capita monthly expenditure (Rs)	Per cent household below poverty line
Baroda	658	698	137	142	76.3
Bhilwara	1080	817	166	131	77.6
Sambalpur	1065	1039	187	182	57.5
Siliguri	919	975	161	171	60.2

Source: Field Survey, ISS, 1992.

The high expenditure and comparatively low level of income have led to the high incidence of poverty in all the slums. In the surveyed slums, the percentage of people below the poverty-line is very high in each city. More than half of the population in each city belongs to this category. This is exceedingly high when compared to the Planning Commission estimate which shows that only 20 per cent of the population in urban areas in the country is poor. This indicates that a majority of the urban poor in any city is concentrated in its slums.

It can be assessed from the above observations that the twin components of lack of sufficient income and inadequate employment opportunities on the one hand and high expenditure on the other have left the slum dwellers with hardly any scope for savings. This not only testifies to an interrelationship between growing poverty and slum formation, but also contributes to their perpetuation and expansion. Thus, a vicious circle of slums being the centres of poverty and poverty as the breeding ground of slums makes it difficult for the people to break out.

Role of Nehru Rozgar Yojana in Poverty Alleviation

In the context of the economic background of the slum households it is necessary to discuss the implementation of the Nehru Rozgar Yojana (NRY) the income generation programme which is being implemented along with the Basic Services Programme as a strategy of integrated poverty alleviation in slums. The NRY though a very new programme has been taken up by all the case study centres. However the components of the programme adopted in the cities are not always uniform. In Siliguri for example only the scheme of Housing and Shelter Upgradation (SHASU) was being implemented at the time of our survey. In the other three cities the Scheme of Urban Micro Enterprise (SUME) has been taken up by the local authority. The spread of the programme however has varied in each case as the Table 6.8 shows.

The access of the programme has been most widespread in Siliguri where 81 per cent of the surveyed households in slums applied for loans and 73 per cent received them. Next is the case of Sambalpur where 38 per cent households applied for loan under SUME but 31 per cent received them. In Bhilwara and Baroda the spread of the programme is minimum where only 4 and 10 per cent households applied for loans though a fewer number received them.

Table 6.8
Awareness About NRY and Access to the Loan Facilities

City	Households aware about NRY (per cent)	Households applied for loan		Households received loan	
		Number	Per cent	Number	Per cent
Baroda	10	40	10	5	12
Bhilwara	29	16	4	16	100
Sambalpur	72	152	38	47	31
Siliguri	92	326	81	237	73

Source: Field Survey, ISS, 1992.

The reasons for the poor access of the people to the loan facility as identified in our survey were mainly lack of information. A relatively better access to the loan facility in Siliguri and Sambalpur were because of the high awareness among the people. While in Sambalpur and Siliguri a very high percentage of households (72 and 92 respectively) knew about the programmes, in Baroda and Bhilwara such percentages were abnormally low (Table 6.7). Despite having very low per capita income and high percentage of below-poverty level population, the city government did not take much initiative to reach the programme to the people even though a significant portion of funds on this account has remained unused.

The success of the shelter upgradation programme in Siliguri however did not verify the fulfilment of the objective of employment generation through shelter related works in the town, though it has definitely improved the shelter condition of the slum households to some extent. In Sambalpur the beneficiaries of loans under SUME stated that their incomes had improved though perhaps only marginally after meeting their monthly instalment payments. In Siliguri where the record of regular instalment payment is impressively high, through the special drive of door-to-door collection by the local government it may be expected that the programme will spread to a larger number of people and employment generation through training activities in shelter related activities will be taken up by the local body in the near future.

Access to Housing and Basic Amenities

The extent of poverty in slums however cannot be measured only in terms of economic deprivation, as manifestation of poverty is 'multi-dimensional' in nature and should include quality of living environment, reflected by quality of housing, access to safe water and sanitation, and physical well-being (Independent South Asian Commission, 1993). Our survey shows that poverty in slums is aggravated by poor shelter and basic service condition.

Despite the fact that the ownership of huts is vested in the households in a majority of cases in all the towns, the ownership of land has not been granted to them. Bhilwara is the only city where the percentage of *pucca* houses is the highest. It must be mentioned here that the standard of *kachcha* houses in Sambalpur differs to a great extent from what those in Siliguri or in Baroda. While in Sambalpur these mud houses have thatched roofs, typically rural in their characteristics, in Siliguri and Baroda they are dilapidated shanties made of rejected tin sheets and tarpaulins. Therefore, it is difficult to use the standard definition of *Kachcha* houses while describing the shelter conditions in slums in the different cities. As Baroda is a metropolitan city, the congestion in houses is much more as the average number of rooms for a household consisting of five members is only 1, while in the other three cities it is 2 (Table 6.9).

Table 6.9
Housing Conditions of Households

(*Per cent households*)

City	Type of Housing					
	Pucca	Semi-*pucca*	*Kachcha*	Ownership of huts	Average No. of rooms	Per cent electrified
Baroda	3	41	56	96	1	69
Bhilwara	71	16	13	86	2	71
Sambalpur	5	24	71	77	2	50
Siliguri	18	13	68	96	2	23

Source: Field Survey, ISS, 1992.

Access to basic amenities being provided under different government sponsored programmes including the UBS also differ from city to city. The most critical need are the sanitation and sewerage facilities which are equally precarious in all the cities. Though water is available to almost all the households in the four cities, the sources vary and depending on source and local condition the adequacy and quality of water also varies.

Table 6.10
Status of Water Supply

(*Per cent household*)

City	Tap water source	Water source inside the premise	Adequate water supply
Baroda	74	12	40
Bhilwara	46	25	75
Sambalpur	56	9	57
Siliguri	11	49	96

Source: Field Survey, ISS, 1992.

In terms of water availability Siliguri households have the best access. The percentage of households having water source inside the premises and having adequate water are quite significant in Siliguri (49 and 96 respectively) (Table 6.10). It is important to note here the observation that in Baroda as in any other metro city the water supply authority does provide protected water supply through taps to almost all the sections of people and also to the poor through community sources, which is almost free, though the quantity of water is mostly insufficient. In smaller cities on the other hand, more households have to fend for themselves in view of the city authorities' inability to reach protected water to the people especially the poor. Therefore they have to spend more on such facilities than their counterparts in large cities.

The surveyed households in the slums of Siliguri are in a better position in terms of toilet facilities also. While 75 per cent of slum households have independent toilets, in Baroda it is only 9 per cent, in Bhilwara 18 per cent and in Sambalpur it is 23 per cent. Over and above this, in the case of Baroda, the percentage of households having no latrine facility is the maximum (above 90 per cent).

In terms of drainage and garbage disposal facilities also the condition in Baroda slums is the worst - only 13 per cent households have some kind of drainage facilities while this percentage is 54, 24 and 60 of Bhilwara, Sambalpur and Siliguri respectively. Therefore the overall service condition is critical in the slums of all the cities, but in the metro city it is the worst.

The availability of social infrastructure such as health and non-formal education facilities which are being provided especially under the UBS programme say a great deal about the nature of implementation and the degree of people's reaction and awareness about these programmes.

Immunisation is carried out under different central and state sponsored health programmes in the cities besides UBS and it is worth noting that though percentages of children immunised in the surveyed slums clusters vary from city to city, and across slum clusters within a city, the involvement of the people and also the local authorities determine the degree of success of these programmes. In Siliguri, for example, the slum households have to go to the municipal dispensary for getting their children immunised, in Sambalpur and Baroda however, the health workers from the municipality visit the local slums and ensure immunisation. The latter method has led to more immunised (64 per cent) children in Sambalpur and Baroda (77 per cent) than in Siliguri (43 per cent). In Siliguri two reasons were highlighted by the people for not taking children for immunisation. While 34 per cent of them cited shortage of time as the reason, as high as 48 per cent reported that they did not know about the immunisation programme. This is an important aspect which needs more intervention from the local government.

The effect of the family planning programme is the example of the KAP (Knowledge, Attitude and Practice) gap in the slums of the surveyed cities. The awareness or knowledge about contraception is high in all cities the attitude towards it, especially of women is also positive, but very few people adopt the measures and if they adopt it at all it is the women who do so. In the case of Bhilwara 61 per cent couples do not use any contraception, in the city of Baroda it is 67 and in Siliguri and Sambalpur more than 52 per cent couples fall in this category. The reasons for the KAP gap are interesting to note (Table 6.11). Husband's reluctance to allow his wife to use contraception is the most frequently recorded reason highlighted by the women. Sambalpur is the only city where a significant percentage of households responded that they did not need to adopt any family planning measure. Further enquiry revealed that most of the couples in this category had either passed their reproductive age or they were widows.

Pre- and post natal care of mothers is another important concern of the UBS programme. It was observed in all the cities that pregnant mothers have become more concerned about pre and post natal care. A significant percentage of women are going in for pre-natal check-up in the hospital, opting for hospital delivery with the help of trained professional instead of going in for home delivery with untrained hands. The comparative studies in Baroda and Sambalpur with other similar studies conducted at different points of time by other agencies showed a definite improvement in this area.

Table 6.11
Reasons for Not Using Contraception

(Per cent Response from Women)

City	Husband does not allow	Facility not available	Doctor not co-operative	Not Needed	Not aware
Baroda	38	6	0	8	34
Bhilwara	33.0	1	1	14	5
Sambalpur	33.2	11.0	0	46.9	8.5
Siliguri	30.40	8.0	0	22	30

Source: Field Survey, ISS, 1992.

Pre-school education for children and non-formal education for adults are the other important objectives of UBS. However in both these areas the four case studies reveal results that are not so impressive. Involvement by the local bodies in terms of providing the infrastructure does not seem to be lacking as in almost all the slums balwadi schools and adult literacy centres have been opened but the use of these facilities by the target groups is limited. Table 6.12 shows that, although the percentage of illiterates is high in each surveyed area, the percentage of adult illiterates using the ALC facilities is insignificant.

Table 6.12
Use of ALCs by Adults

City	Level of Adult Illiteracy (Per cent)	Using ALC Facilities (Per cent)
Baroda	61.7	N.A
Bhilwara	65	N.A
Sambalpur	56	8
Siliguri	40	19

Note: N.A - Data not available because of negligible response.
Source: Field Survey, ISS, 1992.

The response for not using ALC is also important to note. The most oft-cited reason for not utilising the facilities as highlighted by both men and women respondents was the lack of time. The women were too busy either with their household chores or with their daily work if they were employed and the menfolk wanted to spend their leisure time in some other ways than in literacy classes. There seemed to be not much motivation for joining the classes. Many of them also thought it to be a sheer waste of time without any direct benefit accruing from it in terms of better job prospects.

The extent of use of pre-school facilities for children like Balwadi/Anganwadi schools was also found to be not very impressive in any of the case study centres.

Table 6.13
Use of Balwadi Schools

City	Percentage children going to balwadi centres
Baroda	23
Bhilwara	6
Sambalpur	17
Siliguri	36

Source: Field Survey, ISS, 1992.

In many cases the centres have been opened under the programme of Integrated Child Development Services (ICDS) or UBS but many of those had to be closed down for financial reasons, and even if the centres were functioning parents were not taking sufficient interest in sending children there. In Bhilwara for example more than 40 balwadi/anganwadi centres had been opened but many of them are not functioning now and because of this only 6 per cent children are going to these schools (Table 6.13). The infrastructure facilities like ALCs and balwadis which are being provided are not being used on a sustainable basis and the purpose of the programmes in such cases becomes defeated.

Income Class Variation and Access to Services

The above assessment of the access to facilities at city level gives an overall picture but does not provide any insight into the distributional aspect of basic services across income-classes in any city. The analysis of data on access to amenities over income classes shows that there is a considerable variation in the case of some specific services. Our observation reveal that even in slums the access of households to basic amenities in terms of private facilities, improves with increasing income levels. However community services like drainage and garbage collection and disposal do not improve with increase in income level.

In all the cities, in terms of housing amenities, greater percentages of households belonging to higher income categories have better facilities as regards quality of housing or pucca houses, in space, that is, in the number of rooms and also electrification. Siliguri is one exception where the average number of rooms per household is higher in the lowest income class. However, the number of rooms does not in any way ensure better quality of structure (Table 6.14).

In the same way Table 6.15 reveals that the percentage of households with adequate water supply increases with rising income. For water source inside the premise also the trend is similar. Households in higher income classes have independent water sources like wells or handpumps inside their premises to supplement the inadequate municipal water.

Proportionately higher income classes go in for independent toilets (Table 6.16). These observations indicate that there are income-class variations for some physical services which are available at the individual level with extra expenditure. The same observation holds good in the case of health facilities also (Table 6.17). The poorer among the poor are more dependent on community services which are not always available.

The monthly expenditure pattern of the households reveals that people spend more on individual services (Table 6.18) and those who spend in this manner usually belong to the top two income classes. For facilities like health services howevar the household belonging to all income classes have to spend a considerable amount of their monthly expenditure.

Table 6.18 reflects that in all cities a considerable percentage of average total expenditure on basic amenities is spent on services like electricity and private toilets, private doctors, and education while services like water supply and garbage disposal are expected to be provided by the municipality free of charges. Even the poor localities have shown this preference.

Table 6.14
Housing Condition and Access to Electricity Across Income Classes

Income Class (Rs)	Average number of rooms				Per cent Household with											
					Own house				*Pucca* house				Electricity			
	Ba	Bh	Sa	Si	Ba	Bh	Sa	Si	Ba	Bh	Sa	Si	Ba	Bh	Sa	Si
Less than 100	-	-	-	3	-	-	-	100	-	-	-	-	-	-	-	0
101 - 250	1	2	3	2	0	90	50	100	0	20	0	17	17	0	10	17
251 - 500	1	2	2	2	94	83	83	92	0	46	0	22	66	41	27	12
501 - 1000	2	2	2	2	97	79	77	93	2	67	2	8	72	69	37	14
1001 - 2000	2	3	3	2	98	89	82	97	16	82	4	36	74	90	62	43
Above 2000	-	3	3	3	-	91	92	100	-	82	18	33	-	97	76	22
All Classes	1	2	2	2	96	86	77	96	3	71	5	18	69	71	50	23

Source: Field Survey, ISS, 1992.
Note: Ba = Baroda; Bh = Bhilwara; Sa = Sambalpur; Si = Siliguri.
These abbreviation have been used in all following tables.

Table 6.15
Access to Water Supply Facilities Across Income Classes

(Per cent household)

Income class (Rs)	Water supply adequate				Water source inside & independent				Tap water source			
	Ba	Bh	Sa	Si	Ba	Bh	Sa	Si	Ba	Bh	Sa	Si
Less than 100	-	-	-	100	-	-	-	100	-	-	-	0
101 - 250	41	98	100	100	0	10	0	50	80	48	50	0
251 - 500	34	70	45	89	12	10	2	42	68	35	30	3
501 - 1000	48	95	44	95	15	22	5	78	85	40	51	5
1001 - 2000	37	14	57	97	8	33	12	61	62	52	68	5
More than 2000	-	100	47	100	-	48	11	63	-	55	68	4
All Classes	40	75	57	96	12	25	9	49	74	46	56	11

Source: Field Survey, ISS, 1992.

Table 6.16
Toilet Facilities Across Income Classes

(Per cent household)

Income class (Rs)	Having toilet facilities				Having independent toilet facilities				Toilet with flush system			
	Ba	Bh	Sa	Si	Ba	Bh	Sa	Si	Ba	Bh	Sa	Si
Less than 100	-	-	-	100	-	-	-	100	-	-	-	100
101 - 250	0	10	0	100	0	0	0	100	0	0	0	67
251 - 500	1	12	4	79	1	6	4	73	1	13	0	69
501 - 1000	11	17	13	75	9	13	13	69	9	15	0	73
1001 - 2000	30	30	18	85	18	27	18	78	15	30	9	81
More than 2000	-	42	32	95	-	42	32	93	-	48	0	89
All Classes	9	22	23	93	9	18	23	75	8	21	9	77

Source: Field Survey, ISS, 1992.

Table 6.17
Access to Health Care Facilities Across Income Class

(*Per cent household*)

Income class (Rs)	Government hospital				Private doctor			
	Ba	Bh	Sa	Si	Ba	Bh	Sa	Si
Less than 100	-	-	-	50	-	0	-	0
101 - 250	83	30	100	67	0	0	0	0
251 - 500	79	70	89	70	1	5	62	18
501 - 1000	84	69	94	74	0	11	61	20
1001 - 2000	78	74	91	48	0	17	59	36
More than 2000	-	70	92	48	-	15	47	30
All Classes	78	70	93	66	1	12	56	23

Source: Field Survey, ISS, 1992.

Table 6.18
Pattern of Monthly Expenditure on Amenities

City	Average household income (Rs.)	Average household expenditure (Rs)	Reported average expenditure on basic services (Rs.)	Percentage of expenditure on basic services					
				Electricity	Water supply	Toilet	Rent/ house tax etc.	Education (fees uniform books etc.)	Health
Baroda	658	698	176	26.1	0	0.2	0	31.4	39.3
Bhilwara	1080	817	350	5.3	3.6	36.3	15.0	36.5	6.5
Sambalpur	1065	1039	441	9.1	0	11.6	13.4	11.3	37.3
Siliguri	919	975	194	29.4	0	8.8	10.3	30.2	3.0

Source: Field Survey, ISS, 1992.
* Averages have been calculated on the basis of number of households reported spending on such services

Such types of income bias are not evident in case of the social services which are mainly being provided by the municipal bodies under the UBS programme. The spread of the services like mother and child care, which are the focus of the UBS programme, have been found to be moderate in general, as explained earlier but it is equally so among all the income classes (Table 6.19) in all the case study centres. The access to non-formal education like balwadi schools and Adult

Table 6.19
Utilisation of Mother and Child Care Facilities Across Income Class

Income Class (Rs)	Percent Women: Going for pre-natal check-up				Go to trained personnel for child delivery				Utilising family planning measures				Per cent children immunised			
	Ba	Bh	Sa	Si	Ba	Bh	Sa	Si	Ba	Bh	Sa	Si	Ba	Bh	Sa	Si
Less than 100	-	0	00	100	-	-	-	100	-	-	-	0	-	0	-	0
101 - 250	2	20	50	100	42	0	50	83	100	8	50	47	25	0	50	57
251 - 500	26	27	66	92	53	22	60	80	80	6	26	55	28	8	56	40
501 - 1000	31	40	69	80	55	22	69	79	74	7	35	47	34	30	64	34
1001 - 2000	11	49	81	95	78	28	77	83	100	6	45	50	32	50	74	30
More than 2000	-	73	84	63	-	42	84	79	-	8	32	45	-	60	49	21
All Classes	18	42	75	86	56	25	72	80	79	7	37	48	32	35	64	34

Source: Field Survey, ISS, 1992.

Literacy centres is low on the whole in all cities and there is no definite trend pointing to higher income classes using the facilities more (Table 6.20). These facilities as provided by the local bodies under different programmes if they function well are equally accessible to all income classes

Table 6.20
Utilisation of Educational Facilities under UBS Across Income Class

Income class (Rs)	Per cent children in balwadi				Per cent utilising ALC facility			
	Ba	Bh	Sa	Si	Ba	Bh	Sa	Si
Less than 100	-	-	-	0	-	-	-	0
101 - 250	8	0	0	0	0	0	0	23
251 - 500	18	1	5	33	0	0	2	22
501 - 1000	26	6	22	53	0	0	9	18
1001 - 2000	29	7	19	53	0	0	16	17
More than 2000	-	13	14	24	0	0	13	4
All Classes	22	6	17	36	0	0	8	19

Source: Field Survey, ISS, 1992.

Overall low access to these facilities as has been observed earlier may be attributed to three different factors.

First the non-availability of the facilities, second, the awareness among the people about such facilities and third, the lack of proper education about the necessity for such programmes. In many cases especially in Bhilwara and Siliguri it was observed that balwadi schools were opened under UBS and also under ICDS but they had to be closed down because of non-availability of funds.

The awareness about the UBS programme was also found to be varied among case study centres irrespective of income classes. The Table 6.21 show that the perception about UBS and its activities is still not very clear among the beneficiaries even after the continuation of the programme in these centres for the last five to six years at the time of the survey.

Table 6.21
Awareness about UBS over Income Classes

Income class (Rs)	Awareness about UBS				Awareness of community organiser				Discuss problems with RCUs			
	Ba	Bh	Sa	Si	Ba	Bh	Sa	Si	Ba	Bh	Sa	Si
Less than 100	0	0	0	100	0	0	0	100	0	0	0	100
101 - 250	67	10	100	100	67	20	100	100	42	10	100	67
251 - 500	53	21	53	98	50	17	53	94	70	16	32	86
501 - 1000	58	25	74	95	57	20	75	96	70	13	66	91
1001 - 2000	60	33	89	99	62	17	81	100	86	8	74	94
More than 2000	0	39	87	96	0	21	74	63	10	15	68	93
All Classes	57	28	79	96	55	19	73	95	71	12	64	91

Source: Field Survey, ISS, 1992.

The awareness level is the highest in Siliguri (96 per cent), next comes Sambalpur (79 per cent). In Bhilwara the response is significantly low – only 28 per cent respondents knew about the programmes. In Sambalpur and Siliguri a very high percentage of respondents also know the community organiser in charge of their slums; in the case of Bhilwara only 19 per cent respondents replied that they knew the community organiser; and in Baroda even after the long association of the CO with the local community through the community development programme, only half of the households were aware of the programme and also the CO. In Siliguri, interaction of the local community with the local resident volunteer was maximum. In Baroda and Sambalpur also it was satisfactory. In Bhilwara the response of households in this aspect also was very poor.

Though many other factors like availability of time, enough motivation and so on help in influencing the level of participation, it has been observed that high awareness usually tends to greater cooperation and participation.

In the UBS programme different mechanisms have been developed to facilitate the flow of information. In both directions there is scope for wider interaction. Meetings of Neighbourhood Committees, meetings with COs, with other municipal officials, health functionaries are to be organised under UBS for useful and effective communication among the beneficiaries and the service delivering organisation. In Baroda a significant proportion of allocated funds has been spent on such meetings. In Sambalpur and Siliguri also awareness has been created by the COs and other Volunteers. However there is need for wider interaction at the grassroots level.

UBS as a Strategy for Participatory Development Programme: Inferences from Case Studies

The Urban Basic Services Programme was conceived on the basic tenet of community participation at all levels. Making the local body the nodal implementing and monitoring agency of the programme, democratic decentralisation and participation at the political level was ensured and making the neighbourhood development committee responsible at the slum level, people's representation and involvement at the grassroots level was expected. Besides, participation by local NGOs was also expected to supplement the effort. It is in this context that the roles of local bodies and the role of the people through

Neighbourhood Committees are important to assess. The household surveys conducted in the four case study centres and the interaction with the local officials as presented in the preceding chapters throw light on these issues.

The Neighbourhood Committee at the slum is the formal organisation at the lowest level which is supposed to provide the leadership in a collective form. The leadership in such cases means making people aware of such programmes, identifying basic services needs, seeking consensus from the community, drawing mini plans based on felt-needs, taking them to the local body and being able to get those incorporated with the city plan. The next stage is to help the local bodies in implementing these projects. Once the projects are over, the task is to motivate people in using the facilities and properly maintaining them. It is expected that the NHC will participate in resource generation also through local contribution so that it supplements the allocated funds. A revolving fund is to be generated through contribution from the municipality or the UNICEF and a matching fund from the community which will be used for undertaking some current expenditure and for providing small loans to women for income generating centres and for use in emergencies. This fulfils in one way the participation and the objective of decentralisation and financial empowerment to the grassroots level.

Our survey in the four cities give diverse picture in so far as the above aspects of community involvement are concerned. The formation of NHC is the basic requirement of the UBS programme in any slum. Because of this these committees have been formed in almost all the slums. For example, in Sambalpur there are 47 NHCs in 47 slums. However these committees are not always functioning as expected. At the organisational level involvement of the people in the NHC is very low among surveyed households. Out of all the 1600 households surveyed only 12 per cent in Sambalpur and 7 per cent in Siliguri are directly involved with the programme as resident volunteers. In the other two cities, the responses in this effect were negligible. It has been observed that the president of the NHC once selected has continued to hold the position for a long time and there is very little chances for others to be selected. If the presidents, secretaries and others are selected on a rotational basis for specific periods, then others in the locality may take interest and be involved in the NHC activities.

The aspect of financial empowerment of the grassroots level

organisation that is NHC is however evident to some extent only in Sambalpur. The revolving fund has been created by all the NHCs in Sambalpur, and in some cases it has been working well. Each NHC has a corpus of Rs. 5,000 and additional funds have been allocated in case of those which are functioning better. The NHC provides small loans at nominal interest to women bearing partial expenditures for teachers of ALCs, creches, balwadis and so forth. This type of financial empowerment is however absent in other cities. Therefore when the Constitutional Amendment are being effected to empower local bodies in terms of financial autonomy through proper devolution of fund from the state to the local bodies there is reluctance on the part of the local bodies to part with financial power to the grassroots level. The NHCs under the guidance of the CO can handle financial matters effectively if they are given chance.

The involvement of NGOs and other prominent citizens of the city in the running of the UBS has also been one of the objectives of UBS. It is important to note such involvement in the surveyed cities. Though NGO involvement was negligible, except in Baroda, the participation by outsiders either as volunteers or as paid workers is noticeable in Bhilwara and Siliguri. In Bhilwara the system of "Trainers on Call" who are experts in different fields are providing their services when needed and even the volunteers also come from outside sometimes.

Siliguri however is an exception where the system of involvement of those other than the beneficiaries has been institutionalised by the local government. Local youths are engaged as volunteers on a monthly payment basis. They work as ALC teachers, community volunteers, balwadi teachers and so on.

Involvement of these people by the local body has no doubt helped implementing the programme and it has been observed from our study and also from other evaluative studies on Siliguri. The UBS programme in Siliguri is relatively better in providing some basic physical amenities to the slums. In keeping with its Marxist background the city government wants to use community participation as an instrument of urban development as weell as party-building through popular mobilisation. The experiences of UBS in Siliguri though reveal that the political parties in a democratic polity can easily reach the urban poor and achieve considerable success in political mobilisation and political recruitment (Mukhopadhyaya, 1993), this becomes however a very workable proposition only when the political atmosphere is stable and long sustaining at the state as well as the local level. West Bengal State and the Siliguri municipality may be exceptions in this regard. In the frequently changing power structure in the state and at the local level in the country, any change may bring about total collapse in the system and people at the grassroots level may find it difficult to exert themselves in the changed scenario. Therefore, decentralisation and the "empowerment approach", rather than the "delivery approach" is needed. The people at the grassroots level should be involved not as affiliates but as participants in development for the sustainability of any community based programme.

The Siliguri experiences further show that the democratic decentralisation though percolates up to the local government level so far as the implementation of the programme is concerned, the unwillingness to delegate decision-making powers to the local level on the part of the local body has limited the mass involvement and local initiatives in the programme. The programme has remained still a top-down service delivery programme instead of being the reverse. The municipality is providing more physical amenities and loans for housing upgradation than for committing itself to social development. Therefore the objective of UBS to provide a link between social development and physical development through community involvement is being defeated. As social development needs awareness creation and total involvement of the society, it takes time. Therefore the UBS which was till very recently a very structured programme with specific targets to be achieved within a very short period of time, could not really achieve the kind of success expected. In most cases instead of community development, the local governments have placed emphasis on physical development which is easy to provide. The revised UBSP should try to institutionalise community participation with greater emphasis.

The commitment of the local bodies in the implementation of the programme is however the most important indicator of the success of the programmes. The magnitude of the problems though differing from city to city, the degree of involvement of the local government through financial support, programme formulation staff supports and so forth are important in reaching the services to the people.

As uniform data were not available from municipal sources a clear comparable picture does not emerge. Nevertheless the UBS expenditure pattern of the municipalities as discussed in the previous chapters indicates their prioritisation in goal selection. While Siliguri municipality has placed maximum emphasis on water supply and sanitation and education both formal and non-formal, Bhilwara has spent the maximum on sewerage and toilet construction and hand pump installation. Baroda Municipal Corporation has also spent a relatively higher percentage of its total expenditure on sanitation and drinking water compared to Siliguri and Bhilwara.

It is disturbing to note that a very high percentage of the total expenditure is spent as administrative expenditure in Baroda (53) while it is restricted to 10-12 per cent in the case of Siliguri and in Sambalpur it ranges between 20 and 25 per cent.

Baroda being a metropolitan city with a slum population as much as the total population of the other case study cities like Bhilwara and Sambalpur, has sanctioned a staff strength of 2 POs and 7 COs. Therefore with uniform allocation for the UBS projects in all cities it is difficult to keep the organisational expenditure to a minimum. The revised financing pattern of UBSP on a per capita basis (Rs. 60) may remove this discrepancy in the new project towns. However shifting of the financing responsibility of the old UBS projects to the state sector will be more difficult to continue even at the minimum sustainable level. The state and local governments which are perennially under financial constraint will find it further difficult to arrange funds. The experiences with other programmes like EIUS has shown that with the withdrawal of the central government's financial support the state governments find it difficult to allocate funds from state budget. The central government also on the other hand loses its control over the programme in terms of monitoring and evaluation. Therefore there is need for continuation of central sector financial help in the programme even for the old project towns till it takes its deep root and achieves the level of sustainability without outside help.

Summary

Our study of four cities brings out some important observations, some of which are general and some specific to our household survey on UBS. These observations can be summarised as follows:

1. Although the rates of growth of all urban centres are slowing down, the total population has increased considerably in all the case study centres.
2. The economic background of the cities differs to a great extent.

3. Based on the economic background of the city differ the employment structure workforce participation rates among men and women and economic background of the population.
4. The income generation programme for poverty alleviation though it has started very recently, has not picked up yet. Access to these loans is very limited in all the cities. Though in Siliguri such loans have improved the shelter condition to some extent, they have not helped improve the economic condition as the training component of the shelter upgradation scheme has not been emphasised.
5. Pressure on infrastructure facilities has increased tremendously. All the centres are suffering from inadequate water supply, toilet facilities, educational facilities, health facilities and so forth though the intensity of the problem varies.
6. There has been a tremendous growth in slums and slum population during the last few decades. Even though the rate of growth of the city population has decreased, the rate of growth of the slum population has increased manifold.
7. The shelter structure in the slums varies from city to city, though the slums in all the cities suffer from insufficient basic services and environmental degradation.
8. Contrary to the notion that not all the slum dwellers are poor, our survey shows that even in slums there are disparities. Though the majority are poor a significant proportion of households in our survey belong to the middle-income group.
9. Workforce participation rates are high in slums even among women compared to that in the city as a whole though it varies to a great extent from city to city.
10. The literacy rate among slum households is not very low as compared to the city population.
11. There is differential access to basic services across income-classes. Higher income-classes have more individual services than the poor who are mainly dependent on the community services.
12. Expenditure on some basic amenities is quite significant for all income-classes, and for some services it varies directly with the income.
13. The responses of the local bodies towards solving the problems has been varied. Siliguri municipality has done relatively better in this respect.

14. The responses of non-governmental organisations in helping the city government to solve the problems of the city have been significant in the city of Baroda.
15. The major findings about the functioning of the UBS can be listed according to the principal objectives of the programme namely; (i) providing minimum basic amenities, (ii) focus on women and children (iii) community participation, and (iv) convergence of concurrently running programmes.

(i) *Provision of Basic Amenities*: Municipal responses in the provision of basic amenities through the UBS have been varied. Siliguri and Sambalpur municipalities have done relatively well in the provision of some physical amenities like water and sanitation facilities.

(ii) *Woman and Child Focus*: There has been a significant effect in these aspects. Women have become aware of pre and post natal care and are going in for regular health check-up and opting for hospital delivery. In this case again the effect varies from city to city.

(iii) *Community Participation*: Some social infrastructure like balwadi schools, adult literacy centres, immunisation facilities, though being provided by the local agencies are not being used by the households as expected.

At the organisational level also the participation of the surveyed households is limited. Although the neighbourhood development committees have been set up, they are not very effective always in expressing the felt needs of the community.

Interaction of the local people and the UBS staff at the municipal level is very important for the sustainability of the programme. Siliguri may be cited as the success of the right type of municipal staff while in Sambalpur both the elements are present, but the people's own interest is predominant. In the long run the Sambalpur example is expected to take more firm roots in terms of empowerment to the people which is the main objective of the programme.

As a programme with the objective of involving the local women in all stages, Sambalpur UBS is more successful. All the neighbourhood committees are formed by women who take special interest in the local activities.

(iv) *Convergence of the Programmes*: The facilities like water supply, sanitation, drainage and so forth must be provided by the local government under the programmes of Environmental Improvement of Urban Slums, Low Cost Sanitation, in addition to UBS. However very limited access to these services by the people indicates that there has not been proper convergence of these programmes at the local level.

CONCLUSION

Provision of basic services in poor localities through people's involvement has been an age-old tradition in rural India. An attempt was made to replicate the experience in urban low income localities through the adoption of Urban Community Development Projects during the early years of planned development in the country. However the attempt failed in most of the cities with a few exceptions like Hyderabad, Visakhapatanam and so on. Various other programmes such as Environmental Improvement of Urban Slums, Integrated Development of Small and Medium Towns, Low Cost Sanitation Programmes, Sites and Services Programmes, Slum Upgradation Programmes and others which were launched during the subsequent plan periods, were mainly development programmes planned, implemented by the government authorities. The programmes however did not change the scenario much in terms of the access to shelter and basic services for the urban poor. During the early eighties serious concern was expressed by urban experts on the fast deteriorating conditions in the quality of city life and on environmental degradation. Government seriously considered some policy changes and took some initiatives in setting up a Task Force on Urban Development in 1981 which studied the urban issues in minute detail furnished its report in four volumes in 1983, incorporating concrete suggestions on urban planning, management of urban development, policies for slum and squatter development and so forth. Further initiative was taken in 1986 with the setting up of the National Commission on Urbanisation, which through its various sub-committees did in-depth studies into the urban problems and recommended policy changes in all spheres of urban development.

These reports were important landmarks in the field of government initiatives in urban development. Both the reports recognised that one of the reasons for the failure of the above programmes in ameliorating urban poverty and reaching basic services to the poor was the non-involvement of the community at the grassroots level in the programmes and the inadequacy of the top-down services delivery approach. The reports emphasised the need for community based development programmes with community involvement as agents of development and second, the need for integrated development through the convergence of all the programmes at the local level to reduce the possibility of overlapping.

The Urban Basic Services programme was initiated in the mid-eighties as a strategy for community development with the bottom-up approach based on self-help. The programme has been improved upon and renamed as Urban Basic Services for the Poor in 1990. Its emphasis is on the integration of the programme with other concurrently running urban poverty alleviation programmes at institutional and financial levels.

The analysis of our field survey data relating to the extent of urban poverty, availability of basic services and people's participation in the slums of four cities and the strategy of planned intervention through the community based poverty alleviation programmes shows that these interventions, though successful to some extent, could not make much of a dent in so far as the availability of basic minimum facilities is concerned.

In this context, the question may arise whether merely a greater emphasis on a community-based approach will lead to a better access of the poor to improved facilities such as health care, environmental sanitation, water supply, education etc. This leads to certain issues relating to the strategies adopted for financing, implementing and managing the urban poverty alleviation programmes through participatory approach.

It must be emphasised that the basic tenet of successful project implementation through the self-help approach is the effective combination of software components like community awareness, community institutions (neighbourhood committees), trained human resource (dedicated resident volunteers at the grassroots level and community organisers at the local level), on the one hand and hardware in the form of basic physical and social infrastructure, on the other. While the physical infrastructure includes provision of water supply facilities, roads, electric posts, drainage facilities and such like, the social infrastructure includes community centres, *balwadi* schools, training centres for income generation programmes, health centres and so forth. While the community can play a very important role in contributing to the software, the provision of hardware in poor localities to a great extent depends on the public authorities in charge of various service departments. However, for such departments provision of services to slum localities is of secondary importance because of the structures being unauthorised and other limitations.

In the face of the apathy of the public authorities to provide services to the poor through their regular development works, the programme implementation agencies for poor localities, especially the local bodies, have to increasingly depend on allocations from the government under different programmes which in relation to the requirements are meagre. The shifting of financial responsibilities, partially, on the part of the central and state governments to the local bodies makes the situation worse. Over a period of time the expenditure for development purposes from their own resources has been reduced to a great extent in all local bodies. And often matching grants from the centre are not forthcoming unless the state government fulfils its commitment. In addition, the programmes are so designed that a very large percentage of the allocation amount is taken up by establishment costs. Thus the available funds are too thinly spread over a large number of schemes. And because of the non-availability of adequate funds on many occasions people's participation in terms of creating adequate demand for services through carefully chalked out mini-plans at the neighbourhood committee level does not make much headway. Very few schemes so formulated find their place in the municipal action plans and even those which do, get further diluted at the district level. In such circumstances without proper decentralisation of financial powers to the local government level these programmes may not be expected to make sufficient impact on the quality of life of the poor.

In so far as the strategies for programme implementation are concerned, the basic democratic institutional setting is the local self-government. But within the municipal government this approach faces a major difficulty. First, elected representatives tend to perceive it as a threat to their support base if the objectives of the political and community leaders are not congruent (Malhotra, 1989). In the UBS organisational structure the only link between the UBS and the municipality is the Municipal Chairman. The non-involvement of elected representatives in the project management group at the town level, often creates such conflicts on account of which the programme suffers and the resource allocation cannot be effected in favour of the poor. It is, therefore, important that local elected representatives be involved in all such development programmes which influence the quality of life of their people.

In the participatory development process the poor should operate as conscious "subjects" of change and not as "passive recipients." The underlying assumption is that the poor are creative and are capable of taking initiatives for their development (Independent South Asian Commission, 1993). The neighbourhood committee at the lowest level is expected to provide leadership at the grassroots level and help residents articulate their needs for services in a more effective and organised way. "As participatory urban services are people based, it is not uncommon that strong leadership and successful delivery are positively related" (Yeung and McGee, 1988). Therefore, there is need for proper training of the functionaries. In the revised UBSP system a vast network has been established for training the workers at the grassroots level. State level and national level institutions have also been identified for training the trainers. It is expected that this will change the situation in future and effective leadership through strong neighbourhood committees will emerge from the grassroots level.

In order to provide effective leadership the neighbourhood committees are also to be made financially strong. If all these committees are registered under the Act they can have access to institutional finance. In addition to the funds available under various programmes provision can be made so that supplementary funds can be borrowed by the Committee from the financial institutions at concessional rates of interest. Our analysis of data on access to basic services across income class has confined the observation that the provision of essential infrastructure services such as water supply, sanitation and garbage collection in low-income settlements are very much issues of communities and neighbourhoods. They are problems which are not solved by individual action: nor do improvements in family income necessarily lead to improvements in living conditions (Lee, 1993). Therefore a mechanism should be developed by which a part of the additional income generated through the income generation programme like NRY is contributed by the households to the revolving fund in the NHC for infrastructure development. For the maintenance of the infrastructure provided by the municipality the NHC can charge token fees and the responsibility of collection should be with the committee.

From the management aspect, the strategies of convergence of the programmes and integrated approach of service delivery have been adopted. However, the involvement of multiple authorities makes coordination difficult at the municipal level. Even the state governments department do not always oblige the municipality in terms of priorities. In such cases inter-agency coordination and negotiation with officials become more important for the functionaries at the local level than interaction with the beneficiaries.

In such cases the involvement of NGOs is important. However, an important lacuna in the programmes especially in the UBS is the limited involvement of NGOs. NGO participation is important for effective monitoring of the programme, motivating people, creating effective demand by working as intermediaries between the local government and the beneficiaries. Very few NGOs come forward to play this effective role especially in government funded programmes. There is need for involving voluntary agencies for sustaining development by maintaining the services with active participation from the beneficiaries, once the government agencies withdraw from the project area after providing the basic infrastructure.

REFERENCES

Census of India, (1991a). *Provisional Population Totals: Rural-Urban Distribution,*, Office of Registrar General, New Delhi.

--------, (1991b). *Provisional Population Totals: Workers and Their Distribution*, Office of the Registrar General, New Delhi.

Independent South Asian Commission (1993). *Meeting the Challenge*, Report, SAARC Secretariat, Kathmandu.

Lee Yok Shiu F, (1993), "Community Based Urban Environmental Management; Local NGOs as Catalysts" - Paper prepared for Kitakyushu Conference on Urban Environmental Management in Asia, Japan.

Malhotra, D. D. (1989). "Local Institutional Framework for Programme Implementation", Girish K. Mishra and M. K. Narain, (ed.) in *Development Programme for Urban Poor*, Centre for Urban Studies, Institute of Public Administration, New Delhi.

Mukhopadhyaya Ashok, (1993), "Community Participation in Urban Development" in Bidyut Mohanty (ed.) *Urbanisation in Developing Countries*, Concept, New Delhi.

6. Yeung, Y. N, and McGee, T. G, (1986), 'Conclusion', in Y. N. Yeung and T. G. McGee (eds) *Community Participation in Delivering Urban Services in Asia*, International Development Research Centre, Ottawa.

ABBREVIATIONS

ALC	–	Adult Literacy Centre
BCC	–	Baroda Citizens Council
BMC	–	Baroda Municipal Corporation
CI	–	Composite Index
CO	–	Community Organiser
CSLA	–	Community Savings and Loan Association
CV	–	Coefficient of Variation
DRI	–	Differential Rate of Interest
DUDA	–	District Urban Development Authority
EIUS	–	Environmental Improvement of Urban Slums
ESCAP	–	Economic and Social Commission for Asia and the Pacific
EWS	–	Economically Weaker Section
GIDC	–	Gujarat Industrial Development Corporation
GNP	–	Gross National Product
HUDCO	–	Housing and Urban Development Corporation
IBS	–	Ideal Basic Services
ICDS	–	Integrated Child Development Services
IDSMT	–	Integrated Development of Small & Medium Towns
IMR	–	Infant Mortality Rate
ISS	–	Institute of Social Sciences
IUDP	–	Integrated Urban Development Programme
KAP	–	Knowledge, Attitude and Practice
LCH	–	Low Cost Housing
LCS	–	Low Cost Sanitation
LIC	–	Life Insurance Corporation
LIG	–	Low Income Group
LQ	–	Location Quotient
MAC	–	Mutual Aid Committee

MC	–	Municipal Corporation/Council
MFC	–	Municipal Finance Commission
NCU	–	National Commission on Urbanisation
NGO	–	Non Governmental Organisation
NHC	–	Neighbourhood Committee
NIUA	–	National Institute of Urban Affairs
NRY	–	Nehru Rozgar Yojana
NSS	–	National Sample Survey
ORG	–	Operations Research Group
PHC	–	Primary Health Centre
PO	–	Project Officer
RCUES	–	Regional Centre for Urban and Environmental Studies
SAARC	–	South Asian Association for Regional Cooperation
SC	–	Scheduled Caste
SD	–	Standard Deviation
SEPUP	–	Self-Employment Programme for Urban Poor
SHASU	–	Scheme of Housing and Shelter Upgradation
SJDA	–	Siliguri-Jalpaiguri Development Authority
SMA	–	Sambalpur Municipal Area
SMC	–	Sambalpur Municipal Council
ST	–	Scheduled Tribe
SUA	–	Sambalpur Urban Agglomeration
SUDA	–	State Urban Development Authority
SUME	–	Scheme of Urban Micro Enterprises
SUWE	–	Scheme of Urban Wage Employment
UA	–	Urban Agglomeration
UBS	–	Urban Basic Services
UBSP	–	Urban Basic Services for the Poor
UCD	–	Urban Community Development
UIP	–	Urban Improvement Programme
UN	–	United Nations
UNICEF	–	United Nations Children's Fund
WFPR	–	Work Force Participation Rate

GLOSSARY

Anganwadi	–	Centre for mother and child care
Balsevika	–	Female teachers in pre-school centres
Balwadi	–	Pre-school centre for children of 3-6 years
Barpali Latrine	–	Locally made pit latrine
Basti	–	Local term to describe slums
Chawl	–	A block of tenements in a row on one and the same floor with common amenities
Chulha	–	Mud stove
Dai	–	Mid-wife
Kachcha house	–	Shelter with floor, walls and roof made of materials other than brick and cement
Pucca house	–	Shelter with floor and walls made of brick and roof made of cement/concrete
Semi kachcha house	–	Shelter with floor and walls made of brick and cement and roof made of materials other than cement/concrete

INDEX

H

I

K

L

M

N

O

P

S

U

W